CHIEF RED FOX IS DEAD

➤➤➤➤➤➤➤➤➤➤

A HISTORY OF NATIVE AMERICANS
SINCE 1945

Dedicated
to
The First Americans
of the Twenty-First Century

BOOKS BY JAMES J. RAWLS

California Dreaming

California: An Interpretive History (coauthor)

Dame Shirley and the Gold Rush

Never Turn Back

New Directions in California History: A Book of Readings

America and Its Neighbors (coauthor)

California: A Place, A People, A Dream (coeditor)

Land of Liberty: A United States History (coauthor)

Indians of California: The Changing Image

Dan De Quille of the Big Bonanza (editor)

HARBRACE
BOOKS
ON AMERICA

SINCE 1945

CHIEF RED FOX IS DEAD

$\rightarrow\!\!\rightarrow\!\!\rightarrow\!\!\rightarrow\!\!\rightarrow\!\!\rightarrow\!\!\rightarrow\!\!\rightarrow$

A HISTORY OF NATIVE AMERICANS SINCE 1945

JAMES J. RAWLS
Diablo Valley College

UNDER THE GENERAL EDITORSHIP OF
GERALD D. NASH &
RICHARD W. ETULAIN
University of New Mexico

HARCOURT BRACE COLLEGE PUBLISHERS
Fort Worth   Philadelphia   San Diego   New York   Orlando   Austin   San Antonio
Toronto   Montreal   London   Sydney   Tokyo

PUBLISHER **TED BUCHHOLZ**

EDITOR IN CHIEF **CHRISTOPHER P. KLEIN**

ACQUISITIONS EDITOR **DRAKE BUSH**

DEVELOPMENTAL EDITOR **KRISTIE KELLY**

PROJECT EDITOR **LOUISE SLOMINSKY**

PRODUCTION MANAGER **MELINDA ESCO**

ART DIRECTOR **PEGGY YOUNG**

PHOTO RESEARCHER **LILI WEINER**

Cover illustration: *Osage with Van Gogh* by T. C. Cannon used by permission of Walter Cannon and The Heard Museum, Phoenix, AZ. Chapter openers: Detail of *Osage with Van Gogh* by T. C. Cannon.

Picture credits appear on page 265 and constitute a continuation of this copyright page.

Address for Editorial Correspondence:
Harcourt Brace College Publishers
301 Commerce Street, Suite 3700
Fort Worth, TX 76102

Address for Orders:
Harcourt Brace & Company
6277 Sea Harbor Drive
Orlando, FL 32887-6777
1-800-782-4479, or 1-800-433-0001 (in Florida)

Library of Congress Catalog Card Number: 95-80946

ISBN 0-15-501796-9

Printed in the United States of America

5 6 7 8 9 0 1 2 3 4   016   9 8 7 6 5 4 3 2 1

PREFACE

→ → → → → → →

Indians are unable to get non-Indians to accept them as contemporary
beings. Non-Indians either cannot or will not respond to the problems
of contemporary Indians. They insist on remaining in the last century
with old Chief Red Fox, whoever he may really be, reciting a past that is
basically mythological, thrilling, and comforting.
— Vine Deloria, Jr., *God Is Red* (1973)

It was a wondrously clear and warm spring day in 1992 as I walked
with my new friend Phil George (Nez Perce) up the hill toward the
duck pond. Phil and I were working together on a program sponsored
by the National Endowment for the Humanities commemorating the
quincentennial of the voyage of Christopher Columbus. Accompany-
ing us on our walk was a commercial photographer who was going to
take some publicity shots. Phil was dressed in his fancy beaded and
fringed buckskins, looking for all the world like his great grandfather's
cousin, Chief Joseph. When we reached the duck pond, the photographer began maneuvering Phil into position, telling him to sit "Indian style," by which he meant cross-legged. Phil complied with good
humor and assumed the desired pose. The photographer then asked
Phil to look off into the distance with one hand shading his eyes "like
they all used to do." Suddenly it dawned on me what was happening
here. The photographer thought Phil was *playing* Indian, not *being*
Indian. The photographer had seen so many images of noble savages
and bloodthirsty savages on the silver screen that he couldn't quite
grasp that here—right here in front of him—was a real person who
also happened to be an Indian. I stepped forward to assure the photographer that Phil didn't need any coaching, that whatever pose he
chose to assume would be just fine.

As we returned from the duck pond, I reminisced with Phil about a
similar incident from my own boyhood back in the late 1950s. I recalled attending a meeting of my Boy Scout troop at which our special
guest was an American Indian. Like most of my fellow Scouts, I was
enraptured by the dancing and singing of our guest, resplendent in his
feathers and beads and buckskins. When the meeting was over, I went
up for a closer look and was devastated to see a watch on the wrist of
our guest. "Look, he's not a *real* Indian," I blurted out. How could
he be? Real Indians were from a time long ago, as I knew so well from
watching countless episodes of *The Lone Ranger* and *Red Ryder*.

v

Recalling that story now, on our walk from the duck pond, covered the earlier embarrassments of the day and brought a knowing smile to the face of Phil George.

The purpose of this book is to tell something of the recent history of those real people known as Native Americans or American Indians. It is aimed primarily at the non-Indian reader who may have some difficulty accepting Indians as contemporary beings. At the very least, this book should help non-Indians avoid embarrassing themselves by their ignorance. At best, it should provide them with a better understanding of the problems and a finer appreciation of the achievements of the Indian people. If Native readers find their story well told in these pages too, then I shall be doubly gratified.

The history of Native Americans since 1945 is a story of great complexity, yet the theme of this book is really quite simple: survival and balance. In the face of overwhelming odds, Indians have survived and even increased in number in recent years. According to the 1990 census, almost two million Indians are now living in the United States. This represents a nearly 38 percent increase over the 1980 Indian population (due to natural increase as well as a greater self-identification by Indians). Native Americans can be found in every state of the union, with fewer than half living on or near a reservation. The reservations range from the great sixteen-million-acre homeland of the Navajo Nation to small California rancherias of fewer than a hundred acres. Today there are more than 550 federally recognized tribes, with a hundred others seeking recognition.

Balance is a virtue highly prized in virtually all Native American cultures, and balance has been a key to Indian survival. Achieving and maintaining balance have been extraordinarily difficult during the last half of the twentieth century. The countervailing forces have been tremendous, as Native people were continually buffeted by conflicting pressures of assimilation and tradition, change and continuity. Through it all, Indians have survived as a distinct people because of their remarkable ability to adapt to changing circumstances while remaining deeply rooted in traditional values. Tim Giago (Oglala Lakota), founding editor of *Indian Country Today,* put it this way: "Since 1492, the Indian has adapted in order to survive, but we have not given up those things that have made us a unique people in a unique land."

This book is arranged both chronologically and topically, put together with a full recognition that history is truly a seamless web, and that patterns spun by historians are inevitably artificial and arbitrary. The first chapter begins with a brief retrospective of images of Indians in American popular culture, followed by a discussion of the role of Native Americans during World War II. Because federal Indian policy has been a prime element in the recent history of Native people, the next two chapters are devoted to the tortuous shifts in that policy between assimilationism and cultural pluralism. Chapter 2 provides some deep background and carries the policy story to 1960; chapter 3 brings it through the 1990s.

Persistent social and economic problems are discussed in the fourth chapter, including the continuing challenges in employment, health, and education. The problem of Native American poverty continues to this day, and an acknowledgment of it is essential to any understanding of the concerns of contemporary Indian people. The fifth chapter traces the rise of the Indian rights movement, culminating in such dramatic events as the occupation of the headquarters of the Bureau of Indian Affairs in Washington, D.C., and the bloody confrontation at Wounded Knee, South Dakota. More recent controversies are discussed in chapter 6, including conflicts over economic development and the repatriation of Indian artifacts and skeletal remains. The seventh chapter focuses on the survival and revival of traditional cultures. The resurgence of Native religions, languages, and aspects of material culture is described, as are the achievements of the Native American fine arts movement. In chapter 8, the renaissance of Indian literature is presented in all its glory, surveying the major works of Native novelists, short story writers, and poets. The final chapter returns to the image of the Indian in popular culture, emphasizing the role of the Native people themselves in shaping the image presented to their fellow Americans.

It has been my intention to include the voices of Native Americans throughout the book, allowing them to tell their story in their own words. The voices of "ordinary people" are included as often as possible, but inevitably most of the voices are those of Indian leaders and other public figures. Although Native voices are present in all the chapters, they seem to fade a bit in the two on federal policy. Unfortunately, their relative scarcity there is an accurate reflection of the historical reality in which the expressed desires of the Indian people often were drowned out by a cacophony of other voices.

The reader already will have noticed that in this account the terms *Native American* and *Indian* are used interchangeably to refer to the indigenous people of the United States. Although the former term has come into popular usage in the last couple of decades, especially in academia and the world of publishing, it is less frequently used by the Native people themselves. Most refer to themselves by their tribal name, e.g. *Hopi, Seminole, Passamaquoddy.* When they use a more general term, many prefer *American Indian, Indian people,* or simply *Indian.* In any event, the matter of appellation is not something of critical importance for the vast majority of Indians today. As journalist Robert H. White recently observed, "Maybe they feel that a misnomer applied to their ancestors more than five hundred years ago by an Italian adventurer is the least of their concerns." Nevertheless, if anyone is offended by the usages in this book, I hereby extend my sincere apologies.

Perhaps a note also is in order about the title of the book, *Chief Red Fox Is Dead.* Chief Red Fox was a real person, identified as a nephew of the great Sioux leader Crazy Horse, who defeated Custer at the Battle of the Little Big Horn. His name is invoked here to symbolize that *un*real Indian of the past that Sioux historian Vine Deloria, Jr., said has always captivated non-Indians. As a child long ago, I once was among those who were captivated so, but I say now: Let us leave Chief Red Fox in that "mythological, thrilling, and comforting" past, and look instead to the story of the Native people of this century and the next. Yes, Chief Red Fox is dead, but the Indian people of his land are very much alive. It is to them and to their children that this book is respectfully dedicated.

JAMES J. RAWLS
December 29, 1995

ACKNOWLEDGMENTS

➤ ➤ ➤ ➤ ➤ ➤ ➤ ➤

This book is a synthesis based on the works of the dozens of scholars cited in the text and listed in the bibliographical notes at the end of each chapter. Without their pioneering research in the field of Native American history, this book could not have been written. Properly regarded, this is largely a "tertiary work," drawn from the best available secondary sources. To acknowledge more fully the importance of these sources, I have deposited an annotated typescript of this book in the Special Collections Room of the General Library at Diablo Valley College, Pleasant Hill, California. The annotations on the typescript indicate the sources used for nearly every paragraph.

I also am indebted to the many scholars who generously have shared with me their responses to earlier drafts of this work. I wish to thank especially Professor Colin Calloway of Dartmouth College; Professor Edward D. Castillo (Cahuilla / Luiseño) of Sonoma State University; Professors Richard W. Etulain, Gerald D. Nash, and Margaret Connell Szasz of the University of New Mexico; Professor Steven J. Crum (Western Shoshone) of the University of California, Davis; and Professor Clifford E. Trafzer (Wyandot) of the University of California, Riverside.

Special thanks also are due to JoAllyn Archambault (Standing Rock Sioux), director of the American Indian Program at the National Museum of Natural History, Smithsonian Institution, Washington, D.C.; Allen G. Minker, Arizona Superior Court Judge and Visiting White Mountain Apache Tribal Judge; and Larry Myers (Pomo), executive director of the Native American Heritage Commission.

At Harcourt Brace College Publishers I have had the great pleasure of working with a first-rate team of editors, including Drake Bush, Kristie Kelly, and Louise Slominsky. To them I am deeply grateful for their commitment to excellence.

On the home front, J. W. and Kathleen Rawls served faithfully as research assistants and proofreaders; and Linda, Benjamin, and Elizabeth provided never-failing encouragement and support. Thank you all.

ILLUSTRATIONS

→ ⇒ ⇒ ⇒ ⇒ ⇒ ⇒ ⇒

MAPS

MAP A   Federally Recognized Tribes and Reservations   XII

MAP B   Federally Recognized Tribes and Reservations   XIII

MAP C   Federally Recognized Tribes and Reservations   XIV

These three maps are based on a map prepared by the U.S. Geological Survey in cooperation with the Bureau of Indian Affairs, October 1991. Names on the maps indicate the location of federal reservations and federally recognized tribes, but not all reservations or tribes are included. Within Alaska are more than 200 recognized groups; shown are the names and boundaries of the Alaska Native Regional Corporations.

CHARTS

FIGURE 4.1   Native American Amenities in 1990   80

FIGURE 4.2   American Indian Population in the Area of the United States   89

FIGURE 4.3   Distribution of Native American Students, School Year 1989–1990   100

FIGURE 4.4   High School Dropout Rates by Ethnic Group, 1989   101

CONTENTS

PREFACE   V

ACKNOWLEDGMENTS   IX

CHAPTER 1 *Warriors*   1

CHAPTER 2 *Solving the "Indian Problem"*   23

CHAPTER 3 *Toward Self-Determination*   53

CHAPTER 4 *A National Tragedy*   77

CHAPTER 5 *The Trail to Wounded Knee*   105

CHAPTER 6 *The Struggle Continues*   139

CHAPTER 7 *Between Two Worlds*   171

CHAPTER 8 *Native American Voices*   201

CHAPTER 9 *The Changing Image*   229

CREDITS   265

INDEX   267

FEDERALLY RECOGNIZED
TRIBES AND RESERVATIONS
▼▼▼▼
MAP A

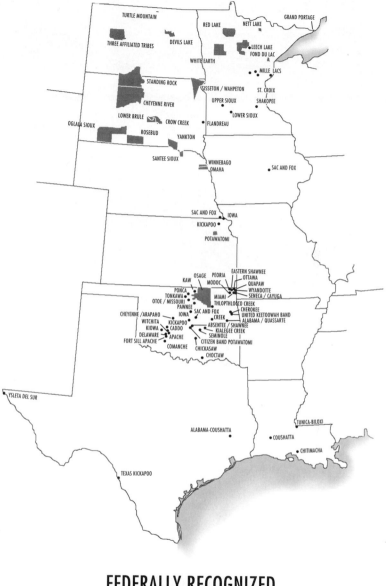

FEDERALLY RECOGNIZED
TRIBES AND RESERVATIONS
MAP B

FEDERALLY RECOGNIZED
TRIBES AND RESERVATIONS

▼▼▼▼
MAP C

HARBRACE
BOOKS
ON AMERICA

SINCE 1945

1

WARRIORS

>→ →→ →→ →→ →→ →→ →→

THE UPRAISED ARMS OF the saguaro cactus stabbed at the sun-bleached sky of Arizona Territory. On a distant ridge puffs of smoke sent a message skyward, its meaning all too clear to the hapless stagecoach driver whose job it was to get his passengers safely through to Lordsburg. This was Apache country, and Geronimo and his marauding band were on the warpath again. Already the driver and his passengers had seen evidence of the destructive fury of these fearsome warriors. The stage had passed through the burned-out ruins of a frontier outpost, its dusty streets littered with the bodies of the dead.

The driver shouted to his eight-horse team, urging it on faster and faster. Suddenly his shouts were drowned out by bloodcurdling yells from Indians charging in hot pursuit. The Apaches were mounted and armed with rifles, spears, and bows and arrows. Their faces were set with a grim determination. An arrow whistled through the open window of the stage, striking one of the passengers in the chest. Next a bullet struck the driver. He winced in pain, pitched forward in his seat, and dropped the reins of his stampeding team. The passengers returned the Indians' fire but their ammunition soon was exhausted. Everything seemed lost when, out of the blue, a troop of United States Cavalry came thundering through the sagebrush and mesquite, bugles blaring and sabers drawn. The hostile Indians turned and fled. The cavalry rescued the stagecoach and its frightened passengers—including the wounded driver—and escorted them safely to Lordsburg.

If this all sounds vaguely familiar, like something you may have seen on late-night television or on a video, you're right. The foregoing bit of purple prose is a synopsis of the climactic scene from John Ford's classic Western film *Stagecoach* (1939). It is an image that has been repeated in countless variations in hundreds of films, an image deeply imbedded within the nation's collective memory. The image is easily recognizable because, like all stereotypes, it depends upon a few familiar clues. The Indians of the silver screen were almost always skilled horsemen, heavily armed, fiercely determined, and adorned with feathered headdresses. Their language was often limited to an unintelligible collection of grunts and "ughs," or a pidgin English punctuated by an occasional "how!" Never mind that this image conveyed little of the vast variety of Native peoples who lived as sedentary fishermen or farmers, who achieved a remarkable degree of peaceful coexistence, who dressed in a wide array of clothing fashioned from local resources, and who spoke hundreds of complex and expressive languages.

Actually, to be fair, there never was a single Hollywood version of the American Indian. Film historians have identified three main stereotypes, each of which was drawn from earlier forms of popular culture. The least common image was that of the Pocahontas figure, the tenderhearted Indian maiden who could be counted on to risk her life to aid the white newcomers in the land of her people. Equally sentimental was the image of the Indian who was virtuous and sublime in his relationship with nature, a tragic figure doomed to extinction by the advance of white civilization. This sympathetic image was essentially an updated version of the noble savage, a literary convention whose roots lay in the writings of Rousseau and other social critics of the Enlightenment. The third image, and the one that predominated, was that of the warrior, a bloodthirsty savage who attempted with all his might to block the westward expansion of white settlement. This was the image that had the most dramatic possibilities and the biggest box-office appeal. It was he who bedeviled those terrorized passengers in *Stagecoach*.

The warrior was the image of choice from the earliest days of the film industry. A band of treacherous Indians in *Kit Carson* (1903) attacked and murdered a band of defenseless trappers, while a press release for *Ogallalah* (1911) warned that the film was as "savage and cruel as Indians are by nature." The most lavish of the early Westerns, suitably entitled *The Indian Wars* (1913), featured the reenactment of five of the bloodiest battles between Indians and the United States Army. The development of the feature film and the low-budget Western of the 1930s and 1940s tended further to emphasize action over sentiment. The Indian warrior thus remained the dominant stereotype. "Not only were bands of marauding savages good adversaries for the heroics of the star," film historians Michael T. Marsden and Jack Nachbar observed, "but also long shots of feathered riders made for exciting action sequences and were eminently reusable."

The quintessential characteristic of the warrior was his opposition to European American civilization. In film after film, masses of armed Indians waged battle against the advance of the frontier, but by the final reel there was never any doubt that their opposition was futile. That was the way it was in their campaigns against the overland pioneers in *The Covered Wagon* (1923), the transcontinental railroad in *The Union Pacific* (1939), and the "singing wires" of the telegraph in *Western Union* (1941). When the warriors did score a victory, as in the Battle of the Little Big Horn, the white protagonists were treated in films such as *The Flaming Frontier* (1926) and *They Died with Their Boots On* (1941) as tragic heroes.

The antecedents of these images can be traced to the first contacts between Europeans and Native Americans in this hemisphere. Images of noble savages and bloodthirsty warriors appeared as stock figures in thousands of travel accounts, novels, poems, and plays; they were reproduced in galleries of paintings, engravings, lithographs, and sculptures. The positive image portrayed the Indians as proud and dignified, possessed of great strength and endurance. The negative image emphasized their incessant warfare, fiendish revenge, and penchant for unspeakable cruelty. Accounts of whites captured by Indians were among the earliest best-sellers in American literature. The first of these so-called captivity narratives, published in 1682, made plain its assessment of Indian character: "Atheistical, proud, wild, cruel, barbarous, brutish, (in one word) diabolical . . . the worse of heathen." Gothic novels in the eighteenth century and dime novels in the nineteenth perpetuated these images endlessly. They were brought to life in Wild West shows that enthralled audiences throughout Europe and the United States in the late 1800s. A favorite attraction of these ersatz historical extravaganzas was a staged Indian attack on—what else?—a runaway stagecoach.

Whether the popular image of the Indian was positive or negative, it was often enveloped in what historian Robert F. Berkhofer, Jr., called "a curious timelessness." European Americans tended to portray Indians in aboriginal times, before white contact, or in the early years of contact. This portrayal neglected the subsequent decades of historical development and the changed conditions among Native Americans. In the white imagination, the only "real" Indians were those who inhabited the distant past. Thus when American audiences viewed John Ford's *Stagecoach* in 1939 they were able to make a nostalgic escape into that past. And Americans surely *needed* an escape, for the news in 1939 was not good. Japanese imperial forces continued their invasion of China, while Great Britain and France declared war on Nazi Germany following Hitler's murderous assault on Poland. The following year the news was no better. The Nazis invaded Denmark, Norway, and the Low Countries; France fell to Germany; and the Battle of Britain began. American audiences witnessed these horrors on newsreels just before settling in to see such films as King Vidor's viciously anti-Indian frontier epic, *Northwest Passage* (1940). As this celluloid drama unfolds, Spencer Tracy as Major Robert Rogers delivers an impassioned speech about the horrors of Indian warfare and commands his valiant Rangers to exterminate the residents of a nearby Native village. The deed is done and Major Rogers is on his way to becoming a frontier saint. The film ends with the major's silhouette dramatically cast against the heavens.

NATIVE AMERICANS IN WORLD WAR II

"Yesterday, December 7, 1941—a date which will live in infamy—the United States of America was suddenly and deliberately attacked by naval and air forces of the Empire of Japan." President Franklin D. Roosevelt thus spoke one of the most fateful sentences in American history. Among the far-reaching effects of the Japanese attack on Pearl Harbor and the subsequent entry of the United States into World War II was a fundamental change in the status of American Indians and their relationship with their fellow Americans. Tens of thousands of Indians served in the armed forces and worked in defense industries during the war, giving many non-Indians their first face-to-face encounters with Native people. These encounters challenged old stereotypes and had profound consequences for all Americans.

Even before the attack on Pearl Harbor, Native Americans had followed closely the news of the struggle raging in Europe and Asia. They watched the same newsreels as their fellow citizens and gathered around loudspeakers to listen to the latest war bulletins. In remote corners of reservations in the Southwest, Indians tuned in shortwave radios to keep informed about troop movements and casualty lists. The news of the war inspired the Navajos to nickname Hitler "Moustache Smeller" and Mussolini "Big Gourd Chin."

Native Americans had special reason to follow closely the news of the war: For the first time in history they were subject to the military draft. About half of all American Indians had been noncitizens during World War I and thus had been exempt from conscription. The dedicated service of 10,000 Indian volunteers in that conflict prompted Congress in 1924 to grant citizenship to all Native people. Thus, when the Selective Service Act of 1940 required all young men to register for the draft, Indians no longer were an exception. By the spring of 1941, more than 7,000 Indians had registered while fewer than 100 had attempted to resist. (The resisters argued that conscription violated tribal sovereignty, but a federal court ruled that tribal membership did not exempt Indians from military service.) Also by the spring of 1941, more than 500 Indians had volunteered for the armed forces and thirty-seven had been inducted, an impressive ratio of fifteen to one. The largest number of volunteers, over 100, came from the Sioux and Assiniboine reservation at Fort Peck in northern Montana. Among the volunteers from Fort Peck were proud descendants of the band that had defeated Custer at the Battle of the Little Big Horn just sixty-five years earlier.

Novelist and ethnologist Oliver La Farge was in a small Pueblo village on December 7, 1941, when the news of Pearl Harbor first arrived. The villagers expressed deep regret, La Farge recalled, "for the many boys, not just their own people, but American boys in general who were going to be killed. . . . There was a general acceptance of the war as their own, deriving from a definite feeling that they were sharers in America and democracy." These sentiments were echoed in villages and on reservations throughout the nation. When asked about the upsurge of patriotism among Native Americans at the outset of the war, one Indian veteran explained simply, "we were fighting for *our country*." To him the attack on Pearl Harbor meant the "enemy was headed this way and we had to stop them. If someone is trying to take something away from us, we fight back. If this is what you call *patriotism*, then we are very patriotic." Another veteran, Cosey Brown (Navajo), remembered his wartime service in similar terms: "I would think, 'I'm doing this for my people.' We protected the American people, also the unborn children which would be the next generation to come. I see young men and women, and I am glad for what I did for them."

Within hours of the attack on Pearl Harbor, Native Americans began preparing themselves for battle. Young men in New Mexico cleaned and oiled their rifles, packed their saddlebags, and rode to Gallup, ready to fight. The superintendent of the Navajo reservation looked out his window on December 7 and saw a large crowd of grim-faced youth gathered nearby. They all were armed and carried their personal effects in bandannas knotted at the corners. When the superintendent asked them what they were doing, they replied, "We're going to fight." The superintendent convinced them to return to their homes and wait for the official call to arms. In the weeks ahead, thousands of Indians rushed to join the armed forces. "I was in school when I heard about Pearl Harbor," recalled Barney Old Coyote, a Crow veteran who had enlisted at age seventeen. "There was revenge in my heart. I joined the Army Air Corps to get back at the Japs." By June 1942 more than 5,000 Indians had volunteered and 4,000 had been inducted. "We would not need the Selective Service if all volunteered like Indians," editorialized the *Saturday Evening Post*.

Native Americans served during the war in all branches of the armed forces and in every major theater of operations. About 25,000 Indians were in uniform, including 21,767 in the army, 1,910 in the navy, 874 in the marines, and 121 in the coast guard. More than 200 Indian women served in the military auxiliaries, the WACS and WAVES, and joined the nurses' corps, Red Cross, and American Women's Voluntary Service. Indian soldiers first saw action in the Pacific, fighting on Bataan and Corregidor. Later they fought on the islands of Guadalcanal and Iwo Jima, across the deserts of North Africa, and on the beaches at Normandy. They served with Douglas MacArthur in the Philippines and with George Patton in Germany. They fought with the Fourth Infantry Division in the liberation of Paris and pursued the enemy across Belgium and into Germany.

Indians served in integrated units throughout the war, in spite of the recommendation by Commissioner of Indian Affairs John Collier that they be placed in a separate division in order to preserve Indian culture. Racial segregation in the armed forces, of course, was nothing new. African Americans had served in segregated units in every war since the American Civil War, and Japanese Americans served during World War II in separate combat units. The War Department insisted,

NAVAJO CODE TALKERS IN THE JUNGLES OF BOUGAINVILLE, THE LARGEST OF THE SOLOMON ISLANDS, DURING WORLD WAR II. THE CODE TALKERS PLAYED A KEY ROLE IN ALLIED VICTORIES THROUGHOUT THE PACIFIC THEATER.

however, that American Indians should be fully integrated in all branches of the military. Several all-Indian training platoons were permitted for Native Americans who failed English literacy tests, but once the recruits were proficient in standard military English, they were assigned to white regiments. The combat unit with the greatest proportion of Native soldiers—about 20 percent—was the Forty-fifth Army Infantry Division from Fort Sill, Oklahoma. This unit had fought in World War I and had taken as its symbol the swastika, a design used by Navajo artisans (and others) for generations. On the eve of World War II, this symbol no longer seemed appropriate and was replaced by another Native image, the thunderbird.

Perhaps the most distinctive contribution of Native Americans in World War II was their service in a Marine Corps signal unit known as the "code talkers." Sending and receiving secret messages were matters of critical importance on any battlefield, and during World War II the Germans and the Japanese proved adept at deciphering American codes. Philip Johnston, a white civilian who had grown up on the Navajo reservation, proposed constructing a new code based on the Navajo language. The Marine Corps approved Johnston's proposal and recruited twenty-nine young Navajos to come to a communication school training center in California to develop the code. These young marines produced an ingenious code that included more than 400 Navajo words for the most frequently used terms in the military lexicon. The Navajo word for "buzzard" became the code name for a bomber, an "owl" was an observation plane, and a "chicken hawk" was a dive bomber. Battleships were known by the Navajo word for "whale," submarines were "iron fish," and destroyers were "sharks." To further confuse the enemy, the code talkers continually changed the code. Each letter of the alphabet also received a Navajo name so that words not in the code could be spelled out. The letter A was the Navajo word for "ant," B was "bear," all the way through "yucca" for Y and "zinc" for Z. The code was so effective that even Navajos who did not know the code were unable to decipher it.

After the initial group of Navajo marines developed the code, they stayed on at California's Camp Pendleton to train new recruits in its use. Navajo instructors drilled their students not only in the code but also in the necessity of defending it with their lives. One instructor later recalled the intense grilling he gave the future code talkers:

> Would you refuse to give away the secret of the code if you had a samurai sword at your throat? If the enemy would ask, "What is your word for *A*?" would you tell them? You begin to bleed; you begin to feel your own blood trickling down . . . warm, with the cutting a little deeper. You *would* lay down your life before you would tell, wouldn't you?

That such training was not just academic was proved during the war when Joe Lee Kieyoomie (Navajo) was captured, imprisoned, and tortured for five months by the Japanese in a futile attempt to force him to reveal the code.

Eventually more than 400 Navajos were recruited for this unique program, and all but thirty served in the Central and South Pacific. When necessary, the code talkers fought alongside their fellow Leathernecks and risked their lives as troubleshooters and stretcher-bearers. Their service was absolutely essential in several key engagements. "Were it not for the Navajos," commented one officer, "the Marines would never have taken Iwo Jima! . . . During the first forty-eight hours, while we were landing and consolidating our shore positions, I had six Navajo radio nets operating around the clock. In that period alone they sent and received over eight hundred messages without an error." Non-Indian veteran Dillon Story's eyes filled with tears as he later recalled the contribution of the code talkers: "They were 100 percent effective, 100 percent. Without them a lot more boys would have died taking those islands."

Native Americans serving in the Pacific, whether as code talkers or not, occasionally suffered the embarrassment and danger of being mistaken for the Japanese enemy. In dozens of cases, the language spoken by the code talkers was mistakenly identified by the uninitiated as Japanese. Far more serious were the cases of mistaken identity in which Indian soldiers were thought to be the enemy in disguise. One Native American marine and his buddies came under fire on Saipan while attempting to make emergency repairs to damaged communication lines. A corporal was killed in the barrage. Later the Indians learned that they had been fired upon by their own men who mistook them for Japanese in marine uniforms. Likewise, an army unit picked up a Native marine on Guadalcanal and sent a message to headquarters: "We have captured a Jap in Marine clothing with Marine identification tags." After several tense exchanges, the Indian marine was properly identified and released. A Navajo had a similar narrow escape on New Georgia Island. He later recalled:

> When we were under fire, one army officer pulled his .45 pistol on me, taking me for a Jap. . . . I had a hard time convincing that officer that I was an American Marine. They threatened to shoot me, but took me to headquarters at my insistence, where I was identified.

Even when they were out of uniform, Native American soldiers ran the risk of being mistaken for the enemy. An MP came upon an Indian soldier bathing in a water-filled crater on an island in the South Pacific. He promptly placed his bayonet between the eyes of the startled bather and adamantly refused to believe the soldier's protestations of innocence—"I'm one of the Marines!"—until he was positively identified by his commanding officer. This same Indian marine later brought back some captured Japanese prisoners. When he arrived at his platoon headquarters, his fellow soldiers treated it as a joke. "Which is the prisoner?" they laughed. "Which are the Japanese?" One field officer said that even the "canine corps" sometimes confused the Indians and the enemy. "We had to watch the war dogs carefully when they were around the Navajos—they couldn't tell them from Japs."

In spite of these occasional lapses of mistaken identity, most Native Americans in the armed forces experienced little overt racial discrimination. Their service in integrated units meant that they faced the same dangers and hardships as other GIs, and from these shared experiences came a mutual respect among Indians and non-Indians alike. The Native American serviceman, regardless of rank, invariably was called "Chief" by his European American buddies. The term often was used in a spirit of playful affection, but it also could signal condescension with derogatory intent. Letters from Indians in the military were filled with accounts of acceptance and friendship across racial lines. Ellison Bowman, a Navajo marine, wrote from the South Pacific, "I am OK here with these people over at South Sea Island. I am swell friend of white soldiers. I am the only one red skin with this outfit. I and them just like a brother now." An Indian tail gunner and radio operator on a B-17 Flying Fortress reported that "members of the crew are swell to me, they are the best fellows after a guy gets to know them." From an army camp in California, Private Amaldo Pino (Tesuque Pueblo) wrote in 1942, "The people here are very friendly to me and treat me mighty fine," and from Fort Bliss, Texas, another Native private wrote simply that "the boys here seems friendly."

Indians who suffered the worst hardships expressed intense feelings of bonding with their white comrades-in-arms. "I would say that all of us who were in Japanese prison camps and survived . . . were closer to each other than even our own brothers could be," recalled one Native American prisoner of war. "The long days of suffering, starving and seeing our buddies die binds us together with bonds of steel." A young Chippewa veteran, reflecting on his wartime experiences, expressed his sentiments in poetry:

> *We bind each other's wounds and eat the same ration.*
> *We dream of our loved ones in the same nation.*

Without question, these shared experiences contributed to the assimilation of Indians into the mainstream of American society. As Alison R. Bernstein, author of *American Indians and World War II* (1991), concluded, "Increased contacts with whites and the outside world in the military stimulated changes in habits and outlooks on the part of Indian soldiers." Indians in the military became enmeshed in the intricacies of a modern bureaucracy, arranging for dependency allotments and applying for veteran's benefits. And the increased pay and benefits of military life meant a substantial rise in the standard of living for Indian soldiers and their families. Consumer goods from European American society that had been beyond the reach of many Native Americans were now readily available. Increased exposure to non-Indian religious traditions also led some non-Christian Native Americans to convert to Christianity. Although the number of conversions is unknown, the traumatic conditions of the battlefield apparently caused Native people to be more open to non-Indian religious practice. "I attend a Catholic mass from the back of a jeep every morning," reported one war-weary Indian private.

Contemporary observers concluded that the wartime experiences of Native Americans would lead inevitably to their complete assimilation. Historian Gerald D. Nash, author of *The American West Transformed* (1985), offered a more balanced appraisal: "If the war had an impact of strengthening acculturation of some Indians, it also had the effect of strengthening various aspects of Indian traditionalism." In spite of the increased exposure to non-Indian religious traditions, many Native Americans continued to practice their traditional religions. Shamans or tribal medicine men conducted sacred rites for the safety of those who were leaving the reservation to enlist in the armed forces. Once overseas, Indians continued to draw strength from traditional beliefs and practices. One Navajo code talker confessed that he always invoked the Great Spirit before transmitting a message. Another said that he had been exposed to the Catholic religion, but had not taken it very seriously. "I *did* pray many times when I was exposed to danger on the main battleline, as a code talker and as a signalman," he recalled. "I prayed as my mother and father had taught me—to the Heavenly Being as well as to Mother Earth." He also learned that while he was away his mother had gone to a sacred hill and prayed for his safety almost every morning using sacred corn pollen. "Maybe that is the reason," mused this grateful marine, "I came back all in one piece."

The continued practice of traditional culture often evoked expressions of great interest from European American observers. War correspondent Richard Tregaskis described the scene among the Indian marines on board ship prior to the landing on Guadalcanal. The senior medical officer found the Indians "doing a war dance. One of them had a towel for a loincloth and a blackened face, and he was doing a cancan while another beat a tom-tom." Likewise, Ernie Pyle described a solemn dance held by Indian marines prior to their landing on Okinawa. The Indians prayed that the strength of the Japanese would be sapped as the marines stormed the beaches. The landing proved to be relatively easy, but the marines later met heavy opposition on the southern part of the island. "O.K., what about your little ceremony? What do you call this?" asked one white marine. An Indian Leatherneck smiled and replied, "This is different. We prayed only for an easy landing." Following the Allied victory, one group of Native Americans celebrated in traditional fashion. "As tom-toms were not items of issue," commented a white officer, "they headed *au naturel* for the bandsmen's tents. Grabbing drums, and later any instruments available, they Indian-danced their way toward the officers' tent."

As these passages suggest, the rhetoric used by European Americans to describe their Indian companions in the armed forces was often filled with clichés drawn from popular culture. Terms such as "war dance," "tom-toms," and "chief" were commonplace. This is hardly surprising since for many whites the war provided them with their first encounters with Indians as real people, living in the here and now, not as flickering images of feathered savages on the silver screen. When whites were called upon to recognize the accomplishments of Native American soldiers, they invariably invoked the popular image that had predominated for generations, the image of the warrior. "The real secret that makes the Indian such an outstanding soldier," concluded Major L. A. Gilstrap, "is his enthusiasm for fight." The same conclusion was reached by journalist Donald C. Peattie in "Lo Takes the Warpath," an article that appeared in *Reader's Digest* in 1943. "The red soldier is tough," commented Peattie. "He takes to commando fighting with gusto. Why not? His ancestors invented it. . . . At ambushing, scouting, signaling, sniping, they're peerless." Even Secretary of the Interior Harold Ickes credited the "warrior traits" of the American Indians for their valor on the battlefields of World War II. It was "the inherited talents of the Indian," he believed, that made him such a good soldier, and those talents included "endurance, rhythm, coordination, sense perception, and enthusiasm for fighting."

Visual representations of Indian soldiers also reflected the warrior image drawn from popular culture. On the cover of the dictionary used for training Navajo code talkers were two cartoon-version Indian warriors, neither of which bore the slightest resemblance to anything Navajo. Military photographers of Native American soldiers sometimes added feathered headdresses—inevitably identified as "war bonnets"—and arranged their subjects in poses reminiscent of stock warrior images from the nineteenth century. At the war's end, the federal government issued a pamphlet, "Indians in the War," which summarized the contributions of Native Americans in the armed forces. On its cover was a painting of a traditional burial of a Plains Indian warrior.

Although these wartime images of Indian warriors clearly revealed their popular culture origins, it is also important to recognize that the images had undergone a fundamental transformation. The warriors of World War II were portrayed as courageous heroes, a far cry from their earlier role as fiendish enemies of the advance of white civilization. These modern warriors were lionized for their abilities as skilled fighters and their willingness to die for their country. "A red man will risk his life for a white as dauntlessly as his ancestor lifted a paleface's scalp," wrote one inspired journalist. Historian Alison R. Bernstein aptly summarized this remarkable shift in attitudes: "It seems as though the Indians' negative image in the nineteenth century as bloodthirsty savages suddenly became a positive image, since they were fighting on the right side. Those supposedly inherent characteristics, which had been formerly despised, now were celebrated."

ON THE HOME FRONT

World War II also had a tremendous impact on the Native Americans who remained on the home front. Forty thousand Indians worked in defense-related jobs during the war, including about half of all the able-bodied Native men who had not joined the armed forces and one-fifth of the women.

The war presented American Indians with an unprecedented array of new job opportunities, some of which were right on the doorstep of their reservations. Manpower shortages at the Phelps-Dodge copper mine in southern Arizona led to the employment of 300 workers from the nearby Tohono O'odham (formerly Papago) reservation. An aluminum plant near the St. Regis Mohawk reservation hired Indian workers as did two large defense construction projects near the Pine Ridge Sioux reservation in South Dakota. More than 3,000 Navajos were employed at the army's Fort Wingate Munitions Depot adjacent to their reservation in western New Mexico. Hundreds of Indians worked on the vast Naval Supply Depot at Clearfield, Utah. This remote facility employed Pueblos from New Mexico, as well as Sho-shones, Arapahos, Apaches, Sioux, and Utes. The labor foreman of the depot praised this multitribal work force in 1945: "I have never had an Indian in my office for disciplinary action."

Some of the new wartime employment opportunities for Native Americans were in cities far from the reservations, and thus thousands left their homes for places like Seattle, Los Angeles, Denver, and Albuquerque. There they worked as machinists, steam fitters, and electricians in munitions factories, aircraft plants, shipyards, machine shops, and military installations. Less-skilled Indian workers also traveled long distances to take advantage of new job opportunities. Members of the Cheyenne and Blackfeet tribes moved to the Northwest and were employed as maintenance workers for the state highway systems. Chippewa tribesmen relocated to Minneapolis and St. Paul to work for the Northern Pacific Railroad on track gangs and construction crews. Indian women joined the ranks of "Rosie the Riveter" and found jobs in defense plants, not only as riveters but also as machinists and inspectors. Women from the Pueblo reservations received training as auto mechanics and worked hauling freight throughout the Southwest. By 1943 more than 12,000 Indian women had left their reservations for war-related work.

Native American defense workers, like their counterparts in the armed forces, faced relatively little discrimination during the war. Defense contractors, desperate for workers, were eager to hire Indians, and Indian workers compiled an enviable record as conscientious and hard-working employees. Relations between Indian and non-Indian workers also were generally free from serious problems, excepting the usual border-town prejudices encountered by Native workers at job sites near their reservations. One of the few reported instances of institutional discrimination was at the Fort Wingate ordnance depot in New Mexico where Indian workers received less pay than whites. The Navajo tribal council filed a formal complaint, but the inequity was not remedied. The local chapter of the Congress of Industrial Organizations (CIO) argued successfully that since Indians did not pay taxes on their land they were entitled to lower wages.

The new wartime employment opportunities proved to be a mixed blessing for Native Americans. The Bureau of Indian Affairs reported in 1945 that the average annual income of Indian families was $1,200, three times what it had been in 1940. At some of the remote wartime job sites, the government provided housing and other social services for Indian employees. But many workers who moved to the cities lived in substandard housing and faced difficult problems of adjustment. Absenteeism, delinquency, and public intoxication were signs of the strain experienced by many rural Indians who had to adjust to the new urban environment. The movement of workers to the cities also depleted the supply of manpower needed to tend the flocks and work the fields back on the reservation. "Few men were left to plow for the women, aged, and children," the All-Pueblo Council of New Mexico reported. On the Mescalero reservation, Apache women worked in the fields for the first time in their history.

Obviously the war was breaking down traditional patterns of life of Native Americans who stayed on the reservations as well as of those who moved away to work in the defense industries. For many who left, it was their first opportunity to be away from their home environment for an extended period of time. They experienced anew the forces of assimilation, conducting their lives in ways that conformed to that of the mainstream culture and compromising traditional values in order to contend with the outside world. And yet the disruptive experiences of the war also encouraged a greater cultural awareness and led many Native Americans to continue traditional lifestyles. Even in the crowded conditions of wartime boomtowns, Indian defense workers retained many of their old attitudes and folkways. Likewise, there was a pronounced strengthening of Indian traditionalism on the reservations even as outside influences were hastening the process of assimilation. Under the stress of war, traditional prayers and dances were performed that had not been practiced for many years. On the Standing Rock reservation in South Dakota in 1942, the Sioux danced their first battle Sun Dance in more than fifty years, praying for victory over the enemies of their country and for the safe return of the 2,000 tribesmen in the armed forces. War chants and prayers for victory also experienced a revival among the Navajo. As one observer commented in 1942, "War has aroused long dormant instincts in the First Americans of our Southwest."

In the midst of these conflicting pressures of traditionalism and assimilation, tribal leaders generally were willing and eager to contribute the resources of their reservations to the war effort. Tribal governments donated funds and bought war bonds, as did thousands of individual Native Americans. Secretary of the Interior Ickes announced in 1943 that Indians had purchased $12.6 million in war bonds. "This," he observed, "equaled the per capita contribution of any racial group including the whites." Meanwhile, Crow leaders in Montana sent a telegram to President Roosevelt volunteering all of their reservation's resources to the War Department with "no strings attached," and the Klamath Indians voted to build an airfield on their Oregon reservation for the training of military pilots. Conflicts occasionally arose between tribal leaders and federal officials over the appropriation of Indian lands for bombing and gunnery ranges. When the army proposed acquiring 400,000 acres from the Tohono O'odham reservation, the chairman of the tribal council asked that alternative sites first be considered. On the Sioux reservation at Pine Ridge, South Dakota, several Indian families were ordered from their homes to make way for an aerial gunnery range for the army. "The War Department was ordering us out," complained one bitter evacuee, "and the superintendent of the reservation said that we would be shot if we didn't leave."

The most controversial use of Indian resources during the war was the leasing of tens of thousands of acres of reservation lands for the internment of Japanese Americans. In 1942 Indian Affairs Commissioner John Collier suggested that the War Relocation Authority build internment camps on reservations for the "colonization of the Japanese." Collier believed the camps would economically benefit the reservations, and he argued further that the Bureau of Indian Affairs was well suited to assist in the relocation of the Japanese Americans because of its "long experience in handling a minority group." Ultimately two relocation camps were built on Indian lands—one along the Colorado River at Poston, Arizona, and the other on the Gila River reservation near Phoenix. Pima tribal leaders at Gila River expressed disappointment that they were not consulted earlier in the decision to locate a camp on their land, and Indians along the Colorado River were openly hostile to the idea of placing Japanese Americans in their midst. In any event, the Japanese Americans were only temporary residents on the reservations. At the war's end, the internment camps were dismantled, and the reservations prepared for the return of tens of thousands of veterans and war workers.

Most of the returning Indian veterans received a hero's welcome when they arrived back on their reservations. Parades, festivals, and public ceremonies celebrated their return. The tribal council of the Cheyenne River Sioux even voted to give each of its 350 veterans a twenty-five dollar bonus. In some instances, however, the veterans were viewed with misgivings. Older residents feared that the returning soldiers had been contaminated by the spirits of enemy soldiers and must undergo purification rites. The Zunis, who had tried desperately to keep their young men out of the war, required every returning veteran to pass through a special ritual before being accepted back into tribal society. One Zuni mother greeted her returning son at Gallup but refused to touch him until he had been decontaminated. Elders and traditionalists also were concerned that those who were returning from the "War of the Whites" had been changed by their experiences and would disrupt tribal values and traditional practices.

The elders were correct in their assessment that the war had changed the returning veterans and defense workers. As anthropologist Peter Nabokov observed, "The Indian veterans who came back to their reservations after World War II were different men. They felt worldly, returning with awareness of lands and people beyond America. They had been brothers-in-arms with non-Indians, and had learned more about their own nation in the process." It is difficult to generalize further about the experiences of those who returned to the reservations. Some returned permanently while others came to regard the reservations as halfway houses between their military service and peacetime assimilation. Many stayed on in the cities, hoping to find jobs in the booming postwar economy. Their numbers swelled the ranks of urban Indians from 24,000 in 1941 to 56,000 by 1950. When these new urbanites failed to find jobs, or were employed only temporarily, they often returned to the reservations until other opportunities became available.

The difficulties of postwar adjustment, for rural and urban Indians alike, were daunting. The war had disrupted the familiar patterns of their lives and changed their expectations in fundamental ways. Stories of maladjustment among Indian veterans became a familiar and tragic refrain in the national press. The story of Ira Hayes (Pima) came to symbolize for many Americans the failure of Indians to make a successful transition to civilian life. Hayes had gained national fame as one of the six marines who had raised the American flag on Mount Suribachi during the battle for Iwo Jima. A photograph of this dramatic scene was reproduced on millions of posters and became one of the most familiar images of the war. After the war, Hayes returned to the Pima reservation in Arizona. There he encountered a series of personal and social problems, having difficulty resuming his place in tribal society and yet unable to cope with life off the reservation. Unemployed, alcoholic, and destitute, Hayes died of exposure on a cold January night in 1955.

Fortunately, the story of Ira Hayes was not typical of the postwar experience of most Indian veterans. Many who returned to the reservations successfully ran for tribal office and became the core of a new generation of Native American leaders. The entire council of elders on the Tohono O'odham reservation resigned after the war, deferring to the leadership of the younger men who were returning home. A former code talker became a tribal judge on the Navajo reservation, and several others were elected to the council. A nineteen-year-old Sioux veteran became tribal chairman on the Lower Brule reservation. These new tribal leaders proved to be a powerful force for change, but they also were intent on preserving many aspects of traditional culture.

Although the leaders' wartime experiences increased immeasurably their exposure to the larger world, the experiences also contributed to a greater awareness and respect for the old ways of their own world. Kiowa veterans in Oklahoma revived the military Black Legs Society (*Tokonga*), singing once again the old songs and dancing the dances of their warrior ancestors. Army veteran Joseph Medicine Crow became a chief on his Montana reservation because of his deeds of heroism in Europe during the war. His deeds were performed in this most modern of wars, far from Crow country, but took on an added significance because they fulfilled the traditional requirements for tribal leadership. He later recalled:

> When I went to Germany I never thought about war honors, or the four "coups" which an old-time Crow warrior had to earn in battle. Those days were gone. But afterwards, when I came back and went through this telling of the war deeds ceremony, why, I told my war deeds, and lo and behold I completed the four requirements to become a chief.

The returning veterans became outspoken advocates for greater access to educational opportunities for Native people. Their training and work experiences during the war had convinced them of the importance of education if they were to compete successfully in the postwar economy. The Serviceman's Readjustment Act of 1944, better known as the GI Bill, provided financial aid for all veterans who wished to continue their education. One Navajo veteran later said, "the most advantageous deal that ever came through was the GI bill, and that gave me an opportunity to go to school." Hundreds of Indians enrolled in agricultural training programs and a wide variety of vocational and technical schools. Others completed their high school diplomas and went on to seek higher education at colleges and universities throughout the United States.

Returning Indian veterans and defense workers, emboldened by their experiences during the war, were impatient to obtain full rights as American citizens. Just as an earlier generation of veterans had won American citizenship following World War I, the veterans of World War II worked to remove any remaining barriers to full equality. At the war's end, provisions in the state constitutions of Arizona and New Mexico still denied Indian citizens the right to vote. Returning veterans found this continued denial of suffrage to be unacceptable. "We went to Hell and back for what?" asked one outraged Navajo veteran. "For the people back home in America to tell us we can't vote!" Other Indian veterans argued cogently, "If we are good enough to fight, why aren't we good enough to vote?" The veterans pressed their case before congressional committees and began litigation to secure their voting rights. During the summer of 1948, courts in Arizona and New Mexico decided in favor of the Indians, ruling that the constitutions of both states had violated the Indians' civil rights under the Fifteenth Amendment.

Victories in other battles were slower in coming but eventually resulted in the removal of two particularly galling barriers to full civil rights for Native Americans. Ever since the early nineteenth century, federal law had prohibited the sale of alcohol to reservation Indians, either on or off the reservation. Likewise, federal laws restricted the sale and use of firearms by Indians. Indian soldiers had been able to order alcoholic beverages in bars around the world during the war and certainly had shown great proficiency in the responsible use of firearms. After the war, Indian veterans were unwilling to have these rights denied at home. "Look," said one disabled veteran, "I have a false eye, cheekbone, a silver plate in my head, but I can't buy liquor in a bar like any American." Legislation to lift the restrictions was introduced in Congress shortly after the war, but not until 1953 did the federal government permit Indians to purchase liquor and firearms on and off the reservation.

These early postwar battles showed the renewed determination of Native Americans to participate fully in the rights and privileges of American society. Yet many Indians were equally determined to preserve and defend their own traditional cultures. At home and abroad, the war unleashed forces that hastened assimilation and also encouraged a revival of traditional cultures. Indians who served in the armed forces and worked in the defense industries were convinced they had demonstrated their loyalty and good citizenship beyond any reasonable doubt. At least 550 Indians had been killed during World War II and another 700 were wounded in action. For their meritorious wartime service, Indians received seventy-one Air Medals, fifty-one Silver Stars, forty-seven Bronze Stars, and two Congressional Medals of Honor. These Indian warriors, who had so valiantly defended their country in its time of greatest peril, expected now to enjoy the full fruits of their victory, to be able to keep what was best from their own world even as they moved into the larger world around them.

SOURCES AND SUGGESTIONS FOR FURTHER READING

The most comprehensive survey of the changing image of Native Americans is Robert F. Berkhofer, Jr., *The White Man's Indian: Images of the American Indian from Columbus to the Present* (1978). Also important for this chapter are two articles in Wilcomb E. Washburn, ed., *History of Indian-White Relations*, vol. 4, *Handbook of North American Indians* (1988): Rayna D. Green, "The Indian in Popular American Culture"; and Michael T. Marsden and Jack G. Nachbar, "The Indian in the Movies." See also Gretchen Bataille and Charles L. P. Silet, eds., *The Pretend Indians: Images of Native Americans in the Movies* (1980); Raymond W. Stedman, *Shadows of the Indian: Stereotypes in American Culture* (1982); and Angela Aleiss and Robert Appleford, "The Indian in Film," in Duane Champagne, ed., *The Native North American Almanac* (1994).

Most of the material in this chapter on the wartime experiences of Native Americans, including many of the direct quotations, is drawn from the definitive study by Alison R. Bernstein, *American Indians and World War II: Toward a New Era in Indian Affairs* (1991). The chapter's discussion of the role of the code talkers is based on the single most complete account of the Navajo contribution to the war, Doris A. Paul, *The Navajo Code Talkers* (1973), available from Dorrance Publishing Co., Inc., 643 Smithfield Street, Pittsburgh, Pennsylvania 15222. See also Lynn Escue, "Navajo Talkers and the Pacific War," *History Today* (July 1991); Margaret T. Bixler, *Winds of Freedom: The Story of the Navajo Code Talkers of World War II* (1993); and the remarkable collection of photographs in Kenji Kawano, *Warriors* (1990).

Gerald D. Nash, *The American West Transformed: The Impact of the Second World War* (1985) provides the larger context for this chapter and was the initial starting point for its conceptualization. Also useful are the firsthand accounts of wartime experiences in Peter Nabokov, ed., *Native American Testimony: A Chronicle of Indian-White Relations from Prophecy to the Present, 1492–1992* (1991). Brief summaries of the changes wrought by World War II appear in Donald L. Fixico, "Dislocated," in Philip Weeks, ed., *The American Indian Experience: A Profile 1524 to the Present* (1988) and William T. Hagan, *American Indians* (1993).

2

SOLVING THE
"INDIAN PROBLEM"

→ → → → → → →

 IN MANY WAYS, THE year 1945 marks the beginning of the modern era in American history. The United States emerged from World War II as the most powerful nation on earth, its military forces having achieved impressive victories around the globe. The old empires of Europe were fast crumbling as the peoples of Asia, the Middle East, and Africa asserted their desire to become independent nations. The United States and its superpower rival, the Soviet Union, engaged in an arms race, stockpiling weapons of mass destruction. Meanwhile, the American economy experienced a postwar boom; the gross national product more than doubled between 1945 and 1960. Yet social tensions increased dramatically as Americans confronted the continuing inequalities of race and class.

In Indian affairs, 1945 was an important year if for no other reason than John Collier resigned as commissioner of the federal government's Bureau of Indian Affairs (BIA). Collier had held the post longer than any other person and was the European American who had the greatest impact on the direction of federal Indian policy in the twentieth century. To appreciate the importance of Collier and his legacy in the second half of the century, it is necessary first to understand something of the background of what came to be called America's "Indian problem": the question of what place (if any) Native Americans should have in the life of the nation.

REMOVAL, RESERVATIONS, AND ALLOTMENT

Proposed solutions to the Indian problem varied tremendously over the decades as competing interests sought to guide American policy. Throughout much of the nation's early history, the dominant interests were European Americans who coveted Indian lands and vigorously supported various strategies of dispossession. Other outspoken European Americans were sympathetic to the Indians and sought to protect them from mistreatment and exploitation; their ardent hope was that the Indian problem could be solved by the assimilation of the Native people into the dominant society. It is hardly surprising that the European Americans who sought to dispossess the Indians and those who wished to protect them were often in conflict, but on many occasions these disparate interests also found themselves in concert, working together in support of the same policy.

During the colonial period, the charters of most English settlements in North America contained instructions to the colonists to convert and "civilize" the Indians. Missionaries and others worked diligently to fulfill these colonial mandates, but they eventually abandoned the effort when they discovered it was far more difficult to separate the Indians from their Native cultures than they had at first imagined. Their early optimism that rapid assimilation was possible soon gave way to policies of segregation and discriminatory legislation. Violent conflicts erupted all along the colonies' western borders as white settlements pressed forward onto Indian lands.

Following the American Revolution and the formation of the new nation, the U.S. Constitution delegated to the federal government the exclusive right to manage Indian affairs. Congress passed a series of acts in the late eighteenth century to regulate trade and intercourse with the Indians and to restrict white encroachment on their lands, but the pressure from settlers and speculators for the opening of new lands was unrelenting. Responding to that pressure, the federal government adopted a policy of removing Indians from areas east of the Mississippi River to new territories in the west. The removal policy originated during the administration of Thomas Jefferson and rested, at first, on the voluntary cooperation of eastern tribes who agreed through treaties to an exchange of territory. The policy later took on a more coercive character under the presidency of Andrew Jackson, culminating in the 1830s with the forced march of the Cherokees of Georgia and other southeastern tribes to lands west of the Mississippi. More than 4,000 Indian men, women, and children—about one-quarter of the Cherokee people—died during the journey. This "trail of tears," as the survivors called their forced removal, became an enduring symbol of white injustice.

Even though the removal policy was often brutal and insensitive to the rights of Native Americans, many sympathetic European Americans regarded it as a necessary step toward Indian assimilation. They believed that the slow process of "civilization and Christianization" could take place only if Indians were removed far from contact with vicious whites on the frontier. Whatever the complex motives that lay behind the removal policy, its effect was to relocate thousands of Indians, either voluntarily or under duress, from lands desired by whites. By the middle of the nineteenth century, most eastern tribes had been moved west of what was called the "permanent Indian frontier," a line extending from Texas to the Great Lakes.

The rapid settlement of the territories on the Pacific slope, following the discovery of gold in California in 1848, suddenly and forever rendered the removal policy obsolete. Just when European Americans believed that they had finally solved the Indian problem, it came roaring back as a matter of pressing national concern. No longer was it possible to remove Indians farther west because beyond California there was no more west. The federal government thus was compelled to design an alternative method for handling its Indian population. That alternative, as it evolved in the 1850s and 1860s, was to concentrate Native people on lands reserved for their exclusive use. Government agents signed treaties with dozens of Indian tribes, guaranteeing them certain rights and privileges in exchange for their surrendering claims to vast stretches of land. The tribes then were required to reside permanently on the government reservations; if they attempted to leave, armed force was used to bring them back. Resistance from zealous Native patriots—like Sitting Bull of the Sioux and Geronimo of the Apaches—was often spectacular but ultimately unsuccessful. Congress in 1871 halted the process of treaty making, bringing to a close an era in which the federal government had negotiated 389 treaties with Indian tribes. By the 1870s the United States had contained its Indian problem on isolated reservations throughout the far west.

The reservation policy, like the removal policy that preceded it, enjoyed for a time the support of European Americans who desired Indian lands as well as those who wished to protect and assimilate the Indians. The concentration of Indians on the reservations opened millions of acres of land for white settlement from the Mississippi to the Pacific, from Canada to Mexico. Once again Indians were moved from lands desired by whites, but at the same time the Indians were being prepared for assimilation. Agents from the Office of Indian Affairs (later the Bureau of Indian Affairs) supervised programs on the reservations to teach Native people basic skills that would enable them someday to take their place in European American society. Teachers arrived on the reservations accompanied by farm implements and instruction booklets to introduce the residents to commercial agriculture as practiced by European Americans. Reservation Indians also were subjected to enormous pressures to divest themselves of their cultural heritage. Government agents cooperated with local missionaries to suppress Native American rituals and religious practices. They banned the Sun Dance on the Ute and Shoshone reservations, prohibited the Pueblos from continuing their initiation rites for the young, and forced the Arapahos to give up their vision quests.

Support for the reservation policy diminished as European Americans became frustrated with both its administration and its accomplishments. It soon became apparent that the management of the reservation system was riddled with fraud and corruption. In an effort at reform, President Ulysses S. Grant in the 1870s adopted the "Quaker policy" of appointing individuals nominated by the Society of Friends and other religious denominations to reservation posts. In spite of some modest improvements, reformers were deeply disappointed at the slow progress the reservation Indians seemed to be making toward assimilation. Many who had originally supported the reservations as a means of achieving Indian assimilation in a single generation were dumbfounded by the Native Americans' tenacity in holding on to their traditional ways of life. Reluctantly they concluded that the reservations were cultural failures. European Americans who came to see the reservations as economic failures also expressed dissatisfaction. Powerful interests that had formerly supported the reservations as a means of opening new lands for white development now sought access to the reservation lands as well. Railroads demanded rights-of-way across reservations, cattle ranchers wanted more grazing land, and speculators found it intolerable that a few impotent tribes should be allowed to monopolize so much valuable real estate.

From these frustrations and disappointments a new federal Indian policy was born. Yet another solution to the perennial Indian problem was to be tried, called *allotment*. Reformers and others in the 1880s began to lobby for breaking up the reservations by allotting a portion of their lands to individual Indians and selling the "surplus" on the open market. Allotment had the enthusiastic support of land-hungry European Americans for obvious reasons. And reformers, who had lost faith in the reservations, supported the new policy as the most effective means yet of achieving their erstwhile goal of Indian assimilation. As historians James S. Olson and Raymond Wilson, authors of *Native Americans in the Twentieth Century* (1984), observed, "By isolating Native Americans on reservations the government was [thought to be] perpetuating tribal values, poverty, and economic dependence. Only in the absence of tribal values and government assistance, the reformers believed, could Native Americans be reasonably expected to shed their own culture."

On February 8, 1887, Congress passed a key piece of legislation in the history of federal Indian policy. Sponsored by Senator Henry L. Dawes of Massachusetts, it was known as the General Allotment Act or simply the Dawes Act. The law called for the allotting of reservation lands to Indian heads of families in 160-acre parcels. Single adults received eighty acres each, and each single youth got forty acres. To prevent Indians from immediately selling their newly acquired property to speculators, the title to their allotted lands was to be held in trust by the federal government for a period of twenty-five years. Once the Indians accepted their allotments, they were granted American citizenship and made subject to the laws of the state in which they lived. All remaining lands not allotted to Indians could be sold to whites by the federal government as "surplus."

To hasten the assimilation process, the Bureau of Indian Affairs intensified its efforts to educate Indians in the ways of European American society. The BIA established off-reservation boarding schools where Indian children were subjected to strict discipline. The children were shorn and dressed in the style of European Americans, forced to speak English and give up their Native languages, encouraged to accept Christianity and deny their own religions, and required to learn new work habits and skills. This triple assault on traditional Indian culture—allotment, citizenship, and education—was greeted with the same enthusiasm that the reservation policy had received earlier. Reformers once again expected full assimilation to be achieved within a single generation.

Allotment was vigorously opposed by many Native Americans who feared it would have a devastating impact on their lands and ways of life. The objections to the act by some tribes—including the Creeks and Cherokees of Indian Territory, the Senecas of New York, and the Sioux in Nebraska—were so strong that they were specifically exempted from its provisions. The fears of the Native Americans were well founded. More than 32,000 allotments were made between 1887 and 1900, granting about 3.3 million acres of former reservation lands to individual Indians. During these same years, 28.5 million acres were declared "surplus" by the federal government and sold to whites. The pace of allotment accelerated in the early twentieth century. Congress in 1906 passed the Burke Act, eliminating the twenty-five year trust period for individual Native Americans who were deemed competent by the secretary of the interior to manage their own affairs. Subsequent legislation made it even easier for Indians to sell their lands. By 1934, when the allotment policy was finally abandoned, the amount of land held by Native Americans had plummeted from 138 million to 48 million acres, a loss of nearly two-thirds in less than fifty years.

The allotment policy was a bonanza for European Americans who gained control of valuable mineral resources, timber lands, and grazing ranges on the former reservations. It was an unmitigated disaster, however, for the Native Americans. The federal government "freed" the Indians from the reservations, but failed to provide them with the financial resources needed for economic survival. About half of the property retained by Indians was arid or desert land not fit for farming. Native people whose allotments included productive lands often were "grafted" out of their holdings by unscrupulous whites whose tactics included everything from deceit to murder. Equally as distressing to those European Americans who had supported allotment as the ultimate solution to the Indian problem, the division of lands seemed to be having no more effect in assimilating Indians than had the reservation policy which preceded it. Historian William T. Hagan sagely observed that allotment "may not have civilized the Indian, but it definitely corrupted most of the white men who had any contact with it."

By the early 1920s the ill effects of allotment were clear: Indian lands and tribal stability had declined dramatically, poverty and disease had increased, and complete assimilation remained only a distant goal. In 1926 the Department of the Interior commissioned a team of respected scholars, headed by anthropologist Lewis Meriam of the University of Chicago, to conduct an independent and comprehensive investigation of Indian affairs. The resulting Meriam report, officially known as *Problems of Indian Administration* (1928), recommended sweeping changes in federal Indian policy. It called for an abandonment of the allotment policy and a phasing out of Indian boarding schools. It also recommended across-the-board improvements in services provided by the BIA and the hiring of more Native Americans to work for the agency. President Herbert Hoover responded in a manner reminiscent of Grant's "Quaker policy" a half century earlier; he appointed two Quakers to head the BIA and charged them with implementing the recommendations of the Meriam report. Unfortunately, the economic collapse of 1929 and the ensuing depression meant that few substantive reforms were achieved during the remaining years of the Hoover administration.

THE COLLIER ERA

One of the most outspoken critics of the federal government's allotment policy was a social worker and community organizer named John Collier. Born in Georgia in 1884, Collier worked among the immigrants of New York City in the early 1900s. There he developed a deep appreciation for the importance of cultural traditions and community values among the city's various ethnic groups. Collier also became increasingly disturbed by many of his fellow European Americans' intolerance and mean-spirited demands for conformity. The destruction unleashed by World War I further convinced him that Western Civilization was bent on destroying itself through the pursuit of such competitive values as individualism and materialism. Propelled by a growing sense of disillusionment and alienation, Collier traveled in 1920 to New Mexico. There he discovered his "Red Atlantis," isolated villages of Pueblo Indians still living communal lives with their ancient traditions intact after centuries of assault by outside influences.

John Collier soon learned that the latest threat to the Pueblos was the federal government's allotment policy. Using his best community-organizing skills, Collier helped establish the All-Pueblo Council to lobby successfully against proposed legislation that would have deprived the Indians of much of their land and water rights without just compensation. Encouraged by this early success, Collier became executive secretary of the newly formed American Indian Defense Association (AIDA) in 1923. Over the next decade, Collier and the AIDA were in the vanguard of the Indian reform movement. They called for a radical change in federal Indian policy: Allotment should be replaced by the preservation of remaining reservation lands through communal ownership, and forced assimilation should be abandoned in favor of the protection of traditional Indian cultures.

The election of Franklin D. Roosevelt to the presidency in 1932 ushered in an unprecedented time of economic and political reform. His selection of Harold Ickes, a charter member of the American Indian Defense Association, to serve as secretary of the interior, and John Collier to head the Bureau of Indian Affairs indicated the new president's desire to reform the nation's Indian policy as well. Commissioner Collier immediately began to redirect the agency under his supervision. He abolished many of the BIA regulations that restricted the civil liberties of Native Americans, insisting that henceforth the federal government would no longer attempt to suppress Indian traditions nor require Indian children to attend Christian religious services. He also reversed the long-standing policy of placing Indian children in boarding schools far from their parents. Collier believed that the children should be educated in day schools on or near the reservations where Native languages and customs would be respected and encouraged, not prohibited.

John Collier realized that the reforms he achieved by administrative decree could easily be reversed by future commissioners. To achieve more lasting change, he drafted and submitted to Congress legislation that would alter fundamentally the nation's Indian policy. Introduced by Senator Burton K. Wheeler of Montana and Representative Edgar Howard of Nebraska, Collier's proposed legislation was revised considerably by a skeptical Congress before it was passed into law on June 18, 1934. The Indian Reorganization Act (IRA), also known as the Wheeler-Howard Act or the Indian New Deal, was the most important statement of federal Indian policy in the twentieth century.

The Indian Reorganization Act contained three key provisions. First, it ended the allotment policy that had been the foundation of federal policy for nearly half a century. Furthermore, all remaining "surplus" lands not yet sold to whites were to be returned to tribal control. To prevent the further loss of lands owned by individuals, the act extended indefinitely the federal government's trust period on ex-

COMMISSIONER JOHN COLLIER OF THE BUREAU OF INDIAN AFFAIRS CONFERS
WITH SEMINOLE LEADERS IN FLORIDA. COLLIER DIRECTED FEDERAL POLICY
AWAY FROM ENFORCED ACCULTURATION AND TOWARD GREATER CULTURAL
PLURALISM. HE SERVED AS BIA COMMISSIONER LONGER THAN ANY OTHER
INDIVIDUAL, FROM 1933 TO 1945.

isting allotments. The second provision of the IRA was its encouragement of Native Americans to reconstitute their tribal governments.
Funds were made available to assist tribes in drafting constitutions and
incorporating themselves for economic development. The powers of
the tribes, however, were not absolute and many of their political and
economic activities remained subject to approval by the secretary of
the interior. The IRA's third major provision was its expansion of educational and employment opportunities for Native Americans. A loan
fund was established for Indian students and school facilities were up-
graded and reoriented. The act also provided for the preferential hiring
of Native Americans within the BIA.

Collier was disappointed that Congress deleted from the final draft
of the IRA an explicit statement that the federal government should
also promote "Indian arts, crafts, skills, and traditions." He did win
passage, however, of separate legislation establishing within the Interior Department an Indian Arts and Crafts Board. This board was
authorized to help Native people form cooperatives of craftsmen and

artists, establish standards of workmanship, and authenticate items of genuine Indian manufacture.

Working through the maze of other New Deal agencies created by the Roosevelt administration, Collier became adept at securing additional aid for Native Americans. He obtained a million acres of "submarginal lands" for Indian use from the Resettlement and Farm Security administrations. From the Public Works Administration he obtained more than $100 million for road building and soil conservation projects on the reservations. The Works Project Administration provided Collier with additional relief funds for unemployed Indians. He also fashioned a separate program for the training and employment of young Indian men, modeled on the Civilian Conservation Corps. The Emergency Conservation Works provided jobs for Indians in resource development, forestry, and soil conservation on the reservations.

In approving the Indian Reorganization Act, Congress stipulated that before the act applied to a reservation it first had to be ratified by the reservation's voters. As usual, Native Americans expressed a wide range of opinions as they debated the pros and cons of the new policy. Assimilationists and mixed-bloods generally (but far from unanimously) favored ratifying the IRA, while many traditionalists and full-bloods argued against it. One hundred and eighty-one tribes, with a combined population of nearly 130,000 individuals, ultimately voted to accept the IRA; and seventy-eight tribes, with a total population of about 86,000, rejected it. Some of the largest tribes—including the Navajos of the Southwest, the Crows of Montana, and the Klamaths of Oregon—were among those who voted against the act. Once a tribe ratified the IRA, the Bureau of Indian Affairs dispatched teams of lawyers to the reservations to assist in the drafting of a formal constitution or charter for incorporation. The Indian bureau also prepared a model tribal constitution, outlining a form of representative government complete with procedures for holding elections and definitions of the powers of the tribal councils.

In assessing the significance of John Collier and the Indian Reorganization Act, it is important to keep several factors in mind. First, the IRA halted the assault on Indian lands that had been underway for three centuries. The earlier policies of removal, reservations, and allotment had all significantly reduced Native lands, opening them for sale and dispersal to European Americans. By contrast, the IRA increased the amount of land under the control of Native Americans. Yet the amount of increase was four million acres, modest in comparison to the enormous losses suffered by Native people in the past. The IRA also was a significant step away from the prevailing "melting-pot" philosophy of assimilationism that had guided all previous policy. Collier brought to the BIA a measure of cultural pluralism that had not been seen before, but he did not abandon assimilation as an ultimate goal. He believed that the preservation of traditional Native cultures, in the critical period before assimilation was complete, was essential for the survival and social stability of the Indian people. The Indian Reorganization Act also was an important step toward self-government for Native Americans. The reconstitution of tribal governments repaired much of the damage caused by the allotment policy and by decades of neglect. Yet the IRA by no means eliminated the paternalism inherent in the long-standing relationship between the federal government and the Indian tribes; the powers of the newly formed tribal governments were still tightly proscribed by federal oversight. Finally, the material conditions of Native Americans improved markedly during Collier's years as BIA commissioner. The expansion of Indian health services halved the mortality rate among Native people and improved methods of cultivation significantly enhanced the productivity of Indian lands.

John Collier's term as commissioner of the Bureau of Indian Affairs was longer than any other in American history. He accomplished a great deal but also incurred the wrath of many enemies. By 1945 he was tired and not a little disgusted; his polices seemed to be under attack from all sides. Powerful economic interests, especially in the states of the far west, opposed Collier's unwavering protection of Native American resources. Mining and timber companies, along with European American ranchers and farmers, complained that Collier was retarding the nation's economic development by making it difficult or impossible to gain further access to Indian lands. Collier could take some comfort from these complaints, for he believed that one of the main responsibilities of the BIA was to protect Indians from the aggrandizing interests that had so often deprived them of their lands in the past. More hurtful to Collier were the criticisms he received from his former colleagues in the Indian reform movement. The Indian Rights Association denounced Collier because his policies seemed to be perpetuating the segregation of Native people, keeping them forever separate from the mainstream of American society. Likewise, the National Council of Churches, another staunch advocate of Indian rights, faulted Collier for hindering rather than promoting Indian assimilation.

Commissioner Collier was pained especially by the criticisms he received from Native Americans. Traditionalists complained that the new tribal governments imposed alien and unacceptable forms of governance. They chaffed under the continuing requirement that tribal decisions had to be approved by the secretary of the interior or other federal officials. From the opposite extreme, Collier faced even stronger censure from assimilated Indians who charged that his policies represented a "return to the blanket." The assimilationists believed that Collier's revitalization of tribal governments hampered the ability of individual Indians to compete successfully in the national economy. John St. Pierre (Yankton Sioux) argued that Collier's policies interfered with the Indians' "right of individual enterprise or private enterprise." Contemporary Native Americans, according to St. Pierre, wanted to "intermingle" and be associated with whites: "We do not want to be segregated and kept off by ourselves because that tends to lead the development of Indians back to the blanket, and that will not be the solution of this Indian problem." Collier's most vocal critics were Alice Lee Jemison (Seneca) and Joseph Bruner (Creek), leaders of the fiercely pro-assimilationist American Indian Federation. Bruner denounced Collier's encouragement of tribal governments as "communistic, subversive, and dangerous to our Nation, not only among the Indians, but all other Americans." Collier's support for Native religious beliefs and practices was denounced by assimilated Indians as unchristian and "Christ-mocking." The assimilationists' attack reached a rhetorical climax when one mixed-blood from Oregon characterized Collier as a "Jew-loving Pink Red."

Throughout his long tenure at the Bureau of Indian Affairs, Collier also faced a steady stream of criticism from hostile members of Congress. BIA programs were routinely underfunded and subjected to close scrutiny by skeptical members of the congressional committees charged with overseeing Indian affairs. Because of a wartime shortage of office space in the nation's capital—and over Collier's vehement objections—the bureau's headquarters were moved to Chicago in the early months of 1942. The following year the Senate Indian Affairs Committee recommended that the BIA be stripped of all its essential functions, and Republican Congressman Karl Mundt of South Dakota called for a thorough investigation of Indian affairs and suggested that the BIA be abolished entirely. In 1944 the House Committee on Indian Affairs handed Collier a stinging rebuff by calling for a complete reversal of the policies he had pursued over the past decade. Disheartened by this constant barrage of criticism, John Collier resigned in January 1945.

In the years since his resignation, John Collier has remained an exceedingly controversial figure. He has been praised and damned with equal fervor, but few deny his central importance. His tenure at the BIA defined an era in American Indian affairs. As Vine Deloria, Jr. (Standing Rock Sioux) and Clifford Lytle, authors of *The Nations Within: The Past and Future of American Indian Sovereignty* (1984), pointed out, in spite of all the withering criticisms endured by John Collier, "the fact remains that the man engineered a complete revolution in Indian affairs." Indeed, much of the subsequent fifteen years of Indian policy may be considered as a "counterrevolution" against Collier's policies, just as the preceding half century may be regarded as the *status quo ante bellum*, or the "pre-revolutionary" era.

THE TRAUMA OF TERMINATION

The resignation of John Collier was followed within three months by the death of President Roosevelt and the departure the next year of Secretary of the Interior Harold Ickes. These three leaders had dominated Indian affairs for more than a decade and their removal signaled a shift in the leadership of federal Indian policy from the executive to the legislative branch. Collier's successor at the BIA, William Brophy, was ill during most of his three years in office. Brophy's replacement, John Nichols, resigned after serving only one year.

The first major statement of postwar Congressional policy for Native Americans was the creation in 1946 of the Indian Claims Commission (ICC). The ICC was a special federal agency before which Indian tribes could file claims against the government of the United States for the settlement of past grievances. Its creation was the result of an odd coalition of Native Americans and European Americans representing a wide range of interests. The Meriam report of 1928 had recommended the establishment of such a commission, and John Collier had lobbied unsuccessfully for its creation throughout his tenure at the BIA. Commissioner William Brophy continued to urge its establishment, observing early in 1946 that for years many Indian tribes had claimed that the United States "has become indebted to them, and that they have just claims against the United States Government." Indeed, the National Congress of American Indians (NCAI) and thousands of individual Native Americans had petitioned the government for just compensation for lands taken from them in the past. Likewise, many organizations of European Americans sympathetic to the Indians joined in the call for the creation of a claims commission as a matter of simple justice.

When Democratic President Harry Truman signed the Indian Claims Commission Act in August 1946, he hailed it as "the beginning of a new era" for Native Americans. "I am glad to sign my name to a measure which removes a lingering discrimination against our first Americans," Truman said. The president cited the wartime service of Indian soldiers as further justification for the creation of the commission. Their loyal and valiant service "on every battle front" proved "the wisdom of a national policy built upon fair-dealing."

The most persuasive voices calling for the creation of the Indian Claims Commission were conservative members of Congress who viewed compensation as the necessary prerequisite for yet another fundamental shift in federal Indian policy. Their watchword was *termination* and they hoped that by settling, once and for all, any remaining grievances of Native Americans, the federal government could terminate its special relationship with Indian tribes and at last "get out of the Indian business." They favored the rapid assimilation of Indians into the mainstream and believed that compensation would provide Indians with the necessary resources for them to survive on their own without any further federal assistance. Compensation and termination were thus enthusiastically embraced as the latest solution to the Indian problem.

The Indian Claims Commission was a three-member board (later expanded to five members) before which any "tribe, band, or identifiable group" could file its claim. The proceedings were conducted according to regular federal court proceedings, with the attorney general defending the government and private attorneys representing the Indians on a contingency fee basis. (Congress limited the attorneys' fees to 10 percent of any final judgment.) The vast bulk of cases the Indian Claims Commission handled were claims that the federal government had taken Indian lands without paying fair market value. The procedure for settling the claims involved several separate stages, each filled with difficulties. The claimants first had to prove they were the descendants of the people who had occupied the land "from time immemorial" or when it was taken by the federal government. Establishing such proof was exceedingly difficult because of the mobility of the tribes and their rivalry with neighboring groups. Once the legitimacy of the claimants was established, the commission had to determine the fair market value of the land when it was appropriated. This too was a complex matter because land values of a century or more ago were open to widely varying interpretations. Finally, the commission had to determine the value of any goods and services provided to the tribe by the federal government over the years. This "offset" was deducted from the amount of the Indians' award.

The Indian Claims Commission originally was scheduled to complete its work in ten years and then cease to exist. The volume of cases, however, required several extensions of the deadline. By the time the commission finally expired in 1978, it had awarded more than $800 million in 285 individual cases out of the approximately 850 filed originally. The average amount per claim was about $3 million, which meant that individual Indians usually received only a few thousand dollars from their tribe's award. In one of the largest cases, the ICC awarded the Indians of California more than $29 million (an amount later increased by interest). Distributed on a per capita basis, this meant that each eligible California Native received a check for $668.51. As anthropologist Nancy Oestreich Lurie observed, "From [the Indians'] point of view, it must appear that the federal mountain labored long and mightily to bring forth a pretty paltry mouse." As paltry as the awards may have seemed to individual Indians, critics of the commission regarded the awards as far too generous. Republican Congressman Blake Clarke asked, "Why must we buy America from the Indians all over again?"

Dispersal of the awards often provoked bitter debate among the tribes. Many full-bloods and traditionalists favored tribal management of the awards, while mixed-bloods and assimilationists (especially those living off the reservation) favored the immediate distribution of the awards on a per capita basis. If a per capita distribution was agreed upon, as most often was the case, the question of tribal membership then had to be resolved. Although each tribe had its own roll of members, the rolls often were incomplete or out of date. Standards of "degrees of blood" also varied, but most tribes required at least one-quarter "blood" to be an enrolled member. Once the Indian Claims Commission announced its awards, tribal roles often expanded dramatically. Shortly before the Miamis were awarded $8 million in 1960, their roll of tribal members included only 317 names. A few years later the list had grown to include more than 3,000 individuals. Naturally enough, many tribal members resented their fellow tribesmen who decided to declare their identity only when a monetary reward was available.

Full-bloods and traditionalists sometimes rejected the claims settlements altogether, arguing that no amount of money could properly compensate them for the lands they had lost. What they wanted was a return of their ancestral lands, not a check from the government. But the Indian Claims Commission Act had expressly provided that all "valid claims would be paid in money. No lands would be returned to a tribe." When the ICC awarded the Taos Pueblo a settlement of $10 million in 1965 for the loss of Blue Lake and surrounding lands in northwestern New Mexico, tribal leaders refused to accept the award. The Taos people believed that the lake was where the spirits of the dead dwelled and where all life originated. "My people will not sell our Blue Lake that is our church," said Taos leader Paul Bernal. "We cannot sell what is sacred. It is not ours to sell." Likewise, the Pit River people of California refused to accept an ICC award of forty-seven cents an acre for lands taken from them in the gold rush. They rejected the cash settlement and insisted on the return of their lands. Evidently what many European Americans had hoped would be a satisfactory (and final) solution to the Indian problem was not acceptable to all Native Americans.

Compensation remained popular among its congressional supporters as an essential first step in the implementation of the termination policy. Termination had many component parts, but it was essentially a withdrawal by the federal government of all relations with the Indian tribes. It sought to "detribalize" or "individualize" Native Americans by phasing out tribal governments and subjecting Indians to the laws and taxes of the states in which they lived. Federal trust protection of Indian lands was to be removed, tribal assets would be transferred or sold, and individual Indians would be granted title to their lands in "fee simple" (meaning they would own their lands with unrestricted rights of disposition). Indians would thus take their place in American society alongside their fellow citizens with the same rights, privileges, and responsibilities. The termination policy was designed to free the Indians from federal control while at the same time it freed the federal government from much of its responsibility for Indian affairs. The policy was at once liberating and destructive. As Native historian Donald L. Fixico (Creek/Seminole/Shawnee/Sac and Fox), author of *Termination and Relocation: Federal Indian Policy, 1945–1960* (1986), concluded, "termination essentially implied the ultimate destruction of tribal cultures and native life-styles, as withdrawal of federal services was intended to desegregate Indian communities and to integrate Indians with the rest of society."

As with so many of the earlier twists in federal Indian policy, termination represented a confluence of many diverse motives and interests. One of the major contributing factors to the drive for termination was the experience of Native people during World War II. Many European Americans concluded that since Indians had adapted so well to the wartime emergency they were ready and able to assimilate fully into mainstream society. Termination also reflected the postwar determination of liberal reformers to end racial discrimination in American life. As the civil rights movement gained momentum to end the segregation of African Americans in the nation's armed forces, schools, and neighborhoods, interest also grew in ending the special status of Native Americans. Reformers came to see the reservations as "rural ghettos" where Indians were unjustly segregated from the rest of American society. The campaign for termination drew support as well from the opposite end of the political spectrum, from conservatives who were caught up in the postwar mania of anticommunism. The McCarthy era was a time when conformity and consensus became synonymous with good citizenship, and the drive to "Americanize" Indians fit neatly into the national mood of fear and intolerance. Conservatives in Congress also were determined to reduce the size and scope of the federal government. Eliminating special programs for Indians seemed to be a good way to begin paring down the costly federal bureaucracy that had proliferated during the years of depression and world war. Termination was related as well to the postwar boom in the American economy. Land developers and other economic interests supported termination because it would make it possible (once again) for European Americans to acquire Indian lands.

The Bureau of Indian Affairs got its first "termination-minded" commissioner in May 1950, when President Truman appointed Dillon S. Myer to the post. Myer had served previously as director of the War Relocation Authority, the agency that operated the wartime internment camps for Japanese Americans. His experiences there convinced him that only complete assimilation would safeguard the nation from future outbreaks of ethnic conflict. Myer's enthusiasm for the rapid assimilation of Native Americans led him to reverse many of the policies of John Collier. He closed reservation day schools and reestabished the practice of placing Indian children in distant boarding schools where they would be separated from their tribal cultures and taught the ways of European Americans. He also attacked the Indian Arts and Crafts Board established by Collier, denying that Native Americans even possessed "legitimate cultures." He regarded tribal governments as anachronisms and sought to diminish their power and influence. Myer removed any BIA personnel whom he suspected of harboring sympathies for "cultural pluralism" and replaced them with appointees who shared his undaunted faith in termination and assimilation.

The election of Republican Dwight Eisenhower as president in 1952 did not mark a dramatic break in the nation's Indian policy. Just before leaving office in March 1953, Dillon Myer worked to insure the continuation of his policies by helping the new administration draft a letter to Congress endorsing termination. Eisenhower's choice for commissioner of the Bureau of Indian Affairs was Glenn Emmons, a banker from New Mexico who shared Myer's commitment to getting the federal government "out of the Indian business."

Termination became official congressional policy on August 1, 1953, with the passage of House Concurrent Resolution 108. Although a concurrent resolution is not enforceable as law, it is binding on Congress as a statement of general intent. Congress unanimously passed the resolution with little apparent consideration of the significance of this fundamental reformulation of federal Indian policy. HCR 108 stated that it was the intent of Congress to make Indians "subject to the same laws and entitled to the same privileges and responsibilities as are applicable to other citizens of the United States." Furthermore, the Indians' status as "wards of the United States" was to be ended as rapidly as possible. The resolution also listed specific tribes and groups of Indians from which federal services were to be withdrawn "at the earliest possible time." The list included tribes located in California, Florida, Texas, and New York, as well as the Menominees in Wisconsin, the Klamaths in Oregon, the Flathead tribe of Montana, and the Potawatomis in Kansas and Nebraska.

One of the key supporters of House Concurrent Resolution 108 was Senator Arthur V. Watkins of Utah. He explained to his congressional colleagues that the removal of federal trust protection over Indian lands also would eliminate their tax exempt status. Indians who opposed termination, he believed, were being selfish. "They want all the benefits of the things we have, highways, schools, hospitals, everything that civilization furnished, but they don't want to help pay their share of it." Watkins compared the resolution to the Emancipation Proclamation, arguing that it would liberate Indians to join the mainstream of American society. Commissioner Emmons heartily endorsed HCR 108 as "one of the most valuable and salutary Congressional measures we have had in Indian Affairs for a great many years."

Two weeks after the passage of House Concurrent Resolution 108, Congress enacted a companion piece of legislation that furthered the process of termination. Known simply as Public Law 280, the act placed many of the Indian lands of California, Nebraska, Oregon, Minnesota, and Wisconsin under the civil and criminal jurisdiction of their respective states. The act also authorized other states unilaterally to extend jurisdiction over the Indians within their boundaries whenever they chose to do so. President Eisenhower signed PL 280 with some reluctance. He hailed it as "another step in granting equality to all Indians in our nation," but he criticized the act for not providing for Indian consent. He urged Congress to amend the law to require the consent of the Indians who were to be placed under state jurisdiction. Congress considered several such amendments, but none was passed.

The implementation of termination began in earnest in 1954 when the Indian subcommittees of the House and Senate met in an unprecedented joint session to consider a number of withdrawal bills. The subcommittees took the extraordinary step of meeting jointly to insure the rapid passage of their proposed legislation in unaltered form. Their strategy was effective, and Congress passed a flurry of termination acts in the mid-1950s. The various termination acts differed in detail, but typically included a statement terminating the federal trust relationship with the former tribal members. Congress routinely revoked the tribal constitutions and dissolved the tribal governments. All laws and agreements of the United States that applied to Indians because of their status as Indians were no longer applicable to the terminated individuals, nor were such individuals entitled to any of the federal services provided to Native people because of their status as Indians. All former tribal members were subject to the jurisdiction of the states in which they lived.

In the critical matter of land ownership, the termination acts usually provided the tribes with a choice. They could either transfer title of tribal properties to a trustee of their own choosing, or they could sell their assets and distribute the proceeds among the former tribal members. Federal trust restrictions also were removed from the lands held by individual tribal members. Once they had title to their land in "fee simple," they were free to dispose of their property in whatever manner they chose. Freedom from federal control, of course, also meant freedom from their former tax-exempt status. Indian property owners were obligated henceforth to pay all applicable taxes on their lands.

The initial reaction of Native Americans to termination varied widely, reflecting intertribal and intratribal differences. As expected, some mixed-bloods and assimilated individuals welcomed the removal of trust status over their lands and the elimination of other federal controls over their lives. But as the results of termination became clear, many Native people came to regard termination as a harmful and destructive policy. Tribal leaders were especially concerned that termination threatened the viability of treaties that had guaranteed Indian rights for decades. Several tribal councils—including those of the Tohono O'odhams, San Carlos Apaches, and Pine Ridge Sioux—voted to condemn the termination policy. "Today some people in Congress and the Department of the Interior would destroy our people with laws which divide us, endanger our property, and violate the provisions of our sacred treaties," observed one Apache leader. "We will not let this happen."

Many individual Native Americans feared that termination would simply set them adrift. Emms Kolina (Montana Chippewa) voiced the concern of many when she testified, "We can't make it without the Federal Government. A few of us have made it maybe but not whole tribes . . . my own tribe could not make it." Among the Osage were dozens of younger tribal members who were confident they could handle termination with little difficulty. But Osage Chief Fred Lookout was concerned that termination would expose older members to exploitation. Opposition to termination was expressed by full-bloods and traditionalists in virtually every tribe. One of the most eloquent statements of opposition came from Earl Old Person, a leader of the Blackfeet:

> It is important to note that in our Indian language the only translation for termination is to "wipe out" or "kill off." . . . How can we plan our future when the Indian Bureau threatens to wipe us out as a race? It is like trying to cook a meal in your tipi when someone is standing outside trying to burn the tipi down.

Opponents summed up their sentiments with the remark that "termination means *ex*-termination."

The fight against termination was led by the National Congress of American Indians (NCAI) and its chairman, Joseph Garry, a World War II veteran and head of the Coeur d'Alene tribal council. In February 1954 Garry organized an emergency conference of more than forty tribes to plan an effective lobbying campaign against termination. The NCAI based its opposition on two fundamental principles. First, it maintained that termination abrogated long-standing treaties between the tribes and the federal government. The NCAI charged that Congress was pursuing "a one-sided approach to free the government of responsibilities and obligations guaranteed in treaties and agreements with [the Indian tribes]." Second, the NCAI asserted that termination violated the principle of the consent of the governed. It argued that Indians had the right to "maintain ownership of the reservations in our own way, and to terminate it only by our consent."

The concerted opposition of Native Americans slowed the pace of termination, but not before several tribes had suffered its disastrous consequences. One of the first tribes to be terminated were the Menominees of Wisconsin. In June 1954 President Eisenhower signed legislation ending all federal services to the Menominee people and removing federal trust restrictions from their lands. The Menominees were a prosperous tribe and appeared to be good candidates for successful termination. They recently had been awarded $8.5 million in claims from the federal government; they also owned valuable timber lands and operated a successful lumber mill.

Although the federal government was not legally obligated to obtain the consent of Indians scheduled for termination, in practice federal officials attempted to secure their voluntary approval. When termination was presented to the Menominees in a special referendum, it was approved unanimously by fewer than 200 tribal members who cast a ballot. Some of those who voted in favor of termination had a clear understanding of the issue and concluded that it was in their best interest to be independent of federal control. Others approved termination under the mistaken belief that they were voting only to accept the $1,500 per capita distribution of the tribe's federal claims settlement. Some were so perplexed by the issue that they thought the federal government would withdraw services to them unless they voted *in favor* of termination. It is probably fair to say that most of the 3,254 members of the tribe wanted to have nothing to do with termination.

DURING THE TERMINATION ERA OF THE 1950S, SECRETARY OF THE INTERIOR J. A. KRUG SIGNED A DOCUMENT PERMITTING THE CONSTRUCTION OF A PROJECT THAT WOULD FLOOD LANDS ALONG THE MISSOURI RIVER THAT HAD BEEN OC-CUPIED FOR MORE THAN A THOUSAND YEARS BY THE TRIBES OF NORTH DA-KOTA. HIDATSA LEADER GEORGE GILLETTE WEEPS AS THE DOCUMENT IS SIGNED.

The Menominee termination act, signed by Eisenhower in June 1954, stipulated that federal supervision over the properties and affairs of the tribe would expire on the last day of 1958. This gave the tribe less than four years in which to establish its own municipalities, schools, health facilities, and other services previously provided by the federal government. The bureaucratic difficulties were enormous, and the Menominees succeeded in having the deadline for termination extended until 1961. At that time the tribal leaders created Menominee Enterprises Incorporated (MEI) to manage the lands and mill formerly owned by the tribe, and they transferred the responsibility for local government to the newly formed Menominee County.

The ill effects of termination soon were apparent. Sales for the Menominees' lumber products plummeted with the end of guaranteed contracts from the federal government, and newly imposed taxes absorbed about half of the remaining profits. In an attempt to remain solvent, MEI sold to European Americans much of the corporation's land, including a large part of the tribe's traditional hunting and fishing grounds. Under the jurisdiction now of state authority, Menominees ended up in jail for hunting and fishing out of season. The Menominee County Hospital was forced to close because it did not have the resources necessary to satisfy state licensing requirements. Health conditions worsened dramatically: By 1965 the infant mortality rate among the Menominees had reached a level 200 percent greater than the national average, and one-third of the tribe had tested positive for tuberculosis. Individuals lost their homes to tax sales, and in five years county welfare costs doubled. The unemployment rate in Menominee County rose to 25 percent, the highest in the state.

The fate of the Menominees was shared by others who underwent termination. Between 1953 and 1960 more than 100 separate tribes or bands were terminated by acts of Congress. California Indians were among the hardest hit. In 1958 Congress passed the "rancheria bill," terminating forty-one California reservations with a single blow. Federal trust protection eventually was removed from 1.3 million acres of Indian land throughout the nation, and 12,000 individuals had their ties with the federal government severed.

It is difficult to escape the conclusion that the termination policy was a calamity for Native Americans. Only about 3 percent of the nation's Indian population was terminated, but the psychological impact of the policy was enormous. Tribes across the country feared that they would be the government's next candidate for termination. Tribes that actually experienced the trauma of termination, such as the Menominees, often were reduced to insolvency and poverty. As a policy to get the federal government "out of the Indian business," termination must also be considered a failure. In the case of the Menominees, their pretermination costs to the government were $144,000 annually; after termination, the high costs of welfare payments and unemployment compensation increased federal expenditures to nearly $3 million in seven years. The overall budget for the Bureau of Indian Affairs continued to grow throughout the 1950s, and the number of agency personnel increased by 20 percent.

Perhaps the only winners of termination were the European Americans who profited from the removal of federal trust protection from Indian lands. Tribes in Montana lost an estimated one-quarter of a million acres to neighboring whites, and lumber companies were the prime beneficiaries of the termination of the Klamaths in Oregon. Local merchants also benefited from the liquidation of tribal assets.

Joseph Garry, head of the National Congress of American Indians, noted in 1958 that real estate offices were mushrooming across the country around reservations scheduled for termination. In a commentary that could have applied to other expressions of federal policy, Garry charged that termination was encouraging a greedy surge in land acquisition by whites even as it was deepening the poverty of Indians.

Bowing to criticism from Native Americans and their European American allies, Secretary of Interior Fred Seaton announced in 1958 that the federal government would no longer terminate tribes without their consent. In a radio broadcast from Flagstaff, Arizona, on September 18, 1958, Seaton declared that it was "absolutely unthinkable . . . that consideration would be given to forcing upon an Indian tribe a so-called termination plan which did not have the understanding and acceptance of a clear majority of the members affected." Seaton pledged that henceforth the government would not end its relationship with any tribe or group "unless such tribe or group has clearly demonstrated—first, that it understands the plan under which such a program would go forward, and second, that the tribe or group affected concurs in and supports the plan proposed." This was a major concession to the critics of termination and a harbinger of a more consensual approach to Indian affairs in the decades ahead.

RELOCATION

A logical corollary to the termination policy was the federal government's concerted effort in the years after World War II to relocate Native Americans from reservations to the nation's cities. The enthusiasm for relocation was fueled in part by the successful experience of Indians in the armed forces and wartime defense industries. At the war's end, government officials were compelled to seek alternative employment opportunities for the more than 100,000 veterans and defense workers who were returning to the reservations. The Bureau of Indian Affairs launched a pilot program in 1948 to provide relocation and job placement services for residents of the great Navajo reservation. Employable Navajos were encouraged to leave the reservation and move to Denver, Salt Lake City, and Los Angeles where special placement offices were available to assist them in finding permanent employment.

The relocation program expanded greatly under the direction of Bureau of Indian Affairs Commissioner Dillon S. Myer, a man who regarded the reservations as little more than "prison camps" and was determined to do all he could to move their residents into the nation's metropolitan centers. (The irony of Myer's role in relocation was duly noted by historian Alison R. Bernstein: As director of the War Relocation Program during World War II, Myer had moved Japanese Americans from urban areas to rural detention centers; after the war, he was engaged in the moving of Native Americans from rural areas to urban ones.) In the fall of 1950, Myer announced that the BIA would provide assistance to any Indians "who wished to seek permanent employment opportunities away from reservations." The following year the BIA's Voluntary Relocation Program began offering a variety of incentives to encourage Indians to move to the cities: travel expenses, free job training and placement services, housing assistance, medical care for one year, and a one-month subsistence allowance. Throughout the early and mid-1950s, the BIA opened Field Relocation Offices in Chicago, St. Louis, Oakland, San Francisco, San Jose, Dallas, Cleveland, Oklahoma City, Tulsa, Phoenix, and Albuquerque. Myer's successor at the BIA, Glenn Emmons, shared the view that the problems of Indian unemployment and poverty could best be solved by convincing large numbers of Native Americans to move from the reservations.

To recruit candidates for the relocation program, the Bureau of Indian Affairs distributed posters and brochures depicting the advantages of life in the city. Illustrations showed happy and contented Indian families living in comfortable homes, surrounded by all the modern conveniences. Unfortunately, the reality for many relocated Native people was far different. Adjusting to an urban environment was often a painful experience, compounded by the difficulty of finding and retaining steady employment. Conforming to rigid work schedules, regulated by the clock, was something that many reservation Indians had not experienced before. In spite of the best efforts of the relocation officers assigned to help them, many newcomers were intimidated and overwhelmed by the sights and sounds of the city.

The experiences of one Creek family from Oklahoma were typical of what awaited many of those who moved to the city in search of a better life. Leonard Bear, Little Light, and their five children were living in a small shanty on the outskirts of Los Angeles in 1956. A

"COME TO DENVER. THE CHANCE OF YOUR LIFETIME!" THE BU-
REAU OF INDIAN AFFAIRS PRODUCED MANY SUCH POSTERS DUR-
ING THE 1950S URGING NATIVE AMERICANS TO LEAVE THEIR
RESERVATIONS AND RELOCATE TO THE CITIES.

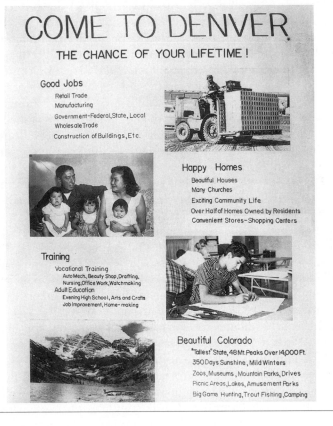

story in the *Atlantic Monthly,* entitled "Uprooting the Indians," described their home:

> The walls were unpainted, the floor a patchwork of linoleum. Through
> an archway, another room was visible where three beds crowded to-
> gether. A two-burner stove stood on a box, and on the only other piece
> of furniture in the room—a battered table—rested the remains of a
> dinner; some white, grease-soaked bags which had contained ham-
> burgers and fried potatoes prepared by the restaurant a few blocks
> away.

Little Light was worried that her husband spent every night drinking, and she was embarrassed by people in stores laughing at her. She would gladly return to Oklahoma, if only she could afford the trip. "They did not tell us it would be like this," she said.

In spite of its evident difficulties, the relocation program continued to attract new recruits. Curiosity about city life and a desperate hope for better economic opportunities were powerful motives for many Native Americans living on the reservations. To improve the chances of successful transition for those who chose to move to the city, tribal councils sought ways of upgrading relocation services. Ben Reifel (Sioux) acknowledged that relocatees needed special help in handling their money. Another tribal leader suggested holding weekly meetings to prepare residents of the reservations for their new lives in the cities and to instruct them in the use of modern household appliances. "Many of our people do not know what these things are," he observed, "and have never had running water in their house and other modern conveniences."

Opposition to relocation came from full-bloods and others who were suspicious that this was just another government program to dispossess Indians of their land and strip them of their culture. Full-blood Cherokees in Oklahoma, as well as elderly Kiowas and Comanches, feared that relocation was aimed at getting rid of Indians altogether. One Bureau of Indian Affairs official on the Colville reservation in Washington reported that the full-bloods there felt that relocation was "a government means to move the Indians from the reservation in order to allow white operators to exploit the reservation and eventually force all Indians from the reservation areas." A similar view was expressed by an Indian in southern California who charged that the government intended to move all the Native people off their land so that whites "could grab it."

Between the end of World War II and 1958, approximately 100,000 Native Americans left the reservations. At least three-fourths of these, however, did so without any assistance from the federal government. By 1960 an estimated 33,000 Indians had participated in the official relocation program. Perhaps as few as 3,000 of the relocatees found permanent employment; most worked in low-paying, unskilled seasonal jobs and were subjected to frequent layoffs. Estimates of the number of Indians who returned to the reservations varied widely. Defenders of relocation claimed that about 30 percent returned to the reservations, while critics claimed that the "return rate" was as high as 60 or 75 percent. As a means of reducing government expenses for Indian affairs, relocation was a disappointment. The budget for the relocation program rose from $575,000 in 1952 to more than $2.8 million in 1957, leading one congressman to complain: "I think the time has come to stop this useless waste of the taxpayers' money in hiring an army of bureaucrats to do something that does not in any way benefit the Indian people."

Nor did relocation produce the degree of assimilation that its supporters had expected. Indian ghettos appeared in places like Chicago's Uptown neighborhood and Bell Gardens in Los Angeles. And Native Americans chose to retain much of their traditional ways of life even in the midst of a radically different environment. As noted by Native historian Donald L. Fixico, "Federal officials failed to comprehend the existing strength of Native American cultures and the tenacity with which Indians would try to preserve their heritage." One of the most comprehensive critiques of the relocation program came from within the government itself. The General Accounting Office in 1958 conducted an extensive evaluation of the program and concluded that many Indians had not been properly prepared for relocation, nor were they placed in areas that offered adequate economic opportunities. After 1958, as it became increasingly clear that substantial numbers of Indians were moving only temporarily to the cities, official support for the relocation program diminished.

Relocation was the last great hope of those who favored assimilation as the ultimate solution to the Indian problem. Assimilation strategies had abounded throughout the nation's history, from the earliest colonial charters and missionary efforts through the removal campaigns and reservation policies of the mid-nineteenth century. Assimilationists from 1880 to 1934 had put their faith in allotment, citizenship, and education as the most effective means of achieving their goal. In the years after World War II, the preferred means became compensation, termination, and relocation. Historians James S. Olson and Raymond Wilson neatly summed up the aspirations of the postwar proponents of assimilation: "With land claims settled, federal authority scuttled, and reservations dwindling in population, the 'Indian problem' would cease to exist." Yet it was abundantly clear by the end of the 1950s that the "problem" had not yet been solved, and the goal of complete assimilation remained as elusive as ever.

SOURCES AND SUGGESTIONS FOR FURTHER READING

The two most important sources for this chapter, ones that supplied the general ideas as well as many of the specific quotations, are James

S. Olson and Raymond Wilson's masterful account, *Native Americans in the Twentieth Century* (1984), and Donald L. Fixico's richly detailed monograph, *Termination and Relocation: Federal Indian Policy, 1945–1960* (1986). See also the comprehensive analysis in Donald L. Parman, *Indians and the American West in the Twentieth Century* (1994).

Many useful surveys of the evolution of federal Indian policy are readily available. The early portions of this chapter are based on Lyman S. Tyler, *A History of Indian Policy* (1973); Lawrence C. Kelly, *Federal Indian Policy* (1990); Wilcomb E. Washburn, "Indian-White Relations," in Eric Foner and John A. Garraty, eds., *The Reader's Companion to American History* (1991); William T. Hagan, *American Indians* (1993); and James J. Rawls, *Indians of California* (1984). The works of Francis Paul Prucha are essential: *American Indian Policy in the Formative Years: The Indian Trade and Intercourse Acts, 1790–1834* (1970), *The Great Father* (1975), and *American Indian Policy in Crisis: Christian Reformers and the Indian, 1865–1900* (1976).

Also of primary importance for this chapter are two articles in Wilcomb E. Washburn, ed., *History of Indian-White Relations*, vol. 8, *Handbook of North American Indians* (1988): Lawrence C. Kelly, "United States Indian Policies, 1900–1980"; and Philleo Nash, "Twentieth-Century United States Government Agencies." Much of the material on the later evolution of federal policy is drawn from articles in J. Milton Yinger and George Eaton Simpson, eds., *American Indians Today* (1978): Raymond V. Butler, "The Bureau of Indian Affairs: Activities Since 1945"; James E. Officer, "The Bureau of Indian Affairs Since 1945: An Assessment"; Vine Deloria, Jr., "Legislation and Litigation Concerning American Indians"; and Nancy Oestreich Lurie, "The Indian Claims Commission."

Vine Deloria, Jr., and Clifford Lytle, *The Nations Within: The Past and Future of American Indian Sovereignty* (1984) is an especially useful guide to the complexities of Indian law and government. The definitive works on the Collier era are Kenneth R. Philp, *John Collier's Crusade for Indian Reform: 1920–1954* (1977); and Lawrence C. Kelly, *The Assault on Assimilation: John Collier and the Origins of Indian Policy Reform* (1983). Among the many recent studies to take a more critical look at individual tribal experiences, see especially Donald L. Parman, *The Navajos and the New Deal* (1976) and Thomas Biolsi, *Organizing the Lakota: The Political Economy of the New Deal on the Pine Ridge and Rosebud Reservations* (1992).

Additional insights are provided by the remarkable synthesis in Alvin M. Josephy, Jr., "Modern America and the Indian," in Frederick E. Hoxie, ed., *Indians in American History: An Introduction* (1988). Also useful on postwar government policy is Alison R. Bernstein, *American Indians and World War II: Toward a New Era in Indian Affairs* (1991).

3

TOWARD
SELF-DETERMINATION

➤➤➤➤➤➤➤➤➤

 FEDERAL INDIAN POLICY in the years since 1960 continued to be buffeted by powerful and often contradictory forces. Periods of relative calm were followed by fierce storms when the winds of change reached gale-force intensity, but through it all the prevailing winds seemed to be moving federal policy in a single direction. Opposition to the assimilationist policies of termination and relocation steadily increased, and the federal government's relationship with Native Americans moved slowly from paternalism toward partnership. In the words of Bureau of Indian Affairs administrator Raymond Butler (Blackfeet):

> The journey from termination, where the federal government was trying to get out of the Indian business, to Indian self-determination, where the federal government is committed to becoming a full partner to the Indian tribes, is the major theme of Indian affairs over the past several decades.

This remarkable change in direction was due, in large measure, to the continued opposition by Native Americans to the discredited policies of termination and relocation. The comment of one Northern Cheyenne in 1971 was typical: "I'm . . . 100 percent against termination, any shape or form, and I've been this way for as far back as I can remember." Tribal leaders across America vigorously objected to any further attempts by the federal government to abandon its treaty obligations to protect Indian rights and property, and individual Native Americans asserted and maintained their right to adapt at their own pace to the ways of the dominant society. "We like to keep our identity as Indians," explained John Cummins, the chairman of the Crow tribal council. "We want to be Crow Indians and at the same time we want to be equal to the white population in the rest of the United States." European Americans increasingly came to recognize both the right and the heartfelt desire of Indians to be Indian.

FROM THE NEW FRONTIER TO THE GREAT SOCIETY

The election of Democrat John F. Kennedy in 1960 ushered in an era of modest reform in American social and political history. Kennedy called his domestic agenda the New Frontier, and he showed an early interest in protecting the rights of the original residents of the old frontier as well. During his presidential campaign, Kennedy pledged to preserve "the Indian land base" and promised that his administration would make no changes in treaty relationships with the tribes without their consent. Nor would his administration take any steps, Kennedy said, to "impair the cultural heritage of any group." Yet Kennedy was forced to move slowly in Indian affairs—as he was in other areas of his moderately liberal legislative agenda—because of conservative opposition in Congress. Much to the disappointment of his Native American constituents, the new president described his Indian policy as simply one of *preparing* Indians for termination.

Shortly after his inauguration in January 1961, President Kennedy appointed a special task force to investigate Indian affairs and to recommend future policy. The task force was headed by W. W. Keeler, principal chief of the Cherokee Nation, and included several future high-ranking officers of the Bureau of Indian Affairs (BIA). After six months of hearings and deliberation, the task force reported that Indian leaders all across America were vigorously opposed to the termination policy. The task force recommended that the federal government emphasize programs of economic development rather than termination, yet it did not go so far as to call for the abandonment of termination altogether. Once the tribes had advanced sufficiently, the task force advised "termination can be achieved with maximum benefit for all concerned." The task force recommended a program, soon dubbed the New Trail, aimed at achieving maximum Indian economic self-sufficiency, full participation of Indians in American life, and equal citizenship rights and responsibilities for all Indians.

In accepting the recommendations of the task force, Interior Secretary Stewart Udall announced that the Kennedy administration intended "to place emphasis on Indian development rather than on termination in the belief that this approach will win the cooperative response from our Indian citizens which is the keystone of a successful program." Udall was vigorous in his criticism of the way termination had been implemented by the Eisenhower administration. "Their so-called termination policy," he said, was to put Native Americans "on their own and let them sink or swim." This callous disregard for Indian welfare had resulted in needless suffering and anxiety. The New Trail of the Kennedy administration, Udall explained, would require the full collaboration of the Indian people.

In early August 1961, Kennedy appointed Wisconsin anthropologist Philleo Nash to serve as commissioner of Indian affairs. Nash had been an outspoken member of the Indian task force and was committed to carrying out its recommendations. He also was sensitive to the growing demand from Native Americans for more control over the federal programs designed for their welfare. At a conference in Chicago in June 1961, several hundred Indian leaders requested that the new administration allow Indians to participate in the decision-making process of designing programs and administering budgets that affected them. Their request was part of the growing consensus among Native Americans that they should have a greater role in the management of their own affairs.

Commissioner Nash concentrated at first on securing for Native Americans the full benefits of the New Frontier, just as John Collier earlier had worked to have Indians included in the social welfare programs of the New Deal. Nash believed that many of the economic and social problems of Indians were sufficiently similar to those of other disadvantaged groups that they did not require special legislative remedies. One of the first of the Kennedy administration's initiatives was the Area Redevelopment Act (ARA) of 1961, providing aid for economic development in chronically depressed areas of the country. During his first year in office, Nash succeeded in having fifty-six reservations and four Alaskan Native regions declared "Redevelopment Areas" eligible for ARA funds. The Native people used their grants-in-aid on a wide variety of projects, including the building of new tribal headquarters and community centers. Nash also was successful in having Native Americans included in the provisions of the Manpower Development and Training Act of 1962. Within a year of its passage, eighty-nine public works and job training programs were operating on reservations in twenty-one states.

In addition to insuring that Native Americans were full participants in the programs of the New Frontier, Philleo Nash also worked to achieve greater economic self-sufficiency for Indian communities by encouraging industries to locate new manufacturing plants on or near the reservations. In 1962 Nash organized within the BIA a Division of Economic Development to encourage business and industrial development, develop reservation natural resources, provide technical assistance to the tribes, and assist with land management practices. The new division experienced limited success in attracting new manufacturing plants, mostly of the light industry type, to the reservations. By the end of 1962, Nash could report that twenty-six plants were operating in predominantly Indian localities, including eight established during the past year. On several reservations, the commissioner noted that "the industrial payrolls have already helped perceptibly to brighten the local economic and social atmosphere."

The federal government's new emphasis on local economic development was supported by many Native Americans who hoped that such development would shield the reservations from termination. If enough large and powerful businesses had a vested interest in the reservations, the tribes could not be terminated without causing major problems for their corporate tenants. With encouragement from Commissioner Nash and the BIA, several tribes negotiated ninety-nine year leases with corporations for the development of reservation resources. When it became apparent that these arrangements amounted to the permanent transfer of some of the most valuable resources of the reservations into the hands of non-Indians, opposition to the long-term leasing plan quickly mounted. Leaders on the Navajo, Northern Cheyenne, and Crow reservations objected to what they called "termination by corporation."

The assassination of John F. Kennedy on November 22, 1963, was a profound shock to Native Americans, as it was to millions of people around the world. This dramatic event, however, did not alter the nation's federal Indian policy. Kennedy's successor, Lyndon B. Johnson, assured the Indian people that they would have an important place in the Great Society just as they had in the New Frontier. A few weeks after becoming president, Johnson proposed an "unconditional war on poverty." The centerpiece of the administration's domestic policy was an ambitious legislative proposal called the Economic Opportunity Act. This omnibus measure would create a powerful new federal agency, the Office of Economic Opportunity (OEO), to coordinate a wide array of antipoverty programs.

As Congress considered the president's proposal, leaders of the National Congress of American Indians (NCAI) and a thousand tribal delegates gathered in Washington, D.C., to attend an American Indian Capitol Conference on Poverty in May 1964. The delegates visited their congressional representatives and respectfully yet forcefully requested that Native Americans be included in the proposed antipoverty legislation. Nineteen sixty-four was an election year and few politicians could avoid responding to such effective lobbying by a group of their constituents. When Congress enacted the Economic Opportunity Act in August 1964, it specifically authorized the creation of a special "Indian desk" within the OEO to insure that the benefits of its many programs were made available to Native Americans. This successful lobbying effort encouraged Native Americans to monitor subsequent legislative proposals and to insist that their eligibility sections include the phrase "and/or Indian tribes" alongside "states and local governments." This persistence paid off, and Indians qualified for nearly every new program of the Great Society. When Congress renewed and expanded the Area Redevelopment Act as the Economic Development Administration in 1964, all federally recognized tribes became eligible for the full range of its programs.

Among the most successful of the Office of Economic Opportunity programs made available to Native Americans were Community Action Projects (CAPs) in which tribal councils were encouraged to design their own plans and apply for grants from the appropriate federal agencies. The stated philosophy of the OEO/CAP administration was that "each individual Indian tribe will operate at its own level of program sophistication and that program development itself will be an educational process." This approach echoed the recommendation of the Meriam Report in 1928 that all federal programs should be aimed at helping Indians make the best possible decisions for themselves. Accordingly, the OEO provided tribal leaders with training and technical assistance in designing CAPs suited to their particular situations. Universities with prior experience working with Indian communities— such as Arizona State University, the University of Utah, and the University of South Dakota—formed a consortium to help the tribal councils create effective projects. Once the CAPs were funded, they were administered by the tribal councils themselves. Thus, Native

Americans assumed additional administrative and decision-making responsibilities previously handled by the BIA.

The range of Great Society programs made available to Native Americans was remarkable. An Indian desk, "headed by a person of American Indian ancestry," was created in the Manpower Administration of the Department of Labor and charged with increasing job training and job placement programs for Native people. In addition, Work Incentive (WIN) projects were developed on reservations in Idaho, New Mexico, Arizona, Montana, and Oklahoma to help welfare recipients find permanent employment. Training and temporary employment also were available to Native Americans at ten Job Corps Conservation Centers and fifty-five Neighborhood Youth Corps projects. The Department of Housing and Urban Development (HUD), created in 1965, assisted in the development of new housing projects on the Rosebud, Pine Ridge, White Mountain Apache, and Blackfeet reservations. HUD's Model Cities program provided additional research and development assistance to communities on other reservations. The Department of Health, Education and Welfare (HEW) formed an Office for Indian Progress in 1967 to coordinate the department's services available to Native Americans through such diverse agencies as the Office of Education, the Public Health Service, and the Social Security Administration.

The Johnson administration's Department of Agriculture offered Indians the widest possible array of services. It established food assistance programs on dozens of reservations, and by 1968 its Needy Family Program was providing 70,000 Native Americans with various surplus commodities. The Rural Electrification Administration (REA) served more than 26,000 Native people, while the Forest Service provided full-time employment for 400 Indians and summer jobs for 500 more through the Youth Opportunity Campaign. The Farmers Home Administration approved $8 million in loans to Indians in 1967 for farm operating expenses and the purchase of new farms and homes. By 1968 the Agricultural Extension Service was offering programs to improve family nutrition and housing conditions on reservations in seventeen states with an Indian population of more than 300,000.

Most (but not all) Native American leaders welcomed the increased flow of federal dollars to the reservations. The administration of federal programs gave tribal councils the experience and self-confidence to demand even greater self-government. Some leaders complained, however, that the flow of federal funds was undercutting the movement toward tribal independence. Native American communities, they argued, were becoming more dependent than ever on the federal government. The president of the National Congress of American Indians, Ed Driving Hawk, observed that "tribal governments have become more administrators of federal programs than tribal governments." And Vine Deloria, Jr., offered an even more biting critique. He charged that the outpouring of federal aid had created a state of "benign confusion, in which Indians seemed more concerned with funding programs than sketching out in broader and more comprehensive terms the ideologies and theories that are necessary for sustained growth."

THE ABANDONMENT OF TERMINATION

Whatever "confusion" the Johnson administration's increase in federal aid may have caused among Native Americans, their opposition to termination remained as clear as ever. The pace of termination had slowed considerably since the late 1950s, but the policy embodied in House Concurrent Resolution 108 had not yet been officially repudiated. Indeed, the Senate Interior Committee in 1964 expressed itself "deeply concerned" about the failure of the Bureau of Indian Affairs to carry out the intent of the resolution. In 1966 the Department of the Interior terminated federal trust relations with four California rancherias, and the following year an additional 100 rancherias were terminated. One of the most powerful advocates of termination was Senator Henry Jackson of Washington, chairman of the Senate Interior Committee. When BIA commissioner Philleo Nash successfully blocked Jackson's attempt in 1966 to terminate the Colville reservation in Washington, a move vigorously opposed by Lucy Covington and other tribal leaders, the senator forced Interior Secretary Udall to remove Nash from his post. Udall then appointed Robert Bennett (Oneida) to head the BIA, the first Native American to serve in that office in nearly a century.

At Robert Bennett's confirmation hearings before the Interior Committee, he was quizzed about his views on termination. Members of the committee complained that in the thirteen years since the passage of House Concurrent Resolution 108 "almost nothing has been done" to implement its provisions. The committee insisted that Bennett submit a written report outlining his understanding of the objectives of federal Indian policy. In a carefully worded statement, Bennett acknowledged that "the Indian leadership" recognized that the federal government would someday change its special relationship with Native Americans. In the meantime, Bennett emphasized, Indians expected the federal government to "meet its responsibilities to them, the same as its national commitment to others." They also expected the federal government to provide them with all the services "to which they are entitled" and to recognize their right "to maintain their Indian identity and culture." Although Bennett's statement was well received by many Native people, it fell short of what some had hoped would be a definitive disavowal of termination.

Shortly after Robert Bennett's confirmation hearings were concluded, Interior Secretary Udall convened a special conference of Bureau of Indian Affairs officials and members of Congress at Santa Fe, New Mexico. Having learned the importance of closely monitoring the actions of federal policy makers, the National Congress of American Indians called its own emergency executive meeting in Santa Fe and insisted on being admitted to the federal conference. Executive Director Vine Deloria, Jr., and other leaders of the NCAI feared that a new era of termination was about to begin. After much deliberation, the federal conferees agreed to allow representatives of the NCAI to speak. In their remarks before the conference, Native leaders first used the term *self-determination* to describe what they sought from the federal government: continuance of the federal trust relationship with the tribes and a transfer of responsibility for administering federal programs to tribal governments.

Udall had called the Santa Fe conference, in fact, to discuss legislative proposals for the development of reservation resources in ways that would allow tribal governing bodies the maximum administrative responsibility. In spite of repeated reassurances that none of these proposals would lead to a revival of the termination policy, many Native Americans remained skeptical. Only slowly, over the next several years, was Udall able to convince Indian leaders that he did not favor a return to the dreaded policies of House Concurrent Resolution 108.

The specter of termination was put to rest most forcefully in a major address by President Johnson on March 6, 1968. Titled "The Forgotten American," it was one of the strongest presidential messages on Indian affairs in the twentieth century. Johnson called specifically for an end to termination and proposed a "new goal" for federal Indian policy. The time had come, he said, to "erase old attitudes of paternalism and [to] promote partnership and self-help." Our goal must be:

> A standard of living for the Indian equal to that of the country as a whole; freedom of choice—an opportunity to remain in their home-lands, if they choose, without surrendering their dignity; an opportunity to move to the towns and cities of America, if they choose, equipped with skills to live in equality and dignity; [and] full participation in the life of modern America, with a full share of economic opportunity and social justice.

In summarizing his goal, Johnson proclaimed "a policy of maximum choice for the American Indian: a policy expressed in programs of self-help, self-development, self-determination." Less than a year had passed since the NCAI leaders in Santa Fe had expressed their prefer-ence for a policy of self-determination. Now the phrase had been taken up by the president of the United States.

Immediately after his speech, Johnson established the National Council on Indian Opportunity to review all current federal Indian programs. The council, similar to the task force Kennedy appointed seven years before, was headed by Vice President Hubert Humphrey and included leaders from the business community, heads of various federal agencies, and several prominent Native Americans. After hiring a staff, the council held hearings and conducted investigations to iden-tify new ways of improving the economic conditions of the Native people and involving Indians in future policy-making decisions.

In 1968 Congress also passed a resolution repudiating (but not formally repealing) the termination policy embodied in House Con-current Resolution 108. Introduced by Democratic Senator George McGovern of South Dakota, the resolution declared that it was the sense of Congress that the federal government should provide its pro-grams and services "to the governing bodies" of the various tribes and that these services should offer "self-determination and self-help . . . for the people involved." Furthermore, the resolution called for the continuation of these services "until the day when the Nation's moral and legal obligations to its first citizens—the American Indians—are fulfilled." The McGovern resolution signaled a further commitment by the federal government to honor its obligations to Native people while at the same time extending to them a greater measure of self-government.

Another legacy from the termination era, Public Law 280, also was repudiated in 1968. Native Americans had come to detest the law, which authorized states to extend their criminal and civil jurisdiction over tribes without their consent, as an assault on tribal identity. Many Indians also opposed PL 280 because the state governments, after assuming jurisdiction over the reservations, often refused to provide effective law enforcement or judicial services. This left Native people without adequate legal protection under either state or federal law. By the early 1960s, tribal leaders throughout the nation were united in their opposition to PL 280.

The movement to have Public Law 280 repealed was coordinated by the National Congress of American Indians. Leaders of the NCAI brought their complaints to Senator Sam Ervin of North Carolina, the powerful chairman of the Constitutional Rights Subcommittee. Ervin consented to hold hearings on the matter and soon became convinced that the states had, indeed, failed to provide sufficient legal protection for Indians after assuming jurisdiction over them. Testimony before the Ervin subcommittee revealed instances of gross neglect in which individuals had been denied assistance by state and local law enforcement personnel. Ervin introduced a series of bills throughout the mid-1960s designed to repeal or amend PL 280, but each failed to win passage.

One month after President Johnson's "Forgotten American" speech, Congress passed the Indian Civil Rights Act (ICRA) on April 11, 1968. Senator Ervin was the primary sponsor of the law, passed as part of the Civil Rights Act of 1968. The ICRA required tribal consent before a state could extend its legal jurisdiction over a reservation and authorized (upon state approval) the retrocession of jurisdiction for tribes already under state authority, thus effectively repealing Public Law 280. The passage of the ICRA prompted optimism among Native Americans that the threat of termination had been removed at last. Wendell Chino (Apache), president of the National Congress of American Indians, commented that the passage of the ICRA significantly eased the apprehension of the Indian people.

The Indian Civil Rights Act did more than just repeal Public Law 280, it also extended to Native Americans (and exempted them from) certain protections guaranteed by the Constitution. As the power of tribal governments increased during the Kennedy and Johnson administrations, questions arose about the relationship between individual tribal members and their tribal governments. The ICRA attempted to resolve these questions by restricting tribal governments in ways comparable to the constraints placed on the federal government by the Bill of Rights. Important concessions were made, however, to tribal leaders who objected that a full extension of constitutional protections would violate traditional practices. Pueblo leaders argued, for instance, that the extension of the provisions of the First Amendment would undermine the Pueblos' traditional form of a religiously established government. The ICRA thus guaranteed tribal members the right to practice their religion freely, but did not prohibit the establishment of a state religion.

Much of the practical effect of the Indian Civil Rights Act was to enlarge the role of the tribal courts. Individual tribal members often exercised their newly guaranteed rights by challenging the actions of tribal governments, and the tribal courts became the arena for settling a wide range of disputes. The courts themselves increasingly came to resemble their counterparts in the federal judiciary. These developments were not universally applauded. Young activists viewed the ICRA as an infringement of tribal privileges, not as a victory for the rights of individuals; and tribal elders were concerned that cultural traditions and customs were being abandoned in favor of the rigid requirements of federal and constitutional law.

In spite of these concerns, many Native Americans welcomed the Indian Civil Rights Act as a major step toward self-determination. One observer went so far as to describe it as the "crowning achievement" of the Johnson administration's Indian policy. It certainly was that administration's *last* achievement in Indian affairs. Beset by mounting opposition to the war in Southeast Asia, Lyndon Johnson announced on March 31, 1968, that he would not seek reelection to a second full term. During his five years in office, Johnson had authorized a significant expansion of federal programs, improving the lives of thousands of individual Indians. The relationship between the tribes and the federal government also had changed in important ways. Tribal leaders had gained valuable experience in designing and administering programs formerly managed by the Bureau of Indian Affairs. Encouraged now to draw upon the resources of the federal government to create programs that best met their needs, Native Americans realized that their success depended largely upon their own initiative and creativity. James Jackson (Quinault) welcomed this new reality:

> We have learned to put outboard motors on our dugout canoes and travel a distance up our river in two hours that formerly took three days. In the same manner we are now trying to put modern governmental procedures behind our great human and natural resources. When we succeed we will travel fast.

AN IRREVERSIBLE TREND

The election of Republican Richard M. Nixon in November 1968 raised fears among Native Americans that the detested policies of the 1950s might yet be revived. But Nixon, to the surprise of many, proved to be a strong supporter of Indian self-determination. "American society can allow many different cultures to flourish in harmony," Nixon proclaimed during his campaign for the presidency. The role of the federal government, he said, should be to provide Indians an opportunity to choose their own path, including the opportunity "to lead a useful and prosperous life in an Indian community." Nixon's campaign rhetoric represented a remarkable acceptance of the principle of cultural pluralism; it was a reassuring sign that federal Indian policy would continue to move toward self-determination and away from the assimilationism of the termination era.

President Nixon's choice of Louis R. Bruce (Mohawk/Sioux), a known opponent of termination, to head the Bureau of Indian Affairs offered further reassurance to Native Americans. Nixon charged Bruce with the responsibility of insuring that "the Indian future is determined by Indian acts and Indian decisions." Bruce soon announced "a fundamental change in policy" that handed even greater authority "to Indian communities and tribes to take part in the planning and operation of activities that touch their everyday lives." Bruce was an eloquent spokesperson for the cause of self-determination; he represented well the consensus that had formed among tribal leaders across the country. "The will for self-determination has become a vital component of the thinking of Indian leadership and the grassroots Indian on every reservation and in every city," he said. "It is an irreversible trend, a tide in the destiny of American Indians that will eventually compel all of America . . . to recognize the dignity and human rights of Indian people."

On July 8, 1970, President Nixon delivered to Congress a Special Message on Indian Affairs. His message was similar to Lyndon Johnson's "Forgotten American" speech two years earlier, but Nixon was even stronger in his denunciation of termination and offered several specific proposals for advancing the cause of self-determination. Nixon condemned termination as "morally and legally unacceptable" and noted that "the mere threat of termination tends to discourage greater self-sufficiency among Indian groups." He therefore called upon Congress to "expressly renounce, repudiate and repeal the termination policy as expressed in House Concurrent Resolution 108 of the 83rd Congress." Nixon proclaimed that the goal of all federal Indian policy should be "self-determination without termination," by which he meant that "Indians can become independent of Federal control without being cut off from Federal concern and Federal support."

The new administration soon took several concrete steps to carry out the president's ambitious agenda for Indian affairs. In October 1970 Secretary of the Interior Walter J. Hickel announced the appointment of fifteen prominent Native Americans to the executive staff of the Bureau of Indian Affairs. Several of these new appointees had participated earlier in the Community Action Programs of the Office of Economic Opportunity, while others had been active in Indian rights organizations, including the National Congress of American Indians. The president also reorganized the National Council on Indian Opportunity, created by Lyndon Johnson in 1968, to include an equal number of Indian and non-Indian members. The intention of these changes in personnel, Nixon explained, was to make federal Indian services more responsive to the needs expressed by Indian leaders.

President Nixon also responded to the decades-long struggle of Native Americans for the return of ancestral lands. In 1906 the land around Blue Lake, New Mexico, had been incorporated into a national forest. The Taos Pueblo people, who considered the lake a sacred place, objected in the strongest possible terms. "We don't have gold temples in this lake," a Taos leader explained in 1961, "but we have a sign of a living God to whom we pray—the living trees, the evergreen and spruce and the beautiful flowers and the beautiful rocks and the lake itself. . . . That is the reason this Blue Lake is so important to us." The Indian Claims Commission had offered $10 million to the Pueblo to compensate them for their loss, but the Indians rejected the offer and demanded the return of the land instead. Powerful forces within the federal government blocked the retrocession of the land, arguing that it would set a dangerous precedent in dealing with future demands. But then, with the backing of President Nixon, Congress passed legislation returning Blue Lake and 48,000 surrounding acres to the Taos Pueblo in December 1970.

Throughout the 1970s, other groups of Native Americans succeeded in having former lands restored to them. The Confederated Tribes of the Warm Springs reservation in Oregon regained approximately 61,000 acres. In Washington state, the Yakama (formerly

TAOS PUEBLO LEADERS LOOK ON APPROVINGLY AS REPUBLICAN PRESIDENT
RICHARD M. NIXON SIGNS LEGISLATION IN 1970 RETURNING SACRED BLUE
LAKE AND 48,000 SURROUNDING ACRES IN NEW MEXICO.

Yakima) Indian Nation recovered 21,000 acres placed in a national
forest reserve in 1908. The Northern Paiutes of Nevada regained control over 27,000 acres. In the Grand Canyon, the Havasupais acquired
trust title to 185,000 acres and permanent access to an additional
95,000 acres of their traditional homeland.

The largest of all the land cessions to Native people during the
Nixon administration—indeed, the largest such cession in American
history—came with the passage in December 1971 of the Alaska Native Claims Settlement Act. This act, like that awarding Blue Lake to
the Taos Pueblo, culminated years of effort by Native people to gain
title to their aboriginal lands. Native Alaskans—including Eskimos,
Aleuts, and Indians—had once occupied and used all of Alaska, but by
the time of Alaskan statehood in 1959 they held title to only a few

hundred acres. In 1966 the Native people formed the Alaska Federation of Natives (AFN), made up of village councils and regional organizations, to demand additional lands and to obtain compensation for lands they had lost. The cause of the AFN was aided by the discovery in 1968 of huge oil reserves on Alaska's north slope and the development of plans to build a pipeline across the interior of the state. Federal authorities thus were powerfully motivated to seek an early settlement of the land claims of the Alaska Natives.

The Alaska Native Claims Settlement Act provided for the transfer of 40 million acres of land and subsurface mineral rights to the Native people, an award of $462 million in cash settlement, and an income of mineral royalties of up to $500 million. The federal government also agreed to assist in the creation of regional corporations to manage the Natives' resources. In the years immediately following the act's passage, the Department of the Interior approved the formation of a dozen Native-owned regional corporations to administer the awards and royalties. The importance of the Alaskan issue was highlighted in November 1973 by the appointment of Morris Thompson (Alaska Athapaskan) as the new commissioner of Indian affairs.

Just three weeks after Thompson's appointment, Congress passed yet another milestone in the movement toward Native American self-determination. The Menominee of Wisconsin were one of the first and the largest of the tribes to be terminated in the 1950s. As the tragic results of termination became increasingly evident, Menominee tribal leaders concluded that their only hope lay in a repeal of the legislation that had terminated their tribe. Spearheading the fight for repeal was a determined Menominee social worker named Ada Deer. She lobbied tirelessly before congressional committees and attracted nationwide publicity to the Menominee cause. On December 22, 1973, Congress passed the Menominee Restoration Act, providing for the "retrocession" of federal trust status over tribal lands and the restoration of tribal access to all federal programs. The act further conceded that the tribe had always remained in existence and that its traditional hunting and fishing rights had never been legally suspended. The Menominee people elected Ada Deer as chairperson of their newly refounded tribal government.

The Menominee Restoration Act was the most convincing evidence yet that the federal government's termination policy was dead. Subsequent legislation restored tribal status to terminated groups in Utah, Arizona, and Oregon. Federal protection was reinstated over the

Modocs, Ottawas, Paiutes, Peorias, and Wyandots; and federal benefits were extended to the Passamaquoddies and Penobscots of Maine. Congress also passed legislation reconstituting the tribal governments of the Five Civilized Tribes of Oklahoma and restoring to them the right to elect their tribal leaders.

The Nixon administration achieved another of its major goals for Indian affairs in April 1974 with the passage of the Indian Financing Act. In his Special Message to Congress in 1970, Nixon called for an increase in funding for economic development programs on the reservations and for additional financing for local Indian enterprises. Many tribal leaders concurred. Their opposition to the relocation policy had only increased over the years, and they urged the administration to enlarge the opportunities for Indian employment on or near the reservations rather than in remote urban centers. The Indian Financing Act established an Indian Business Development Program to provide capital to aid in the formation of independent Indian businesses. It also authorized the guaranteeing of commercial loans to Native Americans and consolidated and increased the money available in the existing Indian Revolving Loan Fund.

Perhaps the most controversial part of the Nixon administration's Indian policy was its expansion of the role of Native Americans within the Bureau of Indian Affairs. Ever since the Indian Reorganization Act of 1934, the federal government had given preference to "qualified persons of at least one-fourth degree or more of Indian blood" in the filling of vacancies at the BIA. The Nixon administration, however, expanded the practice to include the promotion of personnel within the bureau as well. Secretary of the Interior Rogers C. B. Morton anticipated a negative reaction from non-Indian workers and directed that "careful attention" be given to the protection of their rights. In spite of Morton's directive, non-Indian employees at the BIA filed an unfair labor practice suit and took their case to federal court. Relations between Indian and non-Indian employees within the BIA deteriorated to their worst point in the history of the agency.

The issue of Indian preference at the Bureau of Indian Affairs was resolved by the United States Supreme Court in the case of *Morton v. Mancari* (1974). The question before the court was whether an agency of the federal government could discriminate in favor of Indians on the basis of race. The court ruled that the BIA's policy of giving preference to Indian employees was, in fact, based not on race but on the singular political relationship that existed between Indians and the

U.S. government. Thus the court upheld Indian preference at the BIA because it was "tied rationally" to the fulfillment of the government's unique obligation to Indians.

The rapid changes in federal policy during the Nixon years were propelled, in part, by the rise of the militant Indian rights movement (see chapter 5). Young Indian activists formed the American Indian Movement (AIM) in 1968, the year Nixon was elected, and the Indian occupation of Alcatraz Island in San Francisco Bay occurred during Nixon's first year in office. The activists sought to dramatize their concern that many Native Americans continued to live in poverty, in spite of the advances in federal policy. Hundreds of Indian protestors came to the nation's capital, as part of a demonstration known as the Trail of Broken Treaties, and occupied the headquarters of the Bureau of Indian Affairs during election week in November 1972. The following spring, 200 members of AIM occupied the town of Wounded Knee on the Pine Ridge reservation in South Dakota.

Congress responded to the escalation in Indian activism by creating the American Indian Policy Review Commission in the summer of 1974, charged with investigating the conditions responsible for the discontent that had culminated in the occupation of Wounded Knee. The commission included five Native American members, and its various task forces were staffed almost entirely by Indians. The commission conducted extensive field investigations and compiled a list of more than 200 specific recommendations for changes in federal policy. The final report of the commission included a ringing statement in favor of Indian self-determination, referring to the tribes as "sovereign political bodies" and calling for a continuation of the "special trust relationship" between the tribes and the federal government.

The work of the commission was overshadowed, however, by the Watergate scandal that led to the resignation of Richard Nixon on August 8, 1974. In the years that followed, assessments of the Nixon administration's Indian policies varied widely. Many Native observers commended Nixon for his ambitious agenda of Indian reform and acknowledged his specific achievements. Vine Deloria, Jr., praised Nixon especially for his support of the legislation returning Blue Lake to the Taos Pueblo: "A great deal of credit must be given to the Nixon administration for keeping this type of promise to the Indians." Native scholar Jack Forbes (Powhatan/Lenape), author of *Native Americans and Nixon: Presidential Politics and Minority Self-Determination, 1969–1972* (1981), offered a more critical view. Although Forbes described the early years of the Nixon administration as "probably the most exciting, innovative period" in the history of federal Indian policy, he charged Nixon with following a policy of "neocolonialism." The president's endorsement of self-determination, Forbes concluded, was motivated primarily by a desire to destroy Indian militancy "in order to pave the way for the exploitation of Indian resources."

Republican Gerald R. Ford, who became president when Nixon resigned, pledged to continue the Indian policies of his predecessor. "I am committed to furthering the self-determination of Indian communities," Ford announced, "but without terminating the special relationship between the federal government and the Indian people. I am strongly opposed to termination."

The most significant Indian affairs legislation adopted during Gerald Ford's brief presidency was the Indian Self-Determination and Education Assistance Act of 1975. The act included many of the recommendations contained in Nixon's Special Message of 1970 and was widely regarded as the most important Indian legislation since the Indian Reorganization Act of 1934. It expressly repudiated termination and committed the federal government to the achievement of Indian self-determination. The act emphasized the federal government's "unique and continuing relationship with and responsibility to the Indian people," while also recognizing the government's responsibility to assure "maximum Indian participation" in the direction of all federal services to Indian communities. To carry out these responsibilities, the act established new procedures for the tribal governments to contract directly with federal agencies for social welfare programs, including health and educational services. The act also provided that if a tribe wished no longer to administer a particular program it had the right to turn the program back to the federal government. This provision allayed the fears of some Native American leaders that self-determination might yet be termination in disguise.

The Indian Self-Determination and Education Assistance Act culminated the movement toward self-determination that had begun more than fifteen years earlier. It codified the new relationship between the federal government and tribal authorities by allowing the tribal governments to set their own goals, priorities, and administrative procedures for administering federal programs. Tribal governments were empowered to restructure or even reject programs that they determined were not meeting their needs. By 1975 the federal government and the Indian people had traveled a considerable distance down the New Trail announced during the early days of the Kennedy administration. The landmark act of that year, in the words of historians James S. Olson and Raymond Wilson, "swung the great pendulum of relations between Native Americans and European Americans away from overt assimilationist policies toward tribalism and Native American sovereignty."

A NEW DAY

In the years following the passage of the Indian Self-Determination and Education Assistance Act in 1975, the focus of federal Indian policy shifted from the executive and legislative branches to the judiciary. The principle of Native American self-determination raised a host of complex questions about the powers of tribal authorities and their place within the constitutional structure of American government. The Supreme Court decided dozens of cases involving the legal status of Indians during the late 1970s and 1980s; indeed, the court issued more decisions during those years in the area of Indian law than it did in such established fields as antitrust, securities, or international law. Gradually the decisions of the court made it clear that three types of sovereign governments existed within the United States—federal, state, and tribal. As explained by legal scholar Lawrence Baca (Pawnee), any Indian who was a tribal member thus had three citizenships and owed allegiance to each sovereign and derived certain benefits and protections from each.

One of the first of the Supreme Court decisions was *Santa Clara Pueblo v. Martinez* (1978), in which the court upheld the right of a tribe to be governed by its traditional laws, even if those laws conflicted with rights guaranteed under the U.S. Constitution. Specifically, the court prohibited individual Indians from filing federal suits against tribal governments, except in cases involving persons held in tribal custody. In the years since the passage of the Indian Civil Rights Act in 1968, the federal courts had been inundated by lawsuits from individual Indians who claimed their rights were being violated by tribal governments. The court held in *Santa Clara Pueblo v. Martinez* that since Indian tribes were sovereigns, they were immune from suit in federal court, with the sole exception of cases of *habeas corpus.*

This expansive definition of tribal self-determination soon raised the question of whether tribal governments exercised unlimited jurisdiction over non-Indians. In the case of *Oliphant v. Suquamish Tribe of Indians* (1978), the court ruled that an Indian tribe could not try non-Indians for criminal acts, even though they committed the acts on the tribe's reservation. Tribal governments were specifically empowered, however, to exercise authority over non-Indians in civil matters. Tribal courts thus routinely tried cases involving non-Indians in such matters as contract disputes and automobile accidents on the reservations. Tribal governments also regulated non-Indian reservation businesses and zoned non-Indian lands located within reservation boundaries.

The Supreme Court also demonstrated an extraordinary willingness to uphold rights guaranteed to the tribes by treaty. In the Pacific Northwest, Native Americans asserted their right to half of the annual salmon harvest as provided by a treaty signed in the 1850s. After years of protest and litigation, in 1979 the Supreme Court upheld a lower court's decision in favor of the Native people. In the Southwest, the court mandated an equitable distribution of scarce water resources among Native Americans and the states in the case of *Arizona v. California* (1983). And in *County of Oneida v. Oneida Indian Nation* (1985), the court upheld an Indian claim to land in New York state based on treaties negotiated over a century ago, confirming once again that the passage of time had in no way diminished the obligation of the court to redress wrongs done to the first Americans.

No major new legislative proposals for Indian affairs were forthcoming from the executive branch during these years of judicial activism. The only significant innovation in federal policy during the administration of Democratic President Jimmy Carter was the creation in 1977 of the new position of Assistant Secretary of the Interior for Indian Affairs. This change had first been recommended in 1969 by noted historian and journalist Alvin M. Josephy, Jr., as a means of upgrading the status of Indian affairs within the federal bureaucracy; it was endorsed by President Nixon the following year. Carter appointed to the newly created post Forrest J. Gerard (Blackfeet), a former BIA employee who had the support of the National Tribal Chairmen's Association.

Also during the Carter years Congress resolved one of the most emotionally charged issues in Indian affairs. For years private and public agencies had been placing Indian children in non-Indian homes. Organizations of foster parents argued that such placement provided Indian children with the care and support they needed, but many Native people feared it robbed the children of any meaningful contact with traditional culture. In 1978 Congress passed the Indian Child

Welfare Act that restricted the removal of Native children from their families and directed that they be placed in homes reflecting the values of Native American culture. The act further stated that the federal government intended to protect, whenever possible, the integrity of the Indian family unit. The most controversial provision of the act recognized the right of Indian parents to withdraw their consent to the adoption of a child at any time.

The election of conservative Republican Ronald Reagan in 1980 aroused deep concern, once again, among Native Americans about the future of federal Indian policy. The foundation of Reagan's conservative philosophy was a reduction in taxes and government spending, and his "Program for Economic Recovery" included cuts in almost every area of the federal budget except defense. The Reagan administration reserved its heaviest cuts for programs of social welfare, including those for Native Americans. The budget for the Bureau of Indian Affairs was reduced by $76 million in 1981, and other Indian-related programs suffered sweeping budget reductions. Federal funds for Indian higher education were cut by 40 percent; health services for urban Indians were reduced by half. Suzan Shown Harjo (Cheyenne/ Arapaho), head of the National Congress of American Indians, declared that the Reagan administration was the worst for Indians "since the days of outright warfare and termination." In the words of one disgruntled tribal leader, "Trickle-down economics feels a lot like being pissed on."

Reagan administration officials advised Native Americans to turn to the states or the private sector for assistance as federal programs were being reduced. Interior Secretary James Watt suggested that many of the Indians' economic and social problems were the natural result of the federal government's perpetuation of "socialism" on the reservations. Reagan called his domestic program the New Federalism, but to many Native Americans it looked suspiciously like a revival of the termination policy of the 1950s. The president offered reassurances that he would not attempt to alter the basic direction of federal Indian policy, pledging to maintain a "government-to-government" relationship with the tribes. Yet his personal views of Native people were reminiscent of the assimilationists of the late nineteenth century. "Maybe we made a mistake," Reagan mused in 1988, "in trying to maintain Indian cultures. Maybe we should not have humored them in wanting to stay in that kind of primitive lifestyle. Maybe we should have said, 'No, come join us. Be citizens along with the rest of us.'"

The administration of Republican George Bush pursued a more moderate approach to domestic policy and provided a modest increase in funding for Indian affairs. Bush announced in 1991 his intention to build upon the policy of self-determination "first announced by President Nixon." He described "tribal self-government and self-determination" as the cornerstone of his own Indian policy, proclaiming that the "concepts of forced termination and excessive dependency on the Federal Government must now be relegated, once and for all, to the history books." He encouraged tribal governments to assume greater responsibility for federal programs, as provided by the Indian Self-Determination and Education Assistance Act. By the end of 1991, tribal governments were contracting with the federal government to operate more than 30 percent of all Bureau of Indian Affairs programs. Many Native Americans were especially pleased by the creation of an Office of American Indian Trust to insure that nothing was done to reduce tribal lands the federal government held in trust. The Bush administration also continued the policy of Indian preference in the hiring and promotion of bureau personnel; by 1991 about 87 percent of all BIA employees were Native Americans.

Democratic President Bill Clinton, elected in 1992, promised Native Americans a new era of respect and a continuation of the policy of self-determination. His choice of Ada Deer (Menominee) to head the Bureau of Indian Affairs was widely applauded by Native leaders. "The role of the federal government should be to support and to implement tribally inspired solutions to tribally defined problems," Deer testified before the senate committee that conducted her confirmation hearings in 1993. "The days of federal paternalism are over." The president echoed Deer's views precisely. "I pledge to fulfill the trust obligations of the federal government," Clinton told a gathering of Native leaders at the White House in 1994. "I vow to honor and respect tribal sovereignty based upon our unique historic relationship." The White House conference was a sure sign of the new president's commitment. For the first time in history, a Chief Executive had invited the leaders of all the nation's tribes to meet. Gathered at the White House were Native leaders representing 250 of the nation's more than 550 federally recognized tribes. The leaders applauded Clinton's signing of presidential directives safeguarding Indian rights on tribal lands and protecting the use of eagle feathers for ceremonial purposes, but criticized proposed budget cuts in Indian health services. When even more drastic reductions in the budget for Indian affairs were considered by the Republican-dominated Congress, Ada Deer denounced the cuts as "cultural and economic genocide."

Two of the Native leaders at the White House conference—Navajo Nation tribal chairman Peterson Zah and Wilma Mankiller, principal chief of the Cherokee Nation—persuaded President Clinton to convene additional "Indian Listening Conferences" across the country. The first was held in June 1994 at Albuquerque, New Mexico. Leaders of more than 200 tribes met with ninety federal officials, including Attorney General Janet Reno, Interior Secretary Bruce Babbitt, and Housing and Urban Development Secretary Henry Cisneros. Tribal leaders told the federal officials in wrenching detail about the continuing problems of Indian poverty, inadequate health care, and substandard education. Repeatedly they urged federal officials to recognize additional treaty rights, maintain federal trust responsibilities, and deal with the tribes on a government-to-government basis. "Since the very first treaty," said Wilma Mankiller, "our world has been out of balance." And JoAnn Jones (Winnebago) reminded the officials of President Clinton's promise of a new era of respect: "I do want you to remember respect. We ask you to respect our ability to govern ourselves. Respect the treaties your people have signed. Respect our religion. Respect your fiduciary responsibilities."

By the early 1990s, the Indian policy of the United States had changed dramatically from what it was a century before. At the end of the nineteenth century, tribal governments were under assault and the Indian people were undergoing enforced assimilation. By the end of the twentieth century, tribal governments were flourishing and Native Americans were free to choose their own ways. The threat of termination and the pathos of paternalism, ever present, seemed to be banished at last. In the words of Gaiashkibos (Lake Superior Chippewa), the new president of the National Congress of American Indians: "It has taken the United States and the Indian nations 200 years to come to the point where we can begin to deal with one another as sovereign nations. A new day has begun."

SOURCES AND SUGGESTIONS FOR FURTHER READING

Most of the books and articles cited for chapter 2 are the foundation for this chapter as well. The sources most frequently relied on are Vine Deloria, Jr., and Clifford Lytle, *The Nations Within: The Past and Future of American Indian Sovereignty* (1984); James S. Olson and Raymond Wilson, *Native Americans in the Twentieth Century* (1984);

Lyman S. Tyler, *A History of Indian Policy* (1973); and three articles in J. Milton Yinger and George Eaton Simpson, eds., *American Indians Today* (1978): Raymond V. Butler, "The Bureau of Indian Affairs: Activities Since 1945"; Vine Deloria, Jr., "Legislation and Litigation Concerning American Indians"; and James E. Officer, "The Bureau of Indian Affairs Since 1945: An Assessment."

Three articles in Frederick E. Hoxie, ed., *Indians in American History: An Introduction* (1988) provided additional material for this chapter: W. Richard West, Jr., and Kevin Gower, "The Struggle for Indian Civil Rights"; Charles F. Wilkinson, "Indian Tribes and the American Constitution"; and Alvin M. Josephy, Jr., "Modern America and the Indian." Likewise, four articles in Wilcomb E. Washburn, ed., *History of Indian-White Relations,* vol. 8, *Handbook of North American Indians* (1988) are indispensable: Lawrence C. Kelly, "United States Indian Policies, 1900–1980"; Philleo Nash, "Twentieth-Century United States Government Agencies"; Lawrence R. Baca, "The Legal Status of American Indians"; and Arrell M. Gibson, "Indian Land Transfers." See also Sharon O'Brien, *American Indian Tribal Governments* (1989).

Vine Deloria, Jr., ed., *American Indian Policy in the Twentieth Century* (1985) includes several important articles, including especially Deloria's "The Evolution of Federal Indian Policy Making." For a more critical view, see Jack D. Forbes, *Native Americans and Nixon: Presidential Politics and Minority Self-Determination, 1969–1972* (1981). Also useful are Jack D. Forbes, ed., *The Indian in America's Past* (1964); Sar A. Levitan and Barbara Hetrick, *Big Brother's Indian Programs—With Reservations* (1971); Lawrence C. Kelly, *Federal Indian Policy* (1990); Donald L. Fixico, *Termination and Relocation: Federal Indian Policy, 1945–1960* (1986); and Donald L. Parman, *Indians and the American West in the Twentieth Century* (1994).

The stories of two important contemporary Native American leaders are told in George M. Lubick, "Peterson Zah: A Progressive Outlook and a Traditional Style," in L. G. Moses and Raymond Wilson, eds., *Indian Lives: Essays on Nineteenth- and Twentieth-Century Native American Leaders* (1993); and Wilma Mankiller and Michael Wallis, *Mankiller: A Chief and Her People* (1993). See also the extensive biographical entries in Duane Champagne, ed., *The Native North American Almanac* (1994).

HARBRACE
BOOKS
ON AMERICA

SINCE 1945

4

A NATIONAL
TRAGEDY

 IT IS A SOBERING experience to consider the intractable nature of poverty and reflect upon its tragic consequences for Native Americans. In spite of decades of federal programs designed to eradicate poverty from the nation's reservations and urban slums, Indians continued throughout the twentieth century to be the most disadvantaged group of Americans. A report on the United States' compliance with international human rights accords found in 1979 that

> Native Americans, on the average, have the lowest per capita income, the highest unemployment rate, the lowest level of educational attainment, the shortest lives, the worst health and housing conditions, and the highest suicide rate in the United States. The poverty among Indian families is nearly three times greater than the rate for non-Indian families, and Native people collectively rank at the bottom of every social and economic statistical indicator.

This dismal assessment of Native American poverty stands as a dreadful epitaph to a half century of enormous change and evolution in federal Indian policy. Temporary relief was provided by the expansion of public welfare programs during the New Deal of the 1930s, the boom of employment opportunities during World War II, the dispersal of awards from the Indian Claims Commission, and the resolute War on Poverty during the Great Society of the 1960s, but the underlying conditions of poverty for many Native Americans remained unaltered. The median income for reservation Indians in 1939 was less

than one-third that of European Americans; thirty years later the gap
was virtually unchanged. In 1969 half of all Native families on reservations were living in poverty, as were one-fifth of all urban Indians.

NATIVE AMERICAN POVERTY

What is especially striking—and distressing—is the bleak consistency
in surveys of the social and economic conditions of Native Americans
in the twentieth century. The landmark study by anthropologist Lewis
Meriam in 1928, commissioned by the Department of the Interior,
presented a portrait of Native America that was filled with gloom.
Economic conditions, in general, were deplorable. Ranching and
farming were barely meeting the subsistence needs of Indian families,
and employment opportunities were practically nonexistent. The income level of the typical Indian family was incredibly low: Only 2
percent had annual incomes over $500. Housing was appalling, sani-
tary provisions were grossly inadequate, and diets were woefully deficient. On reservations across America, Indian families lived in homes
with dirt floors and had no running water or sewage disposal facilities.
As a consequence, the health of Indians was markedly inferior to the
rest of the population. Infant mortality rates were high and life expectancy was low. Diseases closely associated with poverty, especially tuberculosis and trachoma, were widespread.

Decade after decade, the tragic dimensions of Native American
poverty were repeated in countless surveys and reports. The familiar
refrain of desperate social and economic conditions became a litany of
disaster. In 1957 the Fund for the Republic commissioned a private
investigation of general conditions of the nation's Indian population.
Not surprisingly, the fund's investigation found that conditions among
Indians were far worse than among any other group of Americans. Employment opportunities were inadequate and unstable, median income
was scandalously low, housing conditions were substandard, health was
poor in comparison to the general population, and education was ill-
preparing Indian youth for success either on or off the reservation.

Nearly a decade later, the California State Advisory Commission on
Indian Affairs issued a strongly worded report on the conditions of the
state's Native people. The commission reported in 1966 that by all
standards of economic and social well-being—employment, income
level, housing, health, and education—the Indians of California ranked
below the European American population and significantly below other

THE INTERIOR OF A HOME IN NORTHEASTERN ARIZONA ON THE VAST RESERVA-
TION OF THE NAVAJO NATION. POVERTY AND SUBSTANDARD HOUSING ON
RESERVATIONS PERSISTED THROUGHOUT THE TWENTIETH CENTURY.

ethnic minorities. The unemployment rate among California Indians
was more than 25 percent, four times that of the general population. Those who were employed were concentrated in low-skilled and

low-paying jobs. More than half of all houses occupied by California Indians failed to meet minimum standards for safety and sanitation. Sixty-five percent of the Indians' homes had unsatisfactory sewage disposal facilities, and 45 percent used contaminated water. The majority of diseases attacking the state's Native people were gastrointestinal or respiratory, diseases closely related to deficiences in shelter, sanitation, and diet.

Five years after the appearance of this grim report on the conditions of the California Indians, University of Michigan anthropologist Joseph G. Jorgensen offered the startling observation that the Indians of California "are *much* better off than their counterparts in other states." Drawing upon evidence compiled by the President's Task Force on American Indians, Jorgensen published his own survey of what he called "the endemic poverty of contemporary Indians" in 1971. He found that unemployment rates on almost all reservations were between 40 and 50 percent, and that the average family income of American Indians was $1,500 per year, $2,000 below the federal poverty line. Houses were "grossly dilapidated" on many reservations, with 83 percent having unsatisfactory facilities for the disposal of sewage. Whereas 48 percent of California Indians had to haul their domestic water, the national average for Indians was 81 percent. Gastrointestinal and respiratory diseases among Native Americans were

FIGURE 4.1

NATIVE AMERICAN AMENITIES IN 1990

Native American Communities	Percentage without Complete Plumbing	Percentage without Telephone	Percentage without Motor Vehicle
White Mountain Apache	13.1	64.5	41.1
San Carlos Apache	16.6	83.9	29.5
Pima and Maricopa	15.2	77.8	34.5
Hopi	30.6	49.3	24.0
Navajo	44.3	81.6	27.2
Tohono O'odham	24.8	55.9	47.6
Zuni Pueblo	5.2	32.6	19.4

Source: 1990 United States Census

seven or eight times the national average, while Indian life expectancy was only two-thirds the national average. Educational levels of Indians also fell short of national standards: fully one-third of all adult Indians were illiterate.

Signs of economic progress among Native Americans were evident in the 1970s and 1980s, but severe problems remained. Unemployment among Native people remained at levels considerably higher than those for other ethnic groups, and income levels remained significantly lower. The overall Indian unemployment rate of 40 percent masked the extent of the problem on many reservations where seasonal unemployment was far higher. During the winter months, unemployment averaged 75 percent among the Fort Berthold Mandans in North Dakota, the San Carlos Apaches in Arizona, and the various Pueblos in New Mexico. Wintertime unemployment often reached 90 percent among the Choctaws of Mississippi and the Sioux of Pine Ridge, South Dakota. On and off the reservation, a lack of education and training meant that employed Indians were locked into low-skilled and low-paying positions. During the 1980s, almost 40 percent of all Native American workers were employed in unskilled or semiskilled jobs, in contrast to a national average of less than 15 percent. According to the 1990 census, the median income for reservation Indians was $13,700, compared to $19,000 for the general population.

Housing and health conditions remained seriously deficient, with more than one-third of all Native American homes having fewer than three rooms. The 1990 census reported that 20 percent of all reservation households lacked complete plumbing facilities and more than half did not have telephones. Poor sanitation and diet contributed to rates of tuberculosis and dysentery among Indians many times higher than the national average. Native Americans also had the highest alcoholism and suicide rates. Historians James S. Olson and Raymond Wilson concluded their survey of Indian poverty in 1984 with a formulation that was by then all too familiar: "Taken together, Native American employment, education, income, and health problems make them the poorest people in the United States."

HEALTH PROBLEMS

One of the most devastating consequences of poverty for Native Americans in the twentieth century was the persistence of severe health problems. The tragic irony is that in the millennia before Europeans arrived on this continent, the people of North America enjoyed excellent health. Native physicians maintained individual and communal health through sacred ritual and the knowledge of an extensive pharmacopoeia. Exposure to diseases and ecological changes introduced by European Americans took a heavy toll on the Native people. The Indian population of what is now the United States plummeted from a high of five million (or possibly far more) before white contact to fewer than 250,000 in 1890.

The government of the United States was slow to acknowledge its responsibility for protecting the health of Native Americans. In dozens of treaties negotiated in the nineteenth century, the federal government promised to provide health services to tribes as partial payment for rights and property ceded to the United States. Unfortunately, few services were provided. Following the transfer of the Bureau of Indian Affairs (BIA) from the War Department to the Department of the Interior in 1849, civilian physicians were assigned to reservations and Indian agencies. But by 1880 a total of just four hospitals and seventy-five physicians were serving the nation's entire Indian population.

Only in the early twentieth century did the federal government begin to provide meaningful health services to Native Americans. The Public Health Service conducted the first comprehensive survey of the health of American Indians in 1909. The resulting Trachoma Survey confirmed widespread reports of an unusually high number of cases of blindness among Indians and also found high levels of other infectious diseases such as tuberculosis. Two years later, in 1911, Congress made the first (and one-time-only) appropriation of federal funds specifically earmarked for Indian health services. The Snyder Act, passed by Congress in 1921, authorized regular appropriation of funds for "the relief of distress and conservation of health" of American Indians. To provide such "relief and conservation," the act created an Indian Health Division within the BIA and established district medical directors throughout the country.

Native Americans serving in the armed forces during World War II received extensive medical care from military physicians. This wartime experience raised expectations for the level of care available when they returned to civilian life. A major step toward fulfilling those expectations was taken on August 5, 1954, when Congress removed the Health Division from the Bureau of Indian Affairs and made it part of the Public Health Service within the Department of Health, Education, and Welfare (later known as the Department of Health and Human Services). This so-called Transfer Act created the Indian Health Service (IHS), under the supervision of the Surgeon General of the United States, charging it with providing all services "relating to the maintenance and operation of hospital and health facilities for Indians, and the conservation of Indian health." The quality of services available to Indians was significantly improved because young physicians could now fulfill their military obligation as commissioned public health officers serving in the IHS.

The creation of the Indian Health Service was motivated not only by a desire to improve health care for Native Americans, it also was related to the termination policy of the 1950s. As Bureau of Indian Affairs official Raymond Butler (Blackfeet) observed, the removal of health services from the BIA was part of the larger plan "to dismantle the bureau" by transferring its separate functions to other executive departments. Congressional proponents of termination hoped that such transfers would result in greater efficiency and lower costs. Expenditures for Indian health dramatically increased, however, following the creation of the IHS. During its first year of operations, the IHS had a budget of $34 million and a staff of 2,900 employees; twenty years later, its budget had grown to more than $200 million and its staff had increased to 7,400.

The Indian Health Service wisely concentrated its attention, at first, on preventive measures. Only by attacking the underlying conditions of poverty among Native Americans could the incidence of infectious diseases such as tuberculosis and trachoma be reduced. Teams of IHS civil engineers, sanitarians, medical social workers, and health educators were sent out to reservations to improve existing conditions. Congress initially authorized the IHS to provide water and waste disposal systems for existing Indian homes; subsequent legislation expanded that authority through cooperative programs with the Bureau of Indian Affairs and the Department of Housing and Urban Development for the construction of new homes as well.

The Indian Health Service initiated more than 4,000 projects, beginning in 1959, to upgrade Native American homes and communities. Over the next thirty years, more than 182,000 individual Indian homes (new and existing) were provided with sanitation facilities funded by the IHS. These facilities included running water, sewage disposal, and solid waste disposal systems. By the early 1990s, approximately 85 percent of all American Indian and Alaska Native homes had been provided with improved sanitation through various IHS programs. Nevertheless, the IHS estimated in 1993 that "sanitation deficiencies" totaling nearly $600 million still needed to be alleviated before all Indian homes would have adequate facilities.

To provide comprehensive medical care for Native Americans, the Indian Health Service had to overcome several major difficulties. Although its budget was steadily increasing, the IHS continued to suffer from inadequate funding and chronic shortages of qualified medical personnel. Also, its "service population" included peoples of many distinct languages and cultures scattered in remote and isolated locations across the country. To meet these challenges the IHS developed several innovative programs, the most successful of which was the training and supervision of paraprofessionals. The program began on an experimental basis in 1955 with the creation of the Navajo-Cornell Field Health Project. Teams of Indian "health visitors" were trained to provide first-contact health care, health education, and disease prevention services. The visitors extended the reach of the IHS professional staff and helped overcome cultural and linguistic differences between physicians and patients.

One of the many dedicated IHS health visitors was Annie Wauneka, a member of the Navajo Nation tribal council who had been involved in local health care programs since the late 1940s. As head of the council Health Committee, she conducted an active campaign to convince Navajos suffering from tuberculosis to undergo treatment. She also inspected Navajo labor camps and, with council support, persuaded local employers to improve sanitary conditions for their workers. As part of the health visitor program, Wauneka assisted in the introduction of antituberculosis drug therapy and regularly visited tubercular patients to encourage them to stay under medical care.

The paraprofessional program became a permanent part of the Indian Health Service in 1968 with the establishment of a national training and research center in Tucson, Arizona. Known as Desert Willow, the center trained Community Health Representatives (CHRs) in basic health skills, home nursing, nutrition, and environmental health services. The CHRs were all Native Americans, trained by the IHS but employed and supervised by their own tribes. Because they were familiar with local cultures and customs, the CHRs served as specialists in "cross-cultural health delivery." They advised IHS physicians on ways to accommodate their medical practice to meet the cultural expectations of Native people, and they explained to patients the importance of modern medical procedures. By 1993, more than 1,400 CHRs were serving 250 tribes in 400 rural communities. The Indian Health Service also developed innovative technologies to improve its delivery of medical services. Using the most advanced telemetry, the IHS in the mid-1970s inaugurated its STARPAHC program (Space Technology Applied to Rural Papago Advanced Health Care). This remarkable program allowed physicians in a central location to communicate by radio and television with paraprofessionals in mobile health centers. Physicians thus could assess medical problems and make recommendations for further care of patients in remote locations. The IHS also developed a high-tech information retrieval system in the 1980s called the Resource and Patient Management System (RPMS). Computers at 200 IHS and tribal health offices facilitated the confidential collection and output of a broad range of health data on individual patients, including such items as immunization records, dental charts, and allergies. This centralized health database was an important resource as Native Americans became increasingly mobile and sought medical care at IHS facilities across the country.

Native Americans living in urban areas benefited not only from improved medical care from the Indian Health Service, but also from a growing number of Indian outpatient and social service programs in the cities. The IHS sanitation program, originally conceived as an on-reservation service, was later extended to serve off-reservation communities as well. Indian clinics in cities such as Chicago, Minneapolis, Seattle, San Francisco, and Los Angeles provided a wide array of medical and health services. Many of the clinics started out as volunteer programs, but were later taken over by state or federal agencies. The staffs of many such urban clinics were predominantly Native American, often attracting from the reservations the few highly skilled professionals.

The most chronic health problem affecting urban and rural Native Americans in the twentieth century was alcohol abuse. The IHS Task Force on Alcoholism reported in 1972 that alcohol abuse was a contributing factor to four of the top ten causes of Indian deaths: accidents, cirrhosis of the liver, homicide, and suicide. Alcohol-related accidents were an especially severe problem for Native Americans. Indians were twice as likely to die from accidents as were non-Indians, and 75 percent of all fatal accidents involving Indians were alcohol related. In addition, alcohol was a factor in 80 percent of all Indian suicides and 90 percent of all homicides committed by Indians. The arrest rate of Indians for alcohol-related offenses was ten times higher than for whites and three or four times the rate for other ethnic groups.

Perhaps the most heart-rending problem of all was the high incidence of fetal alcohol syndrome (FAS) among Native Americans. Rates of FAS varied widely for different tribes and regions, but generally were high on reservations and in urban enclaves across America. The condition is caused by mothers who consume large amounts of alcohol during their pregnancy, and its symptoms include varying degrees of physical deformity and mental retardation. With prevention the only "cure" for FAS, tribal leaders were eager to warn their people of its dangers. The Navajo Nation tribal council in 1982 conducted a workshop on FAS during which one participant observed, "Some Navajo elders used to say years back that if a woman about to bear a child drinks crazy water, the newborn will be crazy in the body and the mind." Roberta Ferron (Rosebud Sioux) put the matter more forcefully: "I am convinced that we [must] . . . halt Fetal Alcohol Syndrome among our Indian people or we will cease to exist as Indians." Public understanding of the tragic effects of FAS increased in 1989 following the publication of *The Broken Cord* by Native writer Michael Dorris (Modoc). This moving firsthand account told the story of one family's ongoing struggle to care for an adopted child afflicted with FAS. "Here is a book so powerful it will not only break your heart," wrote one critic, "it will restore your faith."

No one has ever been able to determine, for certain, why Native Americans were unusually susceptible to alcohol abuse. By the late twentieth century, most scholars had abandoned the theory that Indians were genetically or physiologically inclined to alcoholism; the more favored explanations were those that emphasized cultural or social factors. Professor Theodore D. Graves of the University of California, Los Angeles, concluded that the status of Indians as "marginal men," ill-equipped to handle the stresses of modern life, caused them to "seek release from frustration and failure in drunken stupor."

For many Native American alcoholics, the origins of their problem seemed clear enough. Alcohol abuse was already so prevalent among their family and peers that they began drinking without giving it a second thought. "It seems now almost as though I was taught to drink, like children are taught anything by the example of the grownups around them," observed one forty-three-year-old Indian alcoholic in Chicago, who further remarked:

I can remember sitting around the kitchen on weekends, and everyone would come in Friday after work, with beer and sometimes liquor, and they'd start drinking. Me and my little brother, we'd just sit and watch them. I never thought about it, but I guess it always seemed to me the thing to do. Start drinking on weekends. And then, I guess, I just drank other times, too, until it was just out of my control.

The Indian Health Service devoted a great deal of its attention to the reduction of alcohol abuse among Native people, not only because it was such a serious health problem but also because it drained needed resources from the treatment of other diseases. By the early 1990s, 70 percent of all treatment services provided by the IHS were alcohol related. The IHS funded more than 200 alcoholism programs serving urban areas and reservations, often with the full cooperation of tribal officials. One of the most promising new programs, initiated by the Indian Alcohol and Substance Abuse Prevention and Treatment Act of 1986, authorized the establishment of youth treatment centers within each of the IHS service areas. In 1994 fifteen Native American alcohol-treatment programs joined forces, in a project called Healthy Nations, to develop culturally relevant prevention programs for Native people.

Native Americans also took the lead in developing innovative programs to combat the spread of the human immunodeficiency virus (HIV) and the acquired immunodeficiency syndrome (AIDS). Between 1987 and 1991 the number of AIDS cases among American Indians increased nearly sixfold, but remained relatively low compared with other ethnic groups. One noteworthy example of local initiative was the San Diego American Indian Health Center's HIV education and prevention program. The center provided comprehensive services for Indians infected with HIV and published an illustrated AIDS prevention booklet, *Coyote's Penis* (1990), by Native writer Clifford E. Trafzer (Wyandot). In 1994 a Navajo elder, Daniel Freeland, blessed seventeen HIV-infected Native people at a conference in Albuquerque. "You are warriors," said Freeland, lighting a bundle of sage. "Go that way. Don't let anyone else tell you otherwise."

The health care available to Native Americans during the late twentieth century was powerfully affected by the movement in federal policy toward self-determination. Two complementary pieces of federal legislation, passed in the mid-1970s, permitted tribal governments to take greater responsibility for providing health-care services for their people. The Indian Self-Determination and Education Assistance Act of 1975 established the means by which tribes could contract with the federal government for the staffing and managing of health care programs. The following year Congress passed the Indian Health Care Improvement Act, identifying the specific services that tribes could operate under contract. These included health-care facilities, training programs, waste disposal systems, and urban clinics. The inclusion of the latter was significant, as public health educator Patricia Mail observed, because for the first time the federal government formally recognized the health needs of Indians living off the reservation.

Following the passage of these two key pieces of federal legislation, the Indian Health Service dedicated itself to achieving "maximum tribal involvement in developing and managing programs to meet health needs." As a result, increasing numbers of tribal governments contracted with the IHS for the management of hospitals, outpatient clinics, and other health-care programs. By the early 1990s, tribes were operating more than 300 hospitals, health centers, and health stations; twice as many as were managed by the IHS. Existing IHS programs also expanded to include greater Indian participation. Amendments to the Indian Health Care Improvement Act in 1988 acknowledged the Community Health Representative (CHR) program as an essential part of the overall IHS approach. The CHR program was cited as "a prime example of Indian self-determination, embodying all the precepts and managerial goals of the self-determination principle." By 1993, under the policy of preferential hiring, more than 60 percent of the 14,500 employees of the IHS were Native Americans.

The combined efforts of Native Americans and professionals within the Indian Health Service achieved dramatic improvements in several leading indicators of Indian health. Infectious diseases that once had decimated the Indian population were brought under control and their incidence approached that of the general population. The mortality rate among Indians with tuberculosis, for instance, decreased by 96 percent from 1955 to 1990. Likewise, the maternal mortality rate decreased by more than 90 percent. Especially heartening was the reduction in infant mortality during the same period, from a rate of more than 60 per thousand live births to only eleven, a decrease of 85 percent.

As a consequence of improved health conditions, Native Americans enjoyed higher birth rates and greater longevity. According to the 1990 census, the median age of American Indians was just over 22 years, compared to 30 years for the general population. This relatively young population was growing rapidly; in the late 1980s, the Indian birth rate was 78 percent higher than the overall birth rate in the United States. By 1990 the number of Indians had climbed to almost two million, a dramatic increase from the nadir of fewer than 250,000 ninety years earlier. Equally as encouraging was the increase in Indian life expectancy, nearly on par with the general population by 1990. As Native scholar Russell Thornton (Cherokee), author of *American Indian Holocaust and Survival* (1987), concluded, this remarkable population recovery was a tribute to "human survival instincts, perseverance, and hope."

In spite of such significant improvements in Indian health, serious problems remained at the end of the twentieth century. Despite the reduction in tuberculosis among Native Americans, Indians in the 1990s were still twice as likely to contract the disease and five times more likely to die from it than other Americans. The mortality rate for Indians with diabetes was two and one-half times greater than the rest of the nation, and the Pimas and Maricopas of Arizona continued to have the highest rate of diabetes in the world. Alcohol abuse remained the greatest unsolved health problem for Native

FIGURE 4.2

AMERICAN INDIAN POPULATION IN THE AREA OF THE UNITED STATES, 1492–1990

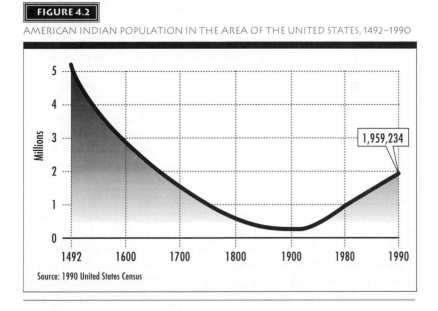

Source: 1990 United States Census

Americans. Alcoholism in the 1990s killed Native people at more than five times the rate that it killed other Americans and killed young Indians, age 25 to 34, at *ten* times the rate of other young adults. Native people also continued to have the highest suicide rate in the nation. Young Indians, age 15 to 24, were committing suicide in the early 1990s at a rate nearly twice that of non-Indians. The highest suicide rate in the nation was among the White Mountain Apaches of Arizona; fifteen tribal members committed suicide in 1992, thirteen of them under age 23.

Surveying the accomplishments of the past few decades, and noting as well the many challenges that still remained, the Indian Health Service offered this balanced appraisal in the 1990s: "Although significant gains have been made, the health status of American Indians and Alaska Natives still lags behind the general United States population."

EDUCATION

Important progress also was made in improving the education of Native Americans, but here, too, major problems persisted. The federal government largely neglected Indian education until the late nineteenth century, even though many earlier treaties had contained provisions for the establishment of schools. The few institutions of learning available to Indian children were provided by missionaries or by the tribes themselves, most notably the Cherokees, Choctaws, and Chickasaws. The federal government in the 1870s began establishing schools for the express purpose of "civilizing" Indians, that is, of eradicating from them all vestiges of Native American culture and transforming them in the mold of European American culture.

The premier institution to achieve this rapid and thoroughgoing assimilation was the off-reservation boarding school, the first of which was established at Carlisle, Pennsylvania, in 1879 by Richard Henry Pratt. Indian students at the Carlisle Indian Industrial School were subjected to enormous pressure to change not only their material culture but also their cultural attitudes and values. "The end to be gained," Pratt explained, "is the complete civilization of the Indian . . . [and] the sooner all tribal relations are broken up; the sooner the Indian loses all his Indian ways, even his language, the better it will be." A similar philosophy imbued the other Indian schools established by the federal government in the late nineteenth century. By 1900, the Bureau of Indian Affairs was operating more than 100 boarding schools, on and off the reservation, as well as nearly 150 reservation day schools. The inadequacy of Indian education was one of the major concerns of the Meriam Report of 1928. This wide-ranging critique of federal Indian policy focused especially on conditions in the boarding schools, charging that students there suffered from insufficient food, overcrowding, harsh discipline, and poor medical care. The Meriam Report called for sweeping changes in the federal government's approach to Indian education, including an upgrading of conditions at the boarding schools, the revision of the schools' curriculum to include elements of Indian culture, and the transformation of reservation day schools into community centers. Many of these recommendations were implemented during the years John Collier headed the Bureau of Indian Affairs in the 1930s. Under Collier's direction, the unrelenting pressure for assimilation was relaxed and the curriculum began to acknowledge the diversity and importance of Native cultures. Courses in tribal history, pottery making, and rug weaving replaced subjects such as algebra and ancient European history. Collier's director of Indian education, Willard Beatty, developed bilingual texts in the Sioux and Navajo languages and instituted one of the nation's first bilingual teacher training programs. One hundred new community day schools were constructed between 1933 and 1941, and enrollment nearly tripled. As Margaret Connell Szasz, author of *Education and the American Indian* (1974), concluded, the era of educational reform during the Collier years resulted in "the most dynamic program of Indian education in the history of the Indian Service."

During the Collier era the federal government also recognized the growing importance of local public schools in the education of Native Americans. By 1930 more than half of all Indian children attending school were enrolled in public schools. Federal authorities had begun contracting with local school districts to provide educational services for Indians in the 1890s, but the process was cumbersome and inefficient. In 1934 Congress passed the Johnson-O'Malley Act, streamlining the funding process by authorizing the federal government to contract with the states, rather than with individual districts. Unfortunately, the act failed to provide adequate supervision of the states' use of Johnson-O'Malley funds; as a consequence, states often used the funds for their general education budgets rather than for special programs to meet the needs of Indian students.

The coming of World War II had both positive and negative effects on the education of Native Americans. Many of the innovative programs of the 1930s were abandoned as budgets and personnel were drained away by wartime demands. On the other hand, experiences of Native Americans during the war led to a renewed appreciation of the value of education and a determination to expand the educational opportunities available. Several tribal councils enacted compulsory education ordinances and offered scholarships to promising high school graduates. Indian veterans eligible for benefits under the GI Bill of Rights enrolled in colleges and vocational training programs in record numbers.

One of the first signs of the stirring of a new interest in education came in the spring of 1946 when a delegation of Navajo leaders went to Washington, D.C. to demand more schools for their people. They pointed out that more than half of all the 22,000 children on the reservation were not in school, most of whom had reached the age of twelve or thirteen without receiving any formal education. Willard Beatty, the director of the Bureau of Indian Affairs' education division, responded by establishing the Navajo Special Education Program in the fall of 1946. The program was designed to meet the needs of overage students, providing them with basic education, vocational training, and the requisite social skills needed for success in European American society. Students were taught the importance of such things as good grooming, proper manners, correct eating habits, and other "elements of white cultural behavior." More than 4,000 students enrolled in the program during its first quarter century of operation.

The curriculum of the Navajo Special Education Program was symptomatic of a fundamental shift taking place in federal Indian policy. The cultural pluralism of the 1930s was giving way to the assimilationism of the postwar era of termination. "The nation's treatment of the Indian had come full circle," historian Margaret Connell Szasz observed. "From the early twenties to the early forties the pendulum had swung toward recognition and encouragement of Indian culture; as the war ended, it began to swing toward assimilation." Willard Beatty's own earlier interest in the preservation of traditional Indian culture had been replaced by a desire to prepare Indians to take their place in the "dominant culture." His assertion that "whatever the [Indian] child learns within the home is contrary to things he needs to know" was nearly identical to the view of Richard Henry Pratt during the heyday of assimilationism in the late nineteenth century.

The swing toward assimilation accelerated with the appointment of Dillon S. Myer as head of the Bureau of Indian Affairs in 1950. Two years later Commissioner Myer replaced Willard Beatty as director of education with Hildegard Thompson, whose success as director of the Navajo Special Education Program had established her credentials as an assimilationist. In pursuit of her goal of preparing Indians for life in an urban and technological society, Thompson expanded adult vocational programs and also altered the curriculum of BIA schools to include more academic courses in science and mathematics.

Working in concert with the policies of termination and relocation, Hildegard Thompson shifted responsibility for Indian education to local public schools whenever possible. This move—part of the terminationists' desire "to get out of the Indian business"—came at the same time the Bureau of Indian Affairs was transferring its health services to the office of the Surgeon General. Under Thompson's direction, the proportion of Indian children who attended public school increased from 52 percent in 1952 to 60 percent a dozen years later. New federal legislation positively encouraged this shift by providing public schools with increased federal aid. In addition to the funds available under the Johnson-O'Malley Act, in 1953 Congress began providing school districts in "federally impacted areas" with funds to furnish education to Indian students. (Districts with Native American students were "federally impacted" because Indians were exempt from paying property taxes, the primary source of revenue for public schools.) Passage of the Elementary and Secondary Education Act in 1965 gave added encouragement to districts to enroll Indian students. The act provided federal aid to school districts to meet the special educational needs of "children of low-income families."

The missing ingredient in the formulation of educational policy for Native Americans throughout the first half of the twentieth century was the voice of the Indians themselves. By the mid-1960s, that voice could no longer be ignored. The emergence of a strong Native American leadership became a powerful new force in Indian education, demanding and achieving a remarkable degree of Indian control over educational policies and institutions. The new leadership first appeared in the battle against termination, but once the tide turned in that conflict, Native people began to focus on educational reform.

The content of textbooks was one of the first of many contentious educational issues to engage the attention of Native American leaders in the mid-1960s. As more and more Indian children enrolled in public schools, parents grew concerned about the negative characterization of Indian cultures often found in instructional materials.

Jeannette Henry (Eastern Cherokee) and Rupert Costo (Cahuilla) first raised the issue in California in 1964, launching a well-documented attack on the demeaning and inaccurate stereotypes of Native Americans found in textbooks used in the public schools. The California Indian Education Association, founded in 1967 by David Risling (Hupa/Yurok), helped carry the fight forward in the next decade. On the Navajo reservation at Shiprock, New Mexico, concerned parents conducted a sit-in at the administration building of the local school district to protest continued use of textbooks that characterized Indians as "savage barbarians." Meanwhile, a survey of more than 100 history texts, conducted by the National Study of American Indian Education, found that "the American Indians have been obliterated, defamed, disparaged, and disembodied. The notion of the blood-curdling, perilous, massacring savage is common."

Native Americans across the country took the initiative in developing dozens of new and innovative educational programs. Stanley Smartlowit, Yakama tribal education chairman in 1963, organized a college preparatory course on the campus of Central Washington State University and established a remedial program at a remote site near the base of Mount Adams. "It's time," Smartlowit said, "we started doing something about education instead of just talking about our problems." Myron Jones (Tuscarora) began teaching Indian parents in New York about federal programs available for their children. The Shoshone-Bannocks in Idaho and the Blackfeet in Montana lobbied for the inclusion of courses in Native American arts and history in the curriculum of local schools. Artist Clarence Pickernell (Quinault) returned to his reservation in western Washington and began offering classes in Indian culture. "A decade ago," Pickerell observed in the late 1960s, "I would have said the culture and traditions were gone, dead. But when I came back . . . a change had taken place. There was a spontaneous reawakening."

Dissatisfaction with the quality of education provided by public schools and schools operated by the Bureau of Indian Affairs led Native Americans in the mid-1960s to establish their own schools. The first of such Indian-controlled schools opened in the fall of 1966 at Rough Rock, an isolated community near Chinle, Arizona. Navajo leaders contracted with the Office of Economic Opportunity (OEO) and the BIA for funding of what was called the Rough Rock Demonstration School. Instruction at this experimental school was in Navajo and English, with special emphasis placed on Navajo history and culture. The school's Navajo Curriculum Center, founded in 1967, published instructional materials drawn from the oral traditions of community members and illustrated by local artists. One of the first publications to appear was Etheloo Yazzie's *Navajo History* (1971).

Although supported by federal funds, control of the school at Rough Rock remained firmly in the hands of an all-Navajo school board. John Dick, one of the first board members, explained the school's purpose:

> We want our children to be proud of being Navajos. We want them to know who they are. . . . In the future they will have to be available to make many choices and do many different things. They need a modern education to make their way, but they have to know both worlds—and being Navajo will give them strength.

The key to the success of Rough Rock was the enthusiastic support it received from the Navajo people. Their identification with the school was evident in the name they gave it. Schools run by the BIA were called, in Navajo, *Washington bi 'olta,* or "school of the federal government"; and public schools were called *Bilagaana Yazhi bi 'olta,* or "white children's school." Only Rough Rock was called *Diné bi 'olta*— "the Navajo school."

The success of Rough Rock soon encouraged other communities to establish similar schools. Navajos in the villages at Ramah and Borrego Pass in New Mexico opened schools based on the Rough Rock model. Likewise, the Chippewa and Cree people in northern Montana assumed control over the Rocky Boy School and began revising its curriculum to include courses in Indian culture and history. Representatives from several such schools banded together in 1971 to form the Coalition of Indian Controlled School Boards, dedicated to the proposition that "if American Indians are to survive as a people, they must develop and control their own schools."

Native American interest in educational reform was not limited to elementary and secondary schools; it extended to the college level as well. Navajo Nation chairman Raymond Nakai and other tribal leaders launched a major fund-raising campaign in the mid-1960s to establish the country's first Indian-controlled college. The campaign succeeded in obtaining grants from both private and public sources, including major funding from the Office of Economic Opportunity. In January 1969 Navajo Community College began offering its first classes at a temporary location in Many Farms, Arizona. The curriculum at NCC

FOUNDED BY THE NAVAJO TRIBAL COUNCIL IN 1968, THE NAVAJO COMMUNITY
COLLEGE AT TSAILE, ARIZONA, WAS THE NATION'S FIRST INDIAN-CONTROLLED
COLLEGE. SHOWN HERE IS THE NED A. HATATHLI CULTURE CENTER, NAMED FOR
THE COLLEGE'S FIRST PRESIDENT.

included academic courses for students intending to transfer to four-
year colleges or universities, as well as vocational courses in such fields
as commercial art, drafting, nursing, welding, and auto mechanics.
The core of the curriculum, however, was the Navajo Studies program
that offered courses in tribal history and culture. Included were
courses in the Navajo language, contemporary tribal issues, and the
history of Indian-white relations taught from an Indian perspective.
For use in the classroom and beyond, the college press began publishing works in tribal history by Navajo writers. As Raymond Brown,
student body president in 1971, observed, "NCC . . . teaches our
young people to become leaders among our own people . . . it teaches
what we, the American Indian, want to learn."

Federal support for the college was put on a permanent basis in
1971 when Congress passed the Navajo Community College Act.

Construction began the following year on a new campus at Tsaile, Arizona, on the eastern edge of scenic Canyon de Chelly. Control of NCC rested with an all-Navajo Board of Regents and an All-Indian Council composed of faculty, students, and administrators. Non-Indian faculty were excluded from participating in the decision making process, a policy that was criticized by some as "reverse discrimination." Ned Hatathli, Navajo president of the college, responded: "This is an Indian owned and an Indian operated institution, and we certainly don't want any people other than Indian to dictate to us what is good for us."

Increased financial aid from the federal government in the 1960s and 1970s led to a significant growth in the number of Indians attending college. Enrollment steadily increased at Indian-controlled colleges— such as those newly established at Standing Rock, North Dakota, and Sinte Gleska, South Dakota—as well as at non-Indian colleges and universities. As their numbers on campus increased, Indian students began to organize and push for the establishment of Indian Studies programs just as African American students were organizing simultaneously to demand programs of Black Studies. At the University of Minnesota, for instance, only five Indian students were enrolled in 1960, whereas 45 were enrolled eight years later. The American Indian Students Association at the university successfully campaigned in 1968 for the inclusion in the curriculum of courses in the Chippewa language, as well as classes in Minnesota Indian history and contemporary Indian affairs. "We never resorted to threats of violence or intimidation," the leader of the Indian students later explained. "We pushed hard, we demanded to be heard, and we were careful to act in a gentlemanly manner so as not to alienate anyone who could help us." By 1970 forty-eight American colleges and universities—most notably in Arizona, California, Montana, Oklahoma, and Washington—were offering Indian Studies programs. The following year, a unique Native American institution of higher learning opened its doors in Davis, California. D-Q University, drawing "upon the strength of Native American culture," offered a full range of academic courses on campus and provided educational programs on reservations throughout the state.

National attention was focused on the issue of Indian education in the late 1960s by the widely publicized findings of the Senate Subcommittee on Indian Education. The subcommittee began its investigation in 1967 under the chairmanship of Democratic Senator Robert

Kennedy of New York, a presidential aspirant who described the condition of American Indians as "a national tragedy and a national disgrace." The subcommittee conducted extensive hearings, interviewing scores of Native Americans and other expert witnesses across the country. Following the assassination of Robert Kennedy in 1968, the chairmanship passed to his brother Senator Edward Kennedy of Massachusetts who issued the subcommittee's final report, *Indian Education: A National Tragedy—A National Challenge* (1969). The Kennedy Report, as it was commonly known, presented a scathing indictment of federal Indian policy and portrayed the condition of American Indians as virtually unchanged from the time of the Meriam Report forty years earlier. It called for a dramatic increase in funding for Indian education at all levels and the adoption of a new national policy for Indian education. The recommendations emphasized the importance of including courses in Native American culture, history, and language in schools where Indian children were in attendance; and of giving tribal leaders and Indian parents a greater role in the local educational process. "The Federal Government must commit itself to a national policy of educational excellence for Indian children," the report concluded, "[with] maximum participation and control by Indian adults and communities."

Native people were particularly encouraged by the Kennedy Report's endorsement of the principle of self-determination. Within a month of the report's publication, in November 1969, Indian educators convened the first meeting of the National Indian Education Association (NIEA). As historian Margaret Connell Szasz pointed out, the NIEA was "the educators' equivalent of the National Congress of American Indians." It was, in other words, a powerful defender of the interests of Native Americans whenever and wherever they might be threatened. The directors of the NIEA described themselves simply as an organization "*by* Indian people *for* Indian people." During the early 1970s, the NIEA became the chief proponent of Indian self-determination in federal education policy.

Leaders of the National Indian Education Association worked closely with members of Congress in drafting what became the Indian Education Act of 1972, an important step toward realizing the goal of self-determination. The act required the participation of parents and tribal leaders in the administration of funds available to public school districts under the "federally impacted" legislation of the 1950s. This important reform was intended to prevent districts from accepting

such funds without providing programs and services specifically designed for Indian students. The act also provided funds to states and
local districts for the development of courses in Native American history and culture. Additional funding was available for the establishment of community-run schools and adult-education projects. All
programs established under the act were to be administered by an
Office of Indian Education, controlled by an (all-Indian) National
Advisory Council on Indian Education. Herschel Sahmaunt (Kiowa),
president of the NIEA, praised the Indian Education Act as the first
law ever to give "Indian people on reservations, in rural settings, and
in the cities control over their own education."

An even more impressive victory for the forces of self-determination
came in 1975 when Congress passed the Indian Self-Determination
and Education Assistance Act. Incorporating language drafted by Native American leaders, the act placed additional control over Indian
education in the hands of the Indians themselves. Specifically, the act
required all states accepting funds under the Johnson-O'Malley Act of
1934 to use those funds exclusively for programs to benefit Indian
students. To guarantee that compliance, the act authorized school
boards controlled by Native Americans to contract directly for Johnson-
O'Malley funds, and it required other districts receiving such funds to
consult a local Indian Parents Committee on all decisions affecting
Indian students. This act had a major impact on Indian education since
the vast majority of Indian children were enrolled in districts receiving
Johnson-O'Malley funds. By the end of the 1970s, fewer than 44,000
Indian students were enrolled in schools operated by the Bureau of
Indian Affairs, whereas more than 171,000 were attending Johnson-
O'Malley–funded public schools.

Even within the schools operated by the Bureau of Indian Affairs,
the move toward self-determination was having a profound effect.
In the late 1970s and early 1980s, the BIA closed several of its off-
reservation boarding schools and opened additional day schools in cooperation with local tribal leaders. On the college level, the Bureau of
Indian Affairs increased its support of institutions like Navajo Community College under the Tribally Controlled Community College
Assistance Act of 1978. By 1984 more than 3,300 Indian students
were enrolled in nineteen such community colleges. Grants from the
BIA also provided aid to two tribally controlled four-year institutions
in South Dakota, Sinte Gleska College and Oglala Lakota College.
The BIA continued to upgrade its own post-secondary schools as well,

offering additional courses in Native American culture and history. The bureau's Institute of American Indian Arts in Santa Fe, New Mexico, offered advanced courses in painting, jewelry, ceramics, sculpture, and other media. Similar changes occurred at the BIA's Haskell Indian Nations University (formerly Haskell Indian Junior College) in Lawrence, Kansas, and its Southwestern Indian Polytechnic Institute in Albuquerque, New Mexico.

After two decades of sweeping changes in educational policy, a special task force of the U.S. Department of Education conducted a comprehensive survey of Native American education. The task force was headed by William G. Demmert, Jr. (Tlingit/Sioux), former treasurer of the National Indian Education Association, and Terrel Bell, former secretary of education. Its final report, *Indian Nations at Risk* (1991), noted the progress that had been made in Indian education but also expressed concern about the serious problems that remained. By 1990 nearly 90 percent of all Native American children were enrolled in public schools, with the remainder in private schools or in schools funded by the Bureau of Indian Affairs. As mandated by federal legislation, Indian parents had an important role in the planning and implementation of programs that affected their children; and instructional materials were available for classroom use that presented history, music, visual arts, and other subjects from a Native American

FIGURE 4.3

DISTRIBUTION OF NATIVE AMERICAN STUDENTS, SCHOOL YEAR 1989–1990

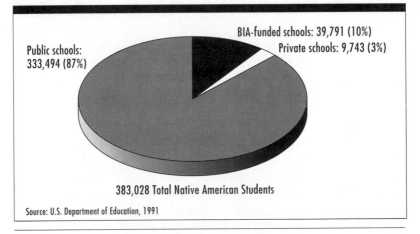

BIA-funded schools: 39,791 (10%)

Private schools: 9,743 (3%)

Public schools: 333,494 (87%)

383,028 Total Native American Students

Source: U.S. Department of Education, 1991

perspective. The percentage of Indian students graduating from high school and attending college steadily increased, while twenty-four tribally controlled colleges offered classes to 5,000 students.

In spite of these positive gains, the task force found convincing evidence that Native American children remained seriously disadvantaged. As many as 60 percent of all Indian students had low academic expectations, were relegated to low ability tracks, and experienced poor academic achievement. A greater percentage of Native American eighth-graders performed at below basic levels in mathematics than did students who were Latin American, African American, European American, or Asian American. Likewise, a higher proportion of Native students repeated a grade than did students of any other group, and their drop-out rates were the highest in the nation. In some areas, Indian drop-out rates were as high as 60 percent, especially in urban schools where Indian students were often the smallest minority. Although Native Americans enrolled in colleges in ever-increasing numbers, only one in four Indian college students graduated.

The task force placed much of the blame for these continuing inequities on the failure of schools to meet the unique needs of Native Americans. In spite of the movement toward self-determination, the task force concluded that many schools "have failed to nurture the intellectual development" of Indian students and have contributed to a weakening of their resolve "to retain and continue the development

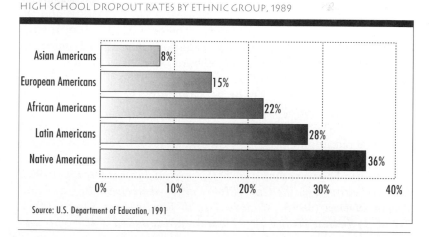

FIGURE 4.4

HIGH SCHOOL DROPOUT RATES BY ETHNIC GROUP, 1989

Asian Americans   8%
European Americans   15%
African Americans   22%
Latin Americans   28%
Native Americans   36%

0%   10%   20%   30%   40%

Source: U.S. Department of Education, 1991

of their original languages and cultures." The challenge was to encourage Native students to retain their distinct cultural identities while preparing them for participation in the larger world. "Schools must enable children and adults," the task force concluded, "to adapt and flourish in the modern environment while maintaining bonds with traditional culture."

The views of the task force were widely shared by Native leaders across the country who agreed that although much had been achieved, much remained to be done. John Woodenlegs, tribal chairman of the Northern Cheyenne, summed up the sentiments of his people: "We feel our children need education which gives the best of both cultures. We feel that many of the values of our past Cheyenne society can still serve us well in this modern world." Achieving and maintaining that balance—taking the best from both worlds—was one sure path transcending America's ongoing national tragedy.

SOURCES AND SUGGESTIONS FOR FURTHER READING

One of the best summaries of economic conditions among Native Americans is Alan L. Sorkin, "The Economic Basis of Indian Life," in J. Milton Yinger and George Eaton Simpson, eds., *American Indians Today* (1978). Much of the material in this chapter on Native American poverty is drawn from two articles in Jack O. Waddell and O. Michael Watson, eds., *The American Indian in Urban Society* (1971): Joseph G. Jorgensen, "Indians and the Metropolis" and Merwyn S. Garbarino, "Life in the City: Chicago." The discussion of more recent conditions is based on the surveys by James S. Olson and Raymond Wilson, *Native Americans in the Twentieth Century* (1986) and W. Richard West, Jr., and Kevin Gover, "The Struggle for Indian Civil Rights," in Frederick E. Hoxie, ed., *Indians in American History: An Introduction* (1988). See also the relevant portions in Duane Champagne, ed., *The Native North American Almanac* (1994), and Arlene Hirschfelder and Martha Kreipe de Montaño, *The Native American Almanac: A Portrait of Native America Today* (1993).

This chapter's discussion of the health of Native Americans is based on several recent publications of the Indian Health Service, a division of the Public Health Service within the U.S. Department of Health and Human Services: *Regional Differences in Indian Health* (1993), *Comprehensive Health Care Program for American Indians and Alaska Natives* (1993), *Indian Health Service Fact Sheet* (1993), *Trends in Indian Health* (1992), and *A Manual on Adolescents and*

Adults with Fetal Alcohol Syndrome with Special Reference to American Indians (1988). Also useful are the historical overviews provided by Patricia D. Mail, "Hippocrates Was a Medicine Man: The Health Care of Native Americans in the Twentieth Century," in Yinger and Simpson, eds., *American Indians Today;* and Harold L. Hodgkinson, *The Demographics of American Indians: One Percent of the People; Fifty Percent of the Diversity* (1990). Additional information is provided by two articles in Wilcomb E. Washburn, ed., *History of Indian-White Relations,* vol. 4, *Handbook of North American Indians* (1988): Lawrence C. Kelly, "United States Indian Policies, 1900–1980" and Philleo Nash, "Twentieth-Century United States Government Agencies."

The discussion of Indian alcoholism is drawn primarily from Theodore D. Graves, "Drinking and Drunkenness among Urban Indians," in Waddell and Watson, eds., *The American Indian in Urban Society;* Edward P. Dozier, "Problem Drinking among American Indians: The Role of Socio-cultural Deprivation," *Quarterly Journal of Studies on Alcohol* (1966); and Nancy Oestreich Lurie, "The World's Oldest On-Going Protest Demonstration: North American Indian Drinking Patterns," in Norris Hundley, ed., *The American Indian* (1974). The twentieth-century increase in the population of Native Americans is described in Russell Thornton, *American Indian Holocaust and Survival: A Population History Since 1492* (1987).

The definitive work on the education of American Indians, and the most important source for the last third of this chapter, is Margaret Connell Szasz, *Education and the American Indian: The Road to Self-Determination, 1928–1973* (1974). Briefer summaries are available in Margaret Connell Szasz and Carmelita S. Ryan, "American Indian Education," in Washburn, ed., *History of Indian-White Relations;* Robert J. Havighurst, "Indian Education Since 1960," in Yinger and Simpson, eds., *American Indians Today;* and Olson and Wilson, *Native Americans in the Twentieth Century.* See also Jon Reyhner, ed., *Teaching American Indian Students* (1988). An impassioned critique of Indian education appears in Vine Deloria, Jr., and Clifford Lytle, *The Nations Within: The Past and Future of American Indian Sovereignty* (1984). This chapter's discussion of the Kennedy Report is based on Edward M. Kennedy, "Let the Indians Run Indian Policy," in Howard M. Bahr, Bruce A. Chadwick, and Robert C. Day, *Native Americans Today: Sociological Perspectives* (1972). The account of Navajo Community College comes partly from Robert W. Young, *A*

Political History of the Navajo Tribe (1978) and Peter Iverson, *The Navajos* (1990). See also Frank C. Miller, "Involvement in an Urban University," in Jack O. Waddell and O. Michael Watson, *The American Indian in Urban Society* (1971). Information on the current status of Indian education is drawn from two publications of the Indian Nations at Risk Task Force of the U.S. Department of Education: *Indian Nations at Risk: An Educational Strategy for Action* (1991) and *Indian Nations at Risk: Solutions for the 1990s* (1991).

5

THE TRAIL TO
WOUNDED KNEE
→ → → → → → → →

 FOR MANY EUROPEAN Americans the first signs of discontent among Native Americans in the 1960s were the bumper stickers carrying such angry slogans as "Custer Had It Coming!" "Red Power!" and "Kemo Sabe Means Honky!" Others got the message when they opened their morning newspapers to read that Indians had taken over the island of Alcatraz in San Francisco Bay or had seized the headquarters of the Bureau of Indian Affairs (BIA) in Washington, D.C. Certainly the message came through loud and clear on that cold winter's day in 1973 when more than 200 Indians occupied a tiny hamlet in South Dakota called Wounded Knee.

At first glance, the causes of the discontent seemed all too obvious. The continuing poverty that plagued the lives of Native Americans made such discontent inevitable: A people could endure substandard housing, health care, and education for only so long. These were the conditions most often cited by contemporary journalists attempting to explain the explosions of Indian rage. But behind the headlines lay other, more complex issues.

MODERATES, TRADITIONALISTS,
AND ACTIVISTS

Among Native Americans were deep divisions that also contributed to the discontent. Intratribal and intertribal rivalries played their part, as did the continuing differences between full-bloods and mixed-bloods, traditionalists and assimilationists, reservation and nonreservation Indians. The divisions were complex and shifting, with few clear lines of demarcation, but three broad groups may be identified. The *moderates* dominated the tribal councils and had a working relationship with the institutions of European American society. The *traditionalists* remained aloof from the tribal governments and maintained the old way of life in remote corners of the reservations. The *activists* were young, college educated, urban, and increasingly impatient. The issues also were complicated, but centered on three fundamental concerns: the preservation of traditional culture, the relationship between the tribes and the federal government, and the nature of the tribal governments themselves.

Native Americans long had been divided by profoundly different views about assimilation and government relations, but these divisions intensified following the formation of new tribal governments under the Indian Reorganization Act (IRA) of 1934. The act granted Indians the right to reconstitute their tribal governments, a right that had been under assault since the days of the Dawes Act a half century earlier. The new governments often were based on model constitutions or corporation charters supplied by the Bureau of Indian Affairs and usually included an elected tribal council and a tribal chairman or president. But the powers of the new tribal governments were far from absolute; their decisions remained subject to the veto power of the secretary of the interior. As new governments were formed and tribal leaders were elected, a natural constituency was created in support of the status quo. Tribal presidents and members of the tribal councils came to have a vested interest in the maintenance of good relations with the federal government.

Vocal opposition to the new tribal governments came from several directions at once. Fiercely pro-assimilation leaders such as Joseph Bruner (Creek), head of the American Indian Federation, feared that the reconstituted tribal governments would impede the acculturation of individual Indians into the dominant European American society. Meanwhile, many full-bloods and traditional Indians boycotted altogether the elections establishing the new tribal governments. The traditionalists preferred the reinstitution of older, consensual models of tribal organization. Many tribes formerly had been ruled by councils of elders who had to agree unanimously on every decision and who could not force their decisions on any dissenting adult tribal member.

Still other Indian leaders objected to the new tribal governments because they remained subject to federal control. The California Mission Indian Federation, led by Adam Castillo (Cahuilla), argued that the tribes should have a direct voice in the removal of reservation superintendents and other BIA employees. One federation member, Rupert Costo (Cahuilla), urged a complete break from BIA control.

As congressional support for the Indian Reorganization Act and other reforms of the Indian New Deal waned during World War II, Commissioner of Indian Affairs John Collier encouraged leaders of the new tribal governments to form their own national organization to defend the gains of the recent past. More than 100 delegates, representing tribes from twenty-seven states, gathered in Denver, Colorado, in November 1944 and founded what became the most important Indian rights organization in the nation's history, the National Congress of American Indians (NCAI). Membership in the NCAI was limited to "persons of Indian ancestry," although non-Indians were allowed to join as nonvoting associates. The NCAI soon came to represent about three-quarters of all Native Americans.

Leaders of the tribal governments dominated the National Congress of American Indians. Its executive council consisted entirely of representatives selected by individual tribal councils. Many of the early NCAI leaders had served in the armed forces during World War II before being elected to positions of responsibility in the tribal governments. As historian Gerald D. Nash observed, "To a large extent the Indian rights movement was led by World War II veterans who actively involved themselves in tribal affairs after the war. Having seen the outside world, they gained a new perspective of themselves and their people." Among this new generation of leaders was Robert Burnette, the outspoken tribal chairman of the Rosebud Sioux who served as an executive director of the NCAI. Burnette had joined the Marine Corps at age seventeen and served in the Pacific during World War II.

During its first two decades of existence, the National Council of American Indians led the fight against termination. In dozens of resolutions adopted at its annual conventions, in the pages of the *NCAI Sentinel,* and in countless appearances before congressional committees, the NCAI waged an unceasing battle against the federal government's attempt to end federal supervision of the tribes. Following the passage of House Concurrent Resolution 108, the NCAI met in an emergency session in the nation's capital for eight weeks in early 1954 to protest the impending termination of tribal trusteeship. Delegates from forty-three tribes adopted a Declaration of Indian Rights demanding the continuation of "federal protection and the promise of certain benefits which our ancestors gave forever to the people of the United States [in return for] title to the very soul of our beloved country." The delegates declared that the reservations "are ancestral homelands, retained by us for our perpetual use and enjoyment."

Typical of the many local battles aided by the National Congress of American Indians was the struggle of the Senecas to preserve their tribal lands. The U.S. government had signed a treaty with the Senecas in 1794 guaranteeing to them lands along the Allegheny River in western New York and Pennsylvania. Flooding along the Allegheny in the twentieth century, however, led to plans to build a dam and reservoir that would inundate more than 10,000 acres of Seneca land, including an ancestral burial ground described by one distraught Seneca woman as "our Arlington." The federal government condemned the land for the reservoir, and the Senecas filed suit in federal court to block the condemnation. "We Indians have a spiritual tie with the earth," explained Harriet Pierce (Seneca), "a reverence for it that whites don't share and can hardly understand." In 1958 a federal court ruled against the tribe, clearing the way for the construction of the Kinzua Dam and the flooding of the Indians' land. Seven hundred people were forced to move from lands their families had occupied for centuries, and 3,000 Seneca graves were relocated. One of the relocated graves was that of the great Seneca chief, Cornplanter.

Meanwhile, outside the conventions and official publications of the National Congress of American Indians, new and more forceful voices were being raised in defense of Indian rights. In upstate New York an articulate and imaginative leader named Wallace "Mad Bear" Anderson (Tuscarora) launched a series of dramatic protests during the 1950s that served as models for similar demonstrations across the country in the following decade. In 1958 Anderson led a successful fight against an attempt by the state of New York to condemn more than 1,000 acres of land on the Tuscarora reservation for the construction of a reservoir. When the state offered to compensate the Tuscarora with $3 million, Anderson rallied his fellow tribesmen with the cry, "This land is your mother. You cannot sell your mother." More than 200 Native people gathered to block the work of the surveyors. Angry Indians threw firecrackers and fired guns over the heads of the surveyors; Indian women and children tackled state troopers and sheriff's deputies. Anderson later led a delegation of 300 sympathizers from across the country to Washington, D.C. There they rallied in front of the White House and attempted to place the secretary of the interior under citizen's arrest. In 1959 a federal commission ruled that the Tuscaroras could not be compelled to sell their land.

New and impassioned Native American leaders also were emerging on the campuses of the nation's colleges and universities. Indian veterans, encouraged by the G.I. Bill of Rights, enrolled in institutions of higher education in record numbers in the years after World War II. Their ranks were swelled further by veterans returning from the Korean War during the 1950s. Attending college gave Indian students valuable skills and new insights into European American society, but it also heightened their sense of separate identity. "Very few of us crossed the gap between the two cultures," observed Herbert Blatchford (Navajo), a young student at the University of New Mexico. "Those who found it difficult to indulge in the new culture developed into a hybrid group, belonging fully to neither culture."

Seeking to preserve their Native American identity on the college campuses, Indian students organized clubs and held "cultural evenings" of traditional dance and song. In 1954 Herbert Blatchford organized a pivotal meeting of college students and tribal elders in Santa Fe, a meeting where he hoped the young could reconnect with the old. Blatchford expressed the concerns of many Indian students who were trying to obtain the benefits of a college education without losing touch with their Indian heritage. "How can we, as young people, help to solve conflicts between cultures?" Blatchford asked. The elders responded that they supported the students' pursuit of their education and assured them that once they had graduated they would be welcomed back to the reservations. "Your people need to know what you know," the elders said. Satisfied with this encouragement, the students persevered in their studies and in their attempts to retain contact with traditional culture. They formed intercollegiate associations of Indian clubs, the most important of which was the Southwestern Regional Youth Conference (SRYC). The SRYC held yearly meetings, including one in 1960 where 350 students from fifty-seven tribes gathered in Santa Fe.

One of the largest and most varied groups of Native American leaders ever to assemble met in Chicago in June 1961. The conference was endorsed by the National Congress of American Indians and organized by Sol Tax, an anthropologist at the University of Chicago. Its purpose was to draft a set of recommendations to guide the Indian policy of the new presidential administration of John F. Kennedy. In attendance were more than 420 Native leaders from sixty-seven tribes, including representatives of the largest and most powerful western tribes as well as spokesmen from eastern tribes unrecognized by the federal government.

Also attending the Chicago conference were several young Native Americans who were recent college graduates. They had not been invited to attend, and they represented no one but themselves. Herbert Blatchford from New Mexico was there, as were Clyde Warrior (Ponca) from Oklahoma and Melvin Thom (Paiute) from Nevada. The young people became increasingly disenchanted with the routine business of the conference. "There was a lot of rigmarole about procedure and all that," recalled Herbert Blatchford. "We weren't interested." Their impatience grew as the elected tribal leaders seemed to dominate the affairs of the convention. "We saw the 'Uncle Tomahawks' fumbling around, passing resolutions, and putting headdresses on people," complained Melvin Thom. "But as for taking a strong stand they just weren't doing it." Clyde Warrior agreed: "It was the old song and dance to a slightly new anthropological tune."

Twelve of the young Native Americans at the conference decided to form their own youth caucus. Chaired by Herbert Blatchford, the caucus met for four days and drafted a comprehensive "Statement of Purpose." The caucus then presented the statement to the entire conference and lobbied to have it adopted. After vigorous and prolonged debate, the caucus succeeded in having its statement overwhelmingly approved by the conference as a "Declaration of Indian Purpose." The declaration contained one of the earliest demands for what became known as the policy of self-determination, the right of the Indians to have greater control over the federal programs designed for their welfare. Furthermore, the declaration proclaimed the Indians' commitment to the defense and preservation of their traditional cultures: "We believe in the inherent right of all people to retain spiritual and cultural values, and that the free exercise of these values is necessary to the normal development of any people."

Emboldened by their success in Chicago, members of the youth caucus made plans to form their own permanent organization. In August 1961 ten young Native Americans gathered in Gallup, New Mexico, and organized the National Indian Youth Council (NIYC). The founding members of the organization—including Herbert Blatchford, Melvin Thom, Clyde Warrior, and Shirley Hill Witt (Akwesasne

LEADERS OF THE NATIONAL INDIAN YOUTH COUNCIL CONFER IN DENVER, COL-
ORADO, IN DECEMBER OF 1964. ON THE LEFT IS MELVIN THOM (PAIUTE), ON THE
RIGHT IS HERBERT BLATCHFORD (NAVAJO), AND STANDING IN THE CENTER IS A
VISITOR FROM CANADA, ALLEN JACOBS (CHIPPEWA).

Mohawk)—were dissatisfied with the cautious tactics and limited
goals of the tribal governments and the National Congress of American Indians. Melvin Thom, elected first president of the NIYC, explained that the new organization was created because "[we] didn't
feel that the older leadership was aggressive enough. And we felt that
Indian affairs were so bad that it was time to raise some hell." The
NIYC criticized the leaders of the NCAI for being too well satisfied
with the status quo. Tribal governments, said Clyde Warrior, were
controlled by "Uncle Tomahawks," his derisive name for "those Indian leaders who are allied with the Bureau of Indian Affairs and who
say what the government wants them to say."

The National Indian Youth Council also criticized tribal leaders for
not adequately defending traditional Native American culture. The
NIYC denounced those who accepted the necessity of assimilation as
"apples," red on the outside but white on the inside. Leaders of the
NIYC called upon Indian people everywhere to regard their cultural
traditions as a source of great strength and power for survival in the
modern world. Herbert Blatchford emphasized the importance of preserving traditional Indian culture in a society dominated by European

Americans. His advice to well-meaning whites who still measured Indian progress by degrees of assimilation was unequivocal: "It is time to face the fact that Indians are skeptical of Anglo-American culture." Clyde Warrior was even stronger in his denunciation of the "American myth" that Indians must someday be assimilated into mainstream society. He was especially troubled by the ready acceptance of assimilation by many young Indians. "I am disturbed to the point of screaming," he confessed, "when I see American Indian youth accepting the horror of 'American conformity' as being the only way for Indian progress."

The defense of traditional culture by the National Indian Youth Council bridged the generation gap between its youthful leaders and tribal elders. A natural alliance thus was formed between the NIYC activists and many (but by no means all) of the traditionalists on the reservations. The leaders of the NIYC expressed great respect for tribal elders, and the elders responded by supporting in varying degrees the young activists. Caught in the middle were the moderates who dominated the tribal governments. Clyde Warrior viewed this alignment as a natural and encouraging development:

> Unrest and resentment have always existed through all the age groups of Indians. But the elders did not think anything could be done. Now they have young people coming home who are somewhat verbal [in English] and who have some knowledge of how the mechanics of government and American institutions work. . . . It's a kind of happy meeting of elders, with power in the community, and these young people who have some idea of how urban America works.

The first concerted action of the National Indian Youth Council was a series of demonstrations to defend Indian fishing rights, in what historian and journalist Alvin M. Josephy, Jr., called "The Great Northwest Fishing War." For many tribes in the Pacific Northwest, fishing was not only an important source of food and income, it was also a traditional activity that contributed to their sense of group identity. They believed that their right to fish had been guaranteed by treaties signed by tribal leaders and representatives of the U.S. government in the 1850s. In the Medicine Creek Treaty of 1854, the Nisquallies, Puyallups, and seven other tribes had ceded vast lands to the federal government. In return, the government recognized the Indians' perpetual right to use their traditional fishing grounds: "The right of taking fish at all usual and accustomed grounds and stations is further secured to said Indians in common with all citizens of the Territory."

As the European American population increased, competition for the dwindling supply of fish intensified. Government officials came under increased pressure from sport fishermen and the commercial fishing industry to restrict Indian fishing. State fish and game regulations were adopted in the early twentieth century and dozens of Indians were arrested for fishing out of season or without a license. Game wardens impounded the Indians' fishing boats and gear as "evidence," thereby depriving them of their means of livelihood. In 1954 Robert Satiacum (Puyallup/Yakama) was convicted of having game fish in his possession during a closed season. Satiacum appealed his conviction on the grounds that his fishing rights were guaranteed by federal treaty and that the state regulations unjustly deprived him of those rights. The state Supreme Court dismissed Satiacum's conviction in a split decision, leaving unresolved the larger issue of state regulations versus Indian treaty rights.

The pace of arrests of Indian fishermen quickened throughout the late 1950s and early 1960s. The Washington State Department of Fish and Game argued that Indian fishermen, using gill nets 600 feet long, were endangering the spawning and survival of several species of Pacific salmon. The state argued further that it had the right to regulate Indian fishing under the provisions of Public Law 280, the federal statute that allowed state governments to extend jurisdiction over Indians even without their consent. The Indians continued to assert their treaty rights and argued that the real threats to the salmon were pollution, the damming of the rivers, and the activities of the non-Indian commercial fishermen. In the case of *Washington v. McCoy* (1963) the state Supreme Court upheld the right of the state government to regulate Indian fishing for conservation purposes. The *McCoy* decision, in effect, nullified the provisions of the Treaty of Medicine Creek signed more than a century earlier. "None of the signatories of the original treaty," the court decreed, "contemplated fishing with a 600 foot nylon gill net, which could prevent the escapement of any fish for spawning purposes."

Following the McCoy decision, the Makah tribal council invited members of the National Indian Youth Council to come to Washington and help organize protest demonstrations. The invitation came at an opportune time for the NIYC. "We . . . were looking for a target area," Melvin Thom recalled. "We were looking for a target area for direct action." The NIYC leaders were especially anxious to work in concert with tribal elders. "We should listen and respect and honor the experience and advice of our elders," said Shirley Hill Witt. In

February 1964 representatives from the NIYC met with elders from more than forty tribes to plan what came to be called "fish-ins." Inspired by the sit-ins of the civil rights movement, a fish-in was an act of civil disobedience in which Indians took direct action to assert their fishing rights guaranteed by treaty. The first fish-in was held in March 1964 on the Quillayute River in western Washington. Hundreds of Indians stood along the banks of the river and watched as fishermen defied the state game wardens by fishing without a license. As the wardens began arresting the Native fishermen, an odd thing happened. "The Indians began to enjoy it," observed Melvin Thom. "They were happy to see some direct action."

Over the next several years, dozens of fish-ins were held on the rivers of Washington state. Not all were as peaceful as the first. As Stan Steiner, author of *The New Indians* (1968), reported, pitched battles were fought along the Puyallup, Yakima, Nisqually, Green, and Columbia rivers. Native fishermen in their boats fought with their fists and were clubbed by game wardens and state police. Women and children along the banks threw sticks and rocks at police and game wardens. More than 1,000 Indians came from across the country to show their support for the embattled fishermen. "It was the first full-scale intertribal *action* since the Indians defeated General Custer on the Little Big Horn," proclaimed the executive director of the NIYC, Herbert Blatchford.

Not all Native Americans in the Northwest supported the fish-ins. Some elected tribal leaders complained that such tactics were undignified and counterproductive; they questioned whether direct action was "the Indian way." But as the number of arrests steadily increased, and as the statements of public officials became more vitriolic, the "moderate" opposition among tribal leaders diminished. The statement of one local prosecutor in Washington's Pierce County was widely reported. "We had the power and force to exterminate these people from the face of the earth, instead of making treaties with them," he exclaimed. "Perhaps we should have! We certainly wouldn't be having all this trouble with them today."

The rhetoric and reality of the fish-ins attracted widespread public attention. Celebrities came to the Northwest to show their support and to join in the acts of civil disobedience. Film star Marlon Brando was arrested along with Robert Satiacum on the Puyallup River in March 1964. Black comedian and civil rights activist Dick Gregory later was arrested and convicted on several counts of illegal

FILM ACTOR MARLON BRANDO AND ACTIVIST ROBERT SATIACUM (PUYALLUP /
YAKAMA) ARE ARRESTED ON THE PUYALLUP RIVER IN MARCH 1964, AS PART OF
THE ONGOING CAMPAIGN TO DEFEND INDIAN FISHING RIGHTS IN WASHING-
TON STATE.

net fishing. Actress Jane Fonda and singer Buffy Sainte-Marie
(Cree) arrived in Washington to show their solidarity with the arrested fishermen.

A significant breakthrough came in May 1966, when the U.S. Department of Justice announced that it was "determined to defend the
treaty rights of the Indian tribes." In a letter to the National Indian
Youth Council, Assistant Attorney General Edwin L. Weisl, Jr., announced that the Justice Department intended to take whatever action
was necessary "to insure that the various tribes are able to pursue their
treaty fishing free from outside interference." The Department of Justice, acting as *amicus curiae* ("friend of the court"), entered one of
the fishing rights cases. In a landmark decision in May 1968, the U.S.
Supreme Court confirmed the treaty rights of the Puyallups and the
Nisquallies. An even more far-reaching decision was handed down six
years later by District Court Judge George H. Boldt. The Boldt decision upheld the rights of the tribes to fish in their traditional fishing
places and ordered that they be allowed to take 50 percent of the

harvestable fish. Judge Boldt also declared many of the existing state regulations of Indian fishing illegal.

With their fishing rights confirmed at last, the tribes of Washington state moved quickly to restore the depleted supply of salmon. They organized the Northwest Indian Fisheries Department and worked closely with the Washington State Department of Fish and Game to develop long-term fish management programs. Individual tribes established fish hatcheries and began releasing millions of salmon fingerlings into Washington streams and rivers. The Northwest tribes had always believed that their survival depended upon the survival of the fish, and they were anxious now to demonstrate that they were devoted and competent conservationists. As one of the fish-in leaders put it, "It wasn't the Indians who killed off the buffalo."

The activism of the National Indian Youth Council challenged the leaders of the National Congress of American Indians to become more assertive in their defense of Indian rights. Clyde Warrior attended the 1964 annual meeting of the NCAI and criticized tribal leaders for allowing federal officials and other non-Indians to control the affairs of the Indian people. Warrior's criticisms were taken to heart by Robert Burnette (Sioux), the executive director of the NCAI. "In fact," said Burnette, "I had wanted to say some of the same things for the past three years." It was also in 1964 that the NCAI got a new executive director, Vine Deloria, Jr., a forceful and eloquent advocate of what became known as "Red Power." Deloria first used the expression at a convention of the NCAI in 1966, declaring that "Red Power means we want power over our own lives. . . . We do not want power *over* anyone. . . . We simply want the power, the political and economic power, to run our own lives in our own way."

The National Congress of American Indians demonstrated its renewed determination to defend the rights of Native Americans by its swift response to the meeting of Bureau of Indian Affairs officials and members of Congress at Santa Fe, New Mexico, in 1966. The leaders of the NCAI held their own emergency conference in Santa Fe to protest what they feared was a renewal of the termination policy. The NCAI leaders for the first time called for a policy of self-determination and insisted upon meeting with federal officials to present their demands. Secretary of the Interior Stewart Udall met with the NCAI leaders and assured them that they would be consulted on the content of future Indian legislation. When the Interior Department subsequently drafted an "Omnibus Bill" for the economic development of

Indian reservations, without first consulting with the NCAI, the Indian leaders charged the federal government with breaking yet another of its promises. The NCAI denounced the proposed legislation as the "Ambush Bill" and the "Ominous Bill" and lobbied successfully to have it defeated.

The National Congress of American Indians put the federal government on notice that the days were over when legislation for the welfare of Native Americans could be drafted without consulting Indian leaders. The NCAI had scored two impressive victories—gaining a hearing at the Santa Fe conference and defeating the Omnibus Bill—yet its days of preeminence as the voice of American Indians were coming to an end. The challenge by young activists was about to increase dramatically. As Vine Deloria, Jr., commented, "The battle over the Omnibus Bill was the last unified resistance by the older tribal leaders."

A SEASON OF DISCONTENT

Several related factors contributed to the increase in Native American activism in the late 1960s and early 1970s. The earlier actions of charismatic leaders such as Wallace "Mad Bear" Anderson were an inspiration to many Indians in the younger generation. Likewise, the success of the fish-ins in Washington state encouraged activists elsewhere to plan their own "direct actions." The growing responsiveness of the federal government also raised expectations and thus contributed to the demand for even greater change. Fundamental to the increase in activism was the growing disenchantment by many younger Indians with elected tribal leaders and the nature of tribal government. The activists dissented from the emerging consensus of tribal leaders and federal officials that the principle of self-determination should be the foundation of federal Indian policy. Self-determination, the activists complained, rendered the tribal governments little more than administrators of federal programs. The activists, often in alliance with reservation traditionalists, increased their demand for a return to traditional forms of tribal organization and a reassertion of unrestricted "tribal sovereignty."

Another potent factor in the rise of Native American activism was the civil rights movement. African Americans in the 1950s and 1960s had captured the nation's attention through a series of widely publicized demonstrations against racial discrimination. Many young Indians could not help being impressed. Martin Luther King, Jr., led a successful boycott in Montgomery, Alabama, to desegregate the city's bus system in the mid-1950s. During the early years of the following decade, black college students conducted sit-ins at lunch counters that served whites only and held "freedom rides" throughout the rural South challenging segregated facilities in bus stations and other places of public accommodation. By the late 1960s, many young African Americans had grown impatient with the pace of progress in achieving equality. They formed more radical organizations, such as the Student Nonviolent Coordinating Committee (SNCC), and demanded "Black Power." Black Power meant different things to different people, but essentially it was a call for greater control by African Americans over their communities, lives, and destinies.

The older generation of Native American leaders showed little enthusiasm for joining, or even supporting, the civil rights movement. Leaders of the National Congress of American Indians carefully avoided involvement in the black struggle for integration and equality, arguing that the goals of the civil rights movement were quite different from the Indians' desire to maintain separate tribal identities and their assertion of special rights. Joseph R. Garry (Coeur d'Alene), elected president of the NCAI in 1953, believed that the status of Native people was fundamentally different from that of other minorities. "As other groups may be pleading for equality," Garry explained in 1956, "the American Indian is fighting to retain his superior rights as guaranteed to him by treaties and agreements as the original inhabitants and the giver in good faith of this rich land."

The younger generation of Native Americans, however, was more inclined to make connections with the civil rights movement. Clyde Warrior, one of the founders of the National Indian Youth Council, spent the summer of 1961 in Mississippi working on a voter-registration project organized by the Student Nonviolent Coordinating Committee. Young Indian activists also participated in the March on Washington, led by Martin Luther King, Jr., in the summer of 1963. Following King's assassination in 1968, several Indians traveled to Atlanta, Georgia, to help plan what came to be called the Poor People's March. Among the thousands of demonstrators who gathered in the nation's capital in the spring of 1968 were more than 100 Indians, some of whom held a brief sit-in at the office of the secretary of interior. Seeing firsthand the enormous publicity generated by the civil rights movement, young Indian activists adopted the rhetoric and tactics used so successfully by African Americans. Thus the young organizers of the

NIYC called themselves "Red Muslims," a term derived from the followers of Malcolm X and the Nation of Islam, the Black Muslims. Likewise, from the term "sit-in" came "fish-in" and "Black Power" was the likely inspiration for the term "Red Power."

Another key factor in the rise of Native American activism was the shift of the Indian population from the reservations to the cities. Wartime employment opportunities, the postwar relocation program, and the desire of individual families to improve their standards of living led to a dramatic redistribution of the nation's Indian population. Only 24,000 Indians lived in metropolitan areas in 1940. The number of urban Indians doubled during each subsequent decade. By 1980 about 740,000 Indians lived in the cities, amounting to more than half the national total. Native Americans living in the cities, far removed from their individual reservations, developed a broader perspective on themselves and the problems of their people. Members of different tribes found themselves living together and interacting in ways that would have been virtually impossible on the reservation. While retaining their own tribal loyalties, they also acquired a transcendent *pan-Indian* identity. They began to see larger issues that affected all Indian people, rather than the narrow concerns of their individual tribes. This broader perspective was nurtured at urban Indian Centers where Native Americans gathered to obtain employment assistance, legal advice, and health care. Intertribal gatherings, or powwows, also served as important vehicles for the emergence of a pan-Indian identity.

From the ranks of the urban Indians came new and more radical Native American leaders and organizations in the late 1960s. This militant wing of the activist movement directly challenged tribal leaders and the existing national Indian organizations. Militants disrupted the convention of the National Congress of American Indians in both 1968 and 1969. As the convention delegates adopted their usual set of resolutions in favor of self-determination, the militants demanded more sweeping changes in federal Indian policy. The delegates denounced the young militants and admonished them to work through "regular organizations and government channels to effect improvements." The militants even challenged the leaders of the National Indian Youth Council. Clyde Warrior in 1968 recognized the irony:

> Five years ago those of us who started off the Youth Council were called the most radical of radicals. Those of us who headed the movement five years ago now are considered Uncle Tomahawks. There is a more and more angry bunch of kids coming up. Which I like. When we started

five years ago I said: It wouldn't be us that do anything. It'll be the ones that come after us. They will be angrier and madder. It's happening. It has happened.

Nineteen sixty-eight was a year of crisis for the United States. American armed forces in Vietnam suffered a severe setback; Martin Luther King, Jr., and Senator Robert Kennedy were assassinated; and antiwar demonstrators plagued the Democratic national convention in Chicago. Also in 1968 three new militant organizations of Native Americans were formed. Each was urban in its origins and pan-Indian in its outlook. Several Indian Centers joined to form American Indians United, and college students in California formed the United Native Americans to "bring together all people of Indian identity and Indian descent . . . [and] all who can identify with the Native American liberation struggle." The most important of the new militant groups was organized in Minnesota. Its name was the American Indian Movement (AIM).

The Native American population of Minneapolis and St. Paul had grown to more than 10,000 by the late 1960s. Suffering from high unemployment, low income, and substandard housing, the Indians of the Twin Cities also complained of police harassment and brutality. Inspired perhaps by the widely publicized activities of the Black Panther Party of Oakland, California, several young Chippewas in Minneapolis organized an "Indian patrol" to monitor the activities of the police. (Two years earlier the Black Panthers, carrying law books and guns, had begun trailing police cars through the streets of Oakland to protect the constitutional rights of African Americans.) The Indian patrol followed police officers through Indian neighborhoods and acted as witnesses whenever a Native American was arrested. During thirty-nine weeks of careful patrolling, the arrest rate of Indians in the Twin Cities declined drastically.

Two of the young Chippewa leaders of the Indian patrol, George Mitchell and Dennis Banks, organized the American Indian Movement in the summer of 1968. Mitchell, the author of the original AIM charter, was a sensitive and quiet young man, whereas Banks was a flamboyant and striking figure who possessed ample charm and an undeniable charisma. The initial purpose of AIM was to protect the rights of Native Americans who had migrated from the reservations to the cities, but it soon took part in demonstrations in cities and on reservations across the country. AIM was truly a militant organization. Its leaders were convinced that the collusion of federal and tribal governments was so complete that it was impossible to achieve reform from within. Among the other early leaders of AIM were two brothers who had served time in prison for felonies, Clyde and Vernon Bellecourt (Chippewa). Clyde became the director of the Minneapolis chapter of AIM, while Vernon headed the Denver chapter. The youngest of the AIM leaders was the energetic and irrepressible Russell Means (Oglala Sioux), born on the Pine Ridge reservation and reared there and in several western cities. After a year in Los Angeles, Means moved to Cleveland where he served as director of the local Indian Center.

The formation of militant groups such as the American Indian Movement was countered by the creation of two new organizations of elected tribal leaders, the National Council on Indian Opportunity (NCIO) and the National Tribal Chairmen's Association (NTCA). The primary function of the NCIO, created by President Johnson in 1968 and chaired by the vice president, was to insure that tribes received the maximum benefits of the social welfare and economic development programs of the federal government. As the policy of self-determination was implemented during the Nixon administration, the council coordinated the contracting of federal programs to the tribal governments for administration. Militants denounced the NCIO because it strengthened the position of the tribal leaders, complaining that it was just another government agency staffed by compliant Indian leaders who "rubber stamped" the decisions of federal officials. The National Tribal Chairmen's Association, organized during the early days of the Nixon administration, acted as a sounding board and national union of elected tribal officials. It vigorously supported the policy of self-determination that was then transferring responsibility and funding for federal programs to the tribal governments. Militants charged that the federal government had formed the NTCA because it wanted "not a sounding board but an echo board, a puppet group that would agree with the government instead of opposing it."

It was at the end of the turbulent decade of the 1960s that the new militant spirit among Native Americans first captured the national headlines when a group of young Indian activists seized Alcatraz Island in San Francisco Bay. This thirteen-acre island had been a military prison and federal penitentiary for decades before it was abandoned in 1963 and declared "surplus property." Largely unnoticed by the national media, a small contingent of Sioux landed on the island in 1964 and claimed settlement rights. Federal agents quietly removed the

Indians the following day. The Sioux responded by filing a claim in federal court, arguing that the Fort Laramie Treaty of 1868 had granted them the right to occupy unused federal property. The court dismissed their case after four years of litigation.

The immediate impetus to the more widely publicized landing on Alcatraz on November 20, 1969, was a convention in San Francisco of American Indians United. The day after the conference ended, a fire destroyed the San Francisco Indian Center, leaving the Native Americans in the San Francisco Bay area without a meeting place. Several militant leaders decided the time was ripe to seize Alcatraz as a site for a new Indian cultural center. An initial landing on November 9 was led by Richard Oakes (Mohawk), a student at San Francisco State University, and Adam Nordwall (Chippewa) from Minnesota. Most of the nineteen Indians who participated in the landing were students at Bay Area colleges and universities. After only one night's occupation, they were removed from the island by federal marshals. Plans were then put in motion to return to Alcatraz with a much larger force. Seventy-eight Native people, organized as Indians of All Tribes, landed on the island on November 20. In addition to Oakes and Nordwall, the leaders included Earl Livermore (Blackfeet), Dennis Hastings (Omaha), Lanada Means (Oglala Sioux), and Grace Thorpe (Sac and Fox/Potawatomi), the youngest daughter of Olympic athlete Jim Thorpe. The number of Indians on the island soon grew to more than 300, drawn from fifty different tribes.

The stated goals of the occupation were to convert the island into a Native American cultural center and to unify Indians everywhere for bolder and more effective action. The leaders of the occupation aligned themselves with traditionalists by issuing a ringing defense of Indian culture. A cultural center on Alcatraz, they explained, would help keep alive "the old Indian ways." The center would include an Indian college, training school, religious and spiritual center, museum, and ecology center. "*This is the first and most important reason we went to Alcatraz Island,*" the leaders proclaimed. Their call for unity was a desperate cry for Indians to overcome the divisions that had so often limited their effectiveness in the past. In a statement issued on December 16, the leaders declared: "While it was a small group which moved onto the island, we want all Indian people to join with us. . . . We are not getting anywhere fast by working alone as individual tribes."

The occupation of Alcatraz also was a dramatic assertion of Native American treaty rights and Indian sovereignty. The leaders of the occupation in 1969, following the lead of the Sioux who had seized the island five years earlier, claimed a pan-Indian treaty right to take over surplus federal property. This bold claim was accompanied by a bitter parody of the broken promises and unwanted paternalism of the federal government. The occupiers declared their own "benevolent policy" for the white caretakers of the island:

> We will give to the inhabitants of this island a portion of that land for their own, to be held in trust by the American Indian Government—for as long as the sun shall rise and the rivers go down to the sea—to be administered by the Bureau of Caucasian Affairs.

The occupation of Alcatraz succeeded brilliantly in gaining national attention for the cause of Native Americans, but it failed to achieve its specific goals. The federal government refused to acknowledge the Indians' claim to the island, and the occupiers were forced to endure a stalemate of many months. At first they enjoyed the enthusiastic support of Indians and non-Indians who regularly visited the island and brought boatloads of supplies. But as the stalemate dragged on support waned. The occupiers of this fog-shrouded rock in San Francisco Bay suffered from shortages of food, water, heat, and electricity. Many left the island to return to their reservations or to take jobs in San Francisco to pay for needed supplies. The occupation ended peacefully on June 11, 1971, when twenty federal marshals landed on the island and removed the fifteen Indians who were still present.

Although the occupation of Alcatraz failed to obtain its goals, it was an event of considerable importance in the history of Native Americans in the twentieth century. During the occupation, the federal government demonstrated a new responsiveness to Indian affairs. In July 1970, President Richard Nixon committed his administration to the policy of self-determination; the following December, Congress voted to return lands around Blue Lake, New Mexico, to the Taos Pueblo. The occupation also deepened the growing cleavage among Native Americans, aligning young activists and many older traditionalists against elected tribal leaders. The activists and traditionalists joined forces as powerful advocates of cultural renewal and tribal sovereignty. The urban activists on Alcatraz gained from the traditionalists a deeper sense of their Indian identity, and traditionalists were energized by their contact with the activists. Caught in the middle were the elected tribal leaders and Indian professionals who were operating the federal programs transferred to the tribes under the policy of self-determination.

FROM THE TRAIL OF BROKEN TREATIES TO WOUNDED KNEE

The peak of Native American activism came in the early 1970s with a series of spectacular demonstrations of Indian anger and discontent. Inspired by the seizure of Alcatraz, a group of young activists in the spring of 1970 occupied Fort Lawton in Seattle, Washington. The fort was scheduled by the army to be decommissioned, and the Indians claimed it under their alleged "right to occupy lands to be declared surplus." More than 100 Indians were arrested by military police and removed. Meanwhile, in Michigan, 250 Chippewas, some wearing war paint, seized a lighthouse and unsuccessfully laid claim to land along the shores of Lake Superior. "If the government doesn't start living up to its obligations," warned one of the protest leaders, "armed resistance and occupation will have to become a regular thing." In June 1970 members of the Pit River tribe in northern California occupied land in Lassen National Park. The tribe earlier had voted to reject payment for this ancestral land under a settlement reached by the Indian Claims Commission. "The Earth is our Mother," the leaders of the occupation proclaimed, "and we cannot sell her." Police arrested more than 150 protestors for trespassing and removed them from the land they claimed.

Activist leaders soon realized that the visibility of their demonstrations was enhanced if the sites they chose had symbolic importance. Thus a small group of Native Americans attempted unsuccessfully to seize Ellis Island in New York Harbor, famous as "The Gateway to the New World." Others temporarily captured the *Mayflower II* and demonstrated at Plymouth Rock on Thanksgiving Day, 1970. One of the most daring of the new wave of demonstrations was held atop the huge stone faces of American presidents at Mount Rushmore in the Black Hills National Monument, South Dakota. The leaders of the demonstration announced that they were protesting the federal government's "many, many broken treaties and promises," and they hoped their action would create "a stronger feeling of unity" among Indians everywhere.

Protests also were aimed directly at the Bureau of Indian Affairs and at elected tribal governments. The activists denounced the BIA ("Bossing Indians Around") for its continuing power over the lives of Indian people. Dozens of demonstrators were arrested in 1970 as they tried to occupy BIA offices in Colorado, Illinois, Minnesota, Pennsylvania, Ohio, California, and New Mexico. In the same year, protests were launched against the head of the Hopi tribal council after it was discovered he had signed secret contracts with energy companies for the strip-mining of sacred lands on Black Mesa. On the Northern Cheyenne and Crow reservations in Montana, angry protests were lodged against tribal leaders who had "sold out" water and mineral rights to corporations under government sponsorship. Similar disclosures on the Navajo reservation pitted traditionalists and activists against the tribal government.

News of such revelations and demonstrations was carried not only in the mainstream media, but also in the pages of Native American newspapers. The American Indian Press Service, founded in 1970 by Charles Trimble (Oglala Sioux), provided extensive coverage and supplied detailed accounts to Indian papers on reservations across the nation. Several new pan-Indian newspapers were particularly significant because they were openly sympathetic to the activists and often critical of elected tribal leaders. The American Indian Historical Society, founded by Jeannette Henry (Eastern Cherokee) and Rupert Costo (Cahuilla), published *Wassaja* from its offices in San Francisco. From the St. Regis reservation in New York came *Akwesasne Notes*, a pro-activist paper that had a national circulation of nearly 50,000.

Understandably, the increase in activism made many elected tribal leaders nervous. They were concerned that their own positions of leadership were being undermined by the growing strength of the activists. They feared also that the demonstrations would provoke a backlash in public opinion, reversing what they regarded as a positive trend in Indian affairs toward self-determination. Local Indian leaders in Massachusetts expressed strong misgivings about the Thanksgiving Day demonstrations at Plymouth Rock. They had planned a more decorous "day of mourning." The elected tribal chairman of the Oglala Sioux denounced the demonstrations atop Mount Rushmore as the work of "out-of-state Indians," an action offensive to the majority of Indians in South Dakota.

What was especially disturbing to many tribal leaders was the growing coalition between activists and traditionalists. In August 1972 several leaders of the American Indian Movement met with elders of the Brule and Oglala Sioux during the annual Sun Dance on the Rosebud reservation in South Dakota. The young activists sought and received a sense of spiritual direction from a Lakota medicine man. "That is actually when the American Indian Movement was first born," one of the AIM leaders later said. In subsequent conversations, the activists and reservation traditionalists shared their grievances against the BIA-approved tribal governments. Among those present was Robert Burnette, former executive director of the National Congress of American Indians. He told of his dream of gathering hundreds of Indians "under the banner of the Trail of Broken Treaties and proceed[ing] to Washington, where we will show the world what Indians truly stand for." It would be a *spiritual* demonstration, Burnette said, and a peaceful one. The idea was quickly approved. Vernon Bellecourt, national coordinator for AIM, agreed to help organize the demonstration.

In late September and early October 1972 dozens of Native Americans met in Denver, Colorado, to plan the Trail of Broken Treaties. Attending the meeting were leaders of nine activist organizations, including the American Indian Movement and the National Indian Youth Council. The plan agreed upon was for three automobile caravans to leave from Los Angeles, San Francisco, and Seattle. The caravans would travel across the country, inviting other Native people to join them along the way, and assemble in Washington, D.C., just before the presidential election in early November. The leaders of the demonstration hoped then to meet with President Nixon and other government leaders.

After the caravans got underway in early October, they converged in St. Paul, Minnesota, to draw up a list of grievances and demands. What emerged from the meeting in St. Paul was a twenty-point document outlining in detail the vision of Indian sovereignty that activists and traditionalists had been formulating for the past decade. This remarkable document called for the repeal of the 1871 federal statute that had prohibited further treaty making with Indian tribes. It demanded the reestablishment of a treaty relationship between the United States and the "Indian Tribes and Nations." Under this new relationship, the tribes would regain the independence and sovereignty they had enjoyed a century earlier. They would be free to reinstate traditional forms of organization and the federal government's power over them would be greatly diminished.

The Trail of Broken Treaties included more than 500 Native Americans when it arrived in the nation's capital on November 3, 1972. By prior arrangement, the participants gathered in the auditorium of the Bureau of Indian Affairs building to await a meeting with government leaders and to receive information on housing arrangements. They soon were disappointed to learn that the only officials willing to meet with them were low-level bureaucrats and that no one had arranged suitable housing. Late in the afternoon, when guards attempted to eject the Indians from the building, a scuffle broke out and several people were hurt. Angry and bitterly frustrated, the Indians decided to barricade themselves in the BIA headquarters. They piled office furniture, file cabinets, copy machines, and typewriters in the doorways and windows. They armed themselves with clubs fashioned from broken table legs, knives made from scissor blades, and spears made out of electrical insulation cable.

The occupation of the Bureau of Indian Affairs building lasted five days. Sympathizers provided the demonstrators with food and other supplies. African American Stokley Carmichael, former head of the Student Nonviolent Coordinating Committee, stopped by to declare that the struggle of the American Indian was an integral part of the civil rights movement. Antiwar activist and pediatrician Dr. Benjamin Spock offered financial support. The demonstrators inside the building were in a constant state of fear that the police were about to storm their barricades. When ordered to vacate the building, one of the defiant occupiers shouted back, "This is a good day to die!" The worst outbreak of violence occurred on the evening of November 6, as the demonstrators were watching a movie about the Washington state fish-ins. One particularly graphic scene of police brutality triggered the audience into spontaneous action. Robert Burnette later recalled:

> Something snapped in the audience and people began to shout that if they were going to be beaten and possibly killed, they'd destroy the hated BIA building first. Men ran amok with clubs and hammers, smashing windows, shattering toilet bowls, and ripping files of records to shreds. In a matter of minutes, the BIA central office was littered with paper and chunks of broken furniture.

Tensions remained high as the leaders of the Trail of Broken Treaties met with federal officials to try to resolve the crisis. Most of the leaders were from the American Indian Movement—Dennis Banks, Russell Means, Clyde and Vernon Bellecourt—but older activists such as Wallace "Mad Bear" Anderson also played a role. Representing the federal government were Leonard Garment, a special assistant to President Nixon, and Commissioner of Indian Affairs Louis Bruce. A tentative settlement was reached on the evening of November 7. The demonstration leaders agreed to leave the building the following day in exchange for assurances that a federal task force would be formed

MEMBERS OF THE TRAIL OF BROKEN TREATIES OCCUPY THE BUREAU OF
INDIAN AFFAIRS BUILDING IN WASHINGTON, D.C., IN NOVEMBER OF
1972. THE OCCUPATION LASTED FIVE DAYS AND ENDED WHEN FEDERAL
OFFICIALS AGREED TO RESPOND TO THE ACTIVISTS' LIST OF TWENTY
DEMANDS.

to respond to their twenty demands. In addition, the government
agreed to provide $66,500 to the demonstrators to transport them
back to their homes. As the activists left the building on November 8,

they took with them files that they later claimed documented the malfeasance of officials in the Bureau of Indian Affairs.

The reaction to the Trail of Broken Treaties revealed once again the deep divisions among Native Americans. The leaders of the demonstration were given a hero's welcome by many young Indians and older traditionalists as they returned home to their reservations. Ceremonies and dances were held in their honor. Many elected tribal leaders, however, condemned the occupation of the Bureau of Indian Affairs building. The leader of the National Tribal Chairmen's Association, Webster Two Hawk (Sioux), blamed the occupation on "irresponsible self-styled revolutionaries." He called upon the federal government to prosecute all those who had participated. Two Hawk also demanded the firing of the federal officials who had failed to protect the building. This demand was met shortly after the occupation ended, when Indian Commissioner Louis Bruce and two other high-ranking officials in the BIA were removed from their posts. A more moderate response came from the National Congress of American Indians. Its executive director deplored the damage to the building, but acknowledged that the NCAI trod "common ground" with many of the twenty demands presented by the leaders of the demonstration. Navajo Nation tribal chairman Peter MacDonald urged the public to focus its attention on the legitimate grievances of the Indian people rather than on the destructive tactics of the militants. Appearing on the television program *Face the Nation,* MacDonald conceded that the Trail of Broken Treaties reflected the "rage and frustration all Indian people feel."

The federal task force formed to consider the demonstrators' twenty demands issued its final report on January 9, 1973. The report rejected as impractical the whole idea of reestablishing a treaty relationship between Indian tribes and the federal government. It pointed out that ever since Indians had become citizens it was no longer possible to make treaties with them. This wholesale rejection of the twenty demands deeply embittered the leaders of the American Indian Movement. They resolved never again to surrender a position of strength without an unequivocal promise from their adversaries to meet their demands.

The American Indian Movement leaders soon had an opportunity to demonstrate their new resolve. Less than two weeks after the federal task force issued its report, a Native American named Wesley Bad Heart Bull (Sioux) was killed in Buffalo Gap, South Dakota. When local authorities arrested a white man for the crime and charged him with second-degree manslaughter—instead of murder in the first-degree—Dennis Banks, Russell Means, and other AIM leaders objected. A demonstration on February 6, 1973, at the county seat of Custer turned violent as Indians and local police engaged in a pitched battle. Demonstrators stoned the courthouse and torched the chamber of commerce building. The police, responding with tear gas and clubs, arrested twenty-seven Indians. Violence also erupted in Rapid City where Indians gathered to protest the double standard of justice that the killing of Bad Heart Bull had come to symbolize. Forty Indians were arrested during several days of demonstrations and violence.

Following the disturbances in Custer and Rapid City, the traditional chiefs, medicine men, and newly formed Oglala Sioux Civil Rights Organization (OSCRO) invited the leaders of the American Indian Movement to come to the Pine Ridge reservation. Many traditionalists and others at Pine Ridge were engaged in a bitter campaign to oust from power the reservation's elected tribal chairman Richard Wilson. The charges against Wilson were typical of the grievances that traditionalists had against tribal leaders on reservations across the country—corrupt dealings with local corporations, election fraud, embezzlement, graft, cronyism, and nepotism. Elected tribal officials were the recipients of millions of dollars in federal funds each year, yet little was done to hold them responsible for the proper dispersal of the funds. This lack of accountability opened the door to corruption by unscrupulous tribal leaders. Wilson also was charged with operating a "goon squad" of special police to intimidate his opponents and maintain his privileged position.

Russell Means and Dennis Banks were among the American Indian Movement leaders who responded to the call to come to the Pine Ridge reservation. They were asked by the traditionalists not only to help them oust the incumbent tribal chairman but also to establish a new form of tribal organization based on traditional forms and free of federal control. The traditionalists even suggested the place where AIM should take its stand, the small reservation hamlet of Wounded Knee. Familiar to millions of European Americans because of Dee Brown's best-seller *Bury My Heart at Wounded Knee* (1971), it was a site sacred to the memory of the nearly 200 Sioux who had been slaughtered there in 1890. "Go ahead and do it, go to Wounded Knee," the elders had told the young activists. "Take your brothers from the American Indian Movement and go to Wounded Knee and make your stand there."

Tribal chairman Richard Wilson was aware of the threat posed by an alliance of the leaders of the American Indian Movement and disgruntled traditionalists. During the Trail of Broken Treaties, Wilson had denounced the leaders of AIM as "a bunch of renegades—nothing but a bunch of spongers" and had banned them from the Pine Ridge reservation. He had even offered to help arrest the AIM demonstrators at Custer and Rapid City. When Russell Means and Dennis Banks came to Pine Ridge, Wilson ordered his special police to keep them under close surveillance. On February 26, 1973, Means was assaulted by members of Wilson's "goon squad." The next day, about 200 armed activists seized control of the village of Wounded Knee. Russell Means was among those who expected a fatal confrontation. "I hope by my death, and the deaths of all these Indian men and women, there will be an investigation into corruption on the reservations and there's no better place to start than Pine Ridge."

The occupation of Wounded Knee lasted for more than seventy days, during which two Native Americans were killed and one federal marshal was paralyzed. The activists fortified the village by building bunkers and digging trenches; they armed themselves with hunting rifles, shotguns, and dynamite. Around the village assembled more than 250 federal marshals and FBI agents, some armed with M-16s and .50-caliber machine guns. The federal forces ringed the village with roadblocks and conducted patrols in armored personnel carriers. Nightly firefights erupted between the two sides with the exchange of thousands of rounds of ammunition. The federal forces soon were joined by a small legion of reporters from across the country. Dramatic scenes of armed combat with Native Americans became a regular feature on the nightly news, an eerie reenactment of the days of Indian warfare a century earlier. As historian Donald L. Parman, author of *Indians and the American West in the Twentieth Century* (1994), observed, the entire episode was characterized by an atmosphere "close to the surreal." Hundreds of Native sympathizers, from more than sixty different tribes, came to Wounded Knee to show their support. Activists from other causes, including African American militant Angela Davis and antiwar attorney William Kuntsler, also made a pilgrimage to this remote South Dakota village.

The two leading organizations of tribal leaders, the National Congress of American Indians and the National Tribal Chairmen's Association, both announced their opposition to the occupation. They viewed it as a dangerous attack on the right of elected tribal governments

OCCUPIERS OF WOUNDED KNEE, SOUTH DAKOTA, FLY THE AMERICAN FLAG UP-
SIDE DOWN AS A SIGNAL OF DISTRESS AND PROTEST. DURING THE TWO MONTH
OCCUPATION OF THE VILLAGE IN 1973, THOUSANDS OF ROUNDS OF AMMUNI-
TION WERE EXCHANGED IN FIREFIGHTS BETWEEN AIM MEMBERS AND FEDERAL
FORCES.

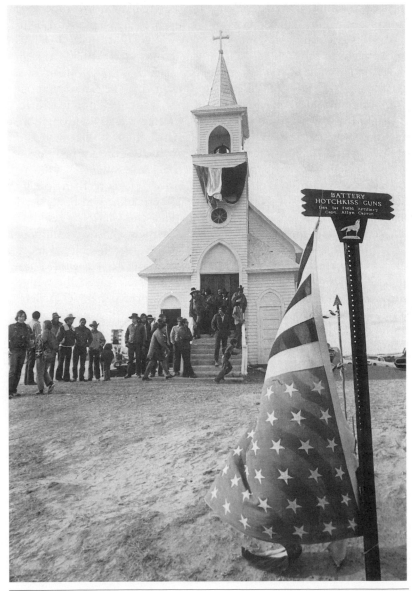

to run their own internal affairs, a right they had fought long and hard to win under the banner of self-determination. If tribal leaders could be overturned by outside activists in league with dissident factions on the reservation, they believed, then the principle of tribal government was seriously endangered.

As the standoff continued, the leaders of the occupation issued a ringing declaration of purpose. On March 11, 1973, the traditional chiefs and headmen at Wounded Knee formed the Oglala Sioux Nation, reasserting the sovereignty that had been recognized by the federal government in the Fort Laramie Treaty of 1868. Russell Means declared on national television that the new Sioux nation was independent from the United States and that its defenders were prepared to shoot anyone who violated its borders. The leaders of the occupation also called for the abolition of the present Pine Ridge tribal government, as created by the Indian Reorganization Act, and the reinstitution of a traditional form of organization free of control by the Bureau of Indian Affairs. They argued that the treaty of 1868 had reserved to the Sioux the exclusive right to choose their own form of government. "*We don't want* tribal council, we *don't want* BIA," exclaimed Irma Rooks (Oglala Sioux). "We want our 1868 treaty!"

This assertion of Indian sovereignty at Wounded Knee, like that made during the Trail of Broken Treaties, was essentially a demand to return to the treaty relationship that had existed between the tribes and the federal government prior to 1871. Such a fundamental change in tribal status was anathema to entrenched leaders such as Richard Wilson, but it enjoyed considerable support among the Indian people. On March 19, 1973, the residents of the Pine Ridge reservation presented federal officials with a petition seeking a referendum to decide whether to disband the present tribal government and to replace it with a traditional form of organization. The petition contained the signatures of 1,400 tribal members. Six of the eight tribal council members subsequently withdrew their support from Chairman Wilson and announced their support for the new free and sovereign Sioux Nation. Three traditional leaders left the reservation to seek recognition and aid from the United Nations.

An agreement to end the crisis was reached in early May 1973. The leaders of the occupation agreed to lay down their arms and abandon their fortified positions. Those who had federal warrants outstanding against them would submit voluntarily to arrest. In exchange, representatives of the Nixon administration promised to send a delegation later in the month to discuss the Sioux treaty of 1868. They also agreed to investigate the alleged corruption of the tribal government and to prosecute all civil and criminal violations. When federal marshals and FBI agents entered Wounded Knee on May 8, they found only 129 of the former defenders still there. The village itself was in a shambles, having suffered millions of dollars in damage during the siege. The only part of the village unscarred was the mass grave of the victims of the 1890 massacre.

The promised meeting to discuss the treaty of 1868 took place on May 17, 1973, on the land of Frank Fools Crow, a respected Sioux elder and spiritual leader. The traditionalist leaders and others in attendance pressed the federal representatives to acknowledge that the Sioux had reverted to their pre-1871 status. They sought recognition of the return to a treaty relationship between the independent Sioux Nation and the United States. They insisted upon a referendum to reinstate a traditional form of tribal organization. The federal representatives replied that no such fundamental change in status was possible. The federal government, they explained, was obligated to continue to recognize the elected tribal government as created by the Indian Reorganization Act of 1934. The meeting ended with the Indian leaders bitterly frustrated. Two weeks later they received a letter from presidential special assistant Leonard Garment reiterating the government's position: "The days of treaty making with the American Indians ended in 1871, 102 years ago."

The leaders of the occupation were also disappointed by the outcome of the federal government's investigation of alleged corruption in the tribal government at Pine Ridge. Federal accountants assigned to audit the financial records of the reservation found the books to be in such disorder that it was impossible to prove any of the allegations of wrongdoing. No charges were filed against tribal chairman Richard Wilson. Russell Means, released after serving thirty-nine days in jail for his part in the occupation, reacted angrily: "The situation is as bad as before the takeover and it only serves to give the suffering Indian people more reason to put their life on the line. We just keep dealing with rhetoric, not action."

In September 1973 Russell Means announced that he would challenge Richard Wilson for the office of tribal chairman. Tremendous bitterness and sporadic acts of violence marked the ensuing campaign between the "BIA faction" supporting the incumbent chairman and the "revolutionary faction" of the challenger. Reservation police shot and killed the president of the Oglala Sioux Civil Rights Organization in October, one of the groups that had invited Means to come to the reservation prior to the occupation of Wounded Knee. When the general election was held on February 7, 1974, Means received strong support from full-bloods and traditionalists in the outlying districts of the reservation, while Wilson won the votes of many mixed-bloods and others who had enjoyed his patronage. The final tally was 1,709 votes for Wilson to 1,530 for Means. Chairman Wilson proclaimed the election a victory for "law and order," while Russell Means interpreted his own strong showing as vindication and exoneration of the American Indian Movement.

Tensions remained high at Pine Ridge the following year when agents of the Federal Bureau of Investigation engaged in a fatal shootout with members of the American Indian Movement on the reservation. In the exchange of gunfire, one Indian and two federal agents were killed. Four AIM members were indicted for murder, but only one, Leonard Peltier, was convicted. Sentenced to consecutive life sentences in a federal penitentiary, Peltier became a *cause célèbre* for Native activists and their supporters who maintained that he had been convicted unjustly and was the victim of a government conspiracy against AIM and its leaders.

The occupation of Wounded Knee was the most important of the expressions of Native American discontent in the 1960s and 1970s. Widely reported at the time, and often recalled since, it marked "a watershed in the relations of American Indians and the Western European peoples," according to Vine Deloria, Jr.

> In demanding independence for the Oglala Nation, the people at Wounded Knee sought a return to the days of pre-discovery, when the tribes of this land had political independence and sovereignty. They sought the recognition by the nations of the world of their rightful status as nations in the community of nations.

Yet the people at Wounded Knee failed to win that recognition, as had those who earlier seized Alcatraz and joined the Trail of Broken Treaties. In subsequent years, several battle-weary activists and traditionalists continued to demand complete tribal sovereignty. But many others made their peace with the existing tribal governments and worked to effect more modest change. Former militants, some of whom had been active in the American Indian Movement and the National Indian Youth Council, won election to positions of leadership in tribal governments. There they dedicated themselves to making their governments more responsive to the needs of the Indian people.

SOURCES AND SUGGESTIONS FOR FURTHER READING

The early background to the Indian rights movement is provided by Hazel W. Hertzberg, *The Search for an American Indian Identity: Modern Pan-Indian Movements* (1971). Later developments are described with great clarity in Hazel Whitman Hertzberg, "Indian Rights Movement, 1887–1973," in Wilcomb E. Washburn, ed., *History of Indian White Relations*, vol. 8, *Handbook of North American Indians* (1988).

Several of the works cited for chapters 2 and 3 also are relied on throughout this chapter. Especially useful are James S. Olson and Raymond Wilson, *Native Americans in the Twentieth Century* (1984); Vine Deloria, Jr., and Clifford Lytle, *The Nations Within: The Past and Future of American Indian Sovereignty* (1984); and Donald L. Parman, *Indians and the American West in the Twentieth Century* (1994).

The discussion of the emergence of Indian activism in the 1950s and early 1960s, including the formation of the National Indian Youth Council (NIYC), is based largely on Stan Steiner, *The New Indians* (1968) and Alvin M. Josephy, Jr., *Red Power: The American Indians' Fight for Freedom* (1971). See also Roy Bongartz, "The New Indian" and Robert C. Day, "The Emergence of Activism as a Social Movement," in Howard M. Bahr, Bruce A. Chadwick, and Robert C. Day, eds., *Native Americans Today: Sociological Perspectives* (1972).

Three books are the main sources for the account of the increase in activism in the late 1960s and early 1970s: Alvin M. Josephy, Jr., *Now That the Buffalo's Gone: A Study of Today's American Indians* (1982); Vine Deloria, Jr., *Behind the Trail of Broken Treaties: An Indian Declaration of Independence* (1974); and Robert Burnette and John Koster, *The Road to Wounded Knee* (1974). On the occupation of Alcatraz, see Adam Fortunate Eagle, *ALCATRAZ! ALCATRAZ!: The Indian Occupation of 1969–1971* (1992) and the forthcoming account by Troy Johnson (1995). Among the many memoirs of the occupation, see especially Richard Oakes in *Ramparts* (December 1972) and Lanada Means and Edward D. Castillo in *American Indian Culture and Research Journal* (1995). The definitive work on the case of Leonard Peltier is Peter Matthiessen, *In the Spirit of Crazy Horse* (1983); for an update see Peter Matthiessen, "Who Really Killed the F.B.I. Men," *The Nation* (May 13, 1991). Rex Weyler, *Blood of the Land: The Government and Corporate War against the American Indian Movement* (1982) and Kenneth S. Stern, *Loud Hawk: The United States versus the American Indian Movement* (1985) offer a broader critique. For an insider's view of the era, see *Where White Men Fear to Tread: The Autobiography of Russell Means* (1995).

HARBRACE
BOOKS
ON AMERICA

SINCE 1945

6

THE STRUGGLE
CONTINUES

➤➤➤➤➤➤➤➤

 NATIVE AMERICAN AFFAIRS faded from the headlines, and from much of the nation's consciousness, in the years after Wounded Knee. Yet the movement toward Indian self-determination continued as Native people across the country worked to achieve greater economic, political, and cultural independence. The struggle in the final quarter of the twentieth century was perhaps less spectacular than it had been in previous years, but it was no less important. It is a struggle that continues to this day.

CONTROL OF ENERGY RESOURCES

One of the attention-grabbing events that dominated the news in the early 1970s was "the energy crisis." Just months after the end of the occupation of Wounded Knee in the spring of 1973, the Organization of Petroleum Exporting Countries (OPEC) announced a sudden and dramatic increase in oil prices. The consequent soaring of the cost of energy affected all Americans, but none so profoundly or unexpectedly as the nation's Indian people. As oil prices skyrocketed, the value of the vast energy resources beneath Indian lands rose accordingly. On the Navajo reservation alone were an estimated 100 million barrels of oil, 25 trillion cubic feet of natural gas, 50 billion tons of coal, and 80 million pounds of uranium.

For decades, American energy corporations had enjoyed access to reservation resources through long-term leases negotiated with tribal governments. The leases provided for the payment of "royalties" to the tribes at rates that were just a small fraction of what the resources were worth. Utah International Corporation, for instance, had signed a twenty-year lease in the mid-1950s for the strip-mining of coal on the Navajo reservation. The lease provided the tribe with a royalty of as little as fifteen cents a ton for coal that sold for more than fifteen *dollars* a ton. Likewise, leases on oil and natural gas reserves typically provided tribes with royalties at rates between 1 and 2 percent of market value. The dramatic rise in energy prices during the early 1970s led many tribes to conclude that such rates were no longer acceptable. The tribal governments of the Navajos, Crows, Northern Cheyennes, and many others demanded a renegotiation of their leases.

In the fall of 1975 leaders of more than twenty of the nation's largest tribes, representing 600,000 Native Americans, organized the Council of Energy Resource Tribes (CERT). Its stated purpose was "to promote the general welfare of energy resource owning tribes and their people through the protection, conservation and prudent management of their oil, natural gas, coal, uranium, geothermal, and oil shale resources." The formation of CERT was a clear signal to the nation's energy corporations that the tribes henceforth would take a more active and aggressive role in the development of their valuable resources.

Along with LaDonna Harris (Comanche) and Charles Lohah (Osage), the prime mover in the formation of the Council of Energy Resource Tribes was Navajo Nation tribal chairman Peter MacDonald. Born in 1928, MacDonald had served in World War II as a Marine code talker and earned a degree in electrical engineering from the University of Oklahoma. After working for several years in the aerospace industry in southern California, he returned to the Navajo reservation in 1963 and soon became active in tribal affairs. MacDonald's main interest was the proper development of the reservation's natural resources. The incumbent tribal chairman, Raymond Nakai, had signed several contracts and leasing agreements with various corporations that proved to be highly unpopular with many reservation residents. The tribal council had granted the Peabody Coal Company— the largest coal producer in the United States—the right to strip-mine a rugged plateau of Arizona desert land known as Black Mesa. The council also had leased reservation property for the construction of several huge coal-fired power plants. Expressing grave concern about the terms of these agreements, MacDonald successfully challenged Nakai for the tribal chairmanship in 1970. In his inaugural address in January 1971, MacDonald pledged that he would never "barter away the Navajo birthright for quick profit." Once in office, MacDonald began the renegotiation of existing contracts and leases on terms more favorable to the Navajos.

Peter MacDonald believed that economic development was the key to true self-determination (meaning greater independence) for Native Americans. This vision led him to become chairman of the Council of Energy Resource Tribes in 1975. As MacDonald explained:

> CERT exists because of a twist of geological fortune. A subsector of American society that has been overlooked for hundreds of years, which inhabits less than 5 percent of the land that was once theirs, today finds itself the owner of a potential energy resource whose wealth is so vast that it has not yet been measured.

At first, many federal officials were leery of CERT. But after MacDonald began meeting with emissaries from OPEC, the international oil cartel, federal authorities decided it was in their best interest to work with this new and powerful Native American organization. The Bureau of Indian Affairs (BIA) and the newly formed Department of Energy began channeling funds to CERT and providing it with technical services. In response, MacDonald pledged his support for the national goal of energy self-sufficiency and promised that the member tribes of CERT were "posed to make a massive contribution to [this] national effort."

The first order of business for CERT was to assist individual tribes in the renegotiation of their leases with energy corporations. One of its earliest victories came when the Crow tribe in Montana successfully renegotiated its coal leasing agreement with Westmoreland Resources Company, winning an increase in the royalty rate from less than seventeen and a half cents to forty cents a ton. CERT also assisted the Crows in invalidating older leases with Shell Oil Company, Gulf Oil Corporation, and Peabody Coal Company, all on the grounds that the terms of the leases were anachronistic in light of increased energy prices. Similar renegotiations were begun on the Fort Berthold reservation in North Dakota and among the Northern Cheyennes in Montana. CERT scored another major victory in 1982 when the Supreme Court ruled that the Jicarilla Apache tribe in New Mexico had the right to impose severance taxes on companies taking oil and natural gas from the reservation. "The power to tax is an essential attribute of Indian sovereignty," the Court ruled. CERT also assisted in the training of Indian professionals to become full-fledged independent producers. Some tribes established partnerships with existing energy corporations while others formed their own tribally controlled energy-development companies.

This new burst of economic activity did not come without controversy. Many residents of the reservations objected to the environmental damage being caused by accelerated economic development. They argued that such development was leaving reservation lands forever despoiled, the air polluted, and scarce water supplies seriously depleted. Spiritual leaders and traditionalists warned that the wholesale development of energy resources was destroying sacred sites and imperiling the survival of traditional culture. The massive extraction of coal and other resources from the depths of the earth was the way of the white man, some said, not the Indian way. One Hopi traditionalist put it this way:

> The white man's desire for material possessions and power has blinded him to the pain he has caused Mother Earth by his quest for what he calls natural resources. And the path of the Great Spirit has become difficult to see by almost all men, even by many Indians who have chosen instead to follow the path of the white man.

The controversy was intense in the area known as the Four Corners region where the states of Arizona, New Mexico, Colorado, and Utah meet. Here was Black Mesa, beneath which lay the nation's richest vein of high-grade, low-sulphur coal. Here, too, was the nation's largest concentration of Native Americans. Both the Navajo and Hopi tribal councils had signed leasing agreements with corporations for the strip-mining of coal on Black Mesa. They also had agreed to the construction of huge coal-fired power plants that generated electricity for the far away cities of Los Angeles, Las Vegas, Phoenix, and Tucson. The leases produced millions of dollars of revenue for the tribes, but also caused significant environmental damage. Strip-mining meant the removal of multiple layers of earth; once the coal was removed, a huge open pit remained. The refining and transporting of the coal required enormous quantities of water, and the burning of the refined coal polluted the air. The environmental damage caused to the area led the federal government to suggest that the Four Corners region be designated a "National Sacrifice Area." Navajo traditionalists and others vehemently objected to the sacrifice of their homeland. Black Mesa, to them, was sacred. "I don't know the white man's ways," said one Navajo elder, "but to us the Mesa, the air, the water, are Holy Elements. We pray to these Holy Elements in order for our people to flourish and perpetuate the well-being of each generation."

The power plants in the Four Corners region produced a pall of yellow-gray haze that covered more than 10,000 square miles. Residents of this vast area were doomed to breathe air laden with a mixture of lead, mercury, sulfuric acid, and other toxic chemicals. Hopi traditionalists complained that their view of the mountains of the *Kachinas*, the San Francisco Peaks north of Flagstaff, was "entirely smudged out." The Sun Watcher at the village of Shongopovi could no longer observe the exact moment of sunrise by which he set the dates for seasonal religious ceremonies. Traditionalists on the Hopi reservation in 1974 challenged the legality of contracts signed by their tribal council for the strip-mining of Black Mesa. Three years later, the Council of Energy Resource Tribes offered legal assistance to the Northern Cheyennes to halt construction of a coal-fired power plant on their reservation in Montana. The Northern Cheyennes were convinced that the plant would cause a significant deterioration in air quality and change their homeland forever. CERT agreed, maintaining that economic development should be balanced by concern for the environment and must be "compatible with tribal cultural values."

The depletion of water supplies was also a serious concern for residents of the Four Corners region. Beginning in the early 1970s, the Peabody Coal Company started pumping more than a billion gallons of water each year from underground aquifers on the Hopi and Navajo reservations. The water was used to transport pulverized coal along a 270-mile slurry line to a power plant in southern Nevada. By the early 1990s, more than twenty billion gallons of underground water had been removed. Hopi and Navajo farmers complained that the groundwater pumping had dried up springs and wells throughout the region, threatening their survival. "The issue here is a culture—the survival of a culture," said Hopi tribal chairman Vernon Massayesva in 1993. "We have no other source of drinking water, and any significant depletion of our groundwater could spell doom for our tribe." The following year, the Peabody Coal Company announced that it would consider using "economically feasible" alternative sources for its slurry operations.

EVEN AS ISSUES OF ECONOMIC DEVELOPMENT AND ENVIRONMEN-
TAL PROTECTION DOMINATED INDIAN AFFAIRS DURING THE LATE
1970S, MANY NATIVE PEOPLE REMAINED IN POVERTY. SHOWN
HERE IS A MAKESHIFT VILLAGE OF THE TRADITIONAL KICKAPOO
TRIBE ON AN ACRE OF BARREN GROUND NEAR EAGLE PASS, TEXAS,
IN NOVEMBER 1980. THE TEMPORARY SHELTERS WERE MADE OF
CANE, RIVER REED, AND CARDBOARD. TRIBAL LEADERS SOUGHT
FEDERAL RECOGNITION AND LAND FOR A PERMANENT
SETTLEMENT.

Similar conflicts over water occurred throughout the western states in the last quarter of the twentieth century. Energy corporations and agribusiness interests often found themselves in conflict with Native Americans over access to the region's scarce water resources. The importance of the issue was underscored in 1978 by Frank Tenorio, Governor of the San Felipe Pueblo:

> There has been a lot said about the sacredness of our land which is our body; and the values of our culture which is our soul; but water is the blood of our tribes, and if its life-giving flow is stopped, or it is polluted, all else will die and the many thousands of years of our communal existence will come to an end.

Dozens of tribes—including the Arapahos, Zunis, Osages, Utes, and Pawnees—battled to regain or preserve tribal water rights. The tribes filed over fifty lawsuits in state and federal courts during the 1970s and 1980s, challenging the water diversions of cities, farmers, and energy corporations. At issue was the interpretation and application of a fundamental principle, established in the landmark case of *Winters v. United States* (1908), that Indian tribes had a "prior and paramount right" to adequate water resources to satisfy the present and future needs of their reservations. One of the most protracted struggles pitted the Paiute tribe of western Nevada against the Newlands Reclamation Project and its diversions of water from the Truckee River. The diversions caused Pyramid Lake to shrink dramatically, thus reducing the fish population upon which the Paiutes depended for their livelihood. In 1981, after years of litigation, a federal court upheld the tribe's right to sufficient water for the maintenance of its fisheries. Ten years later the Paiutes were engaged in a similar struggle over the shrinking waters of nearby Walker Lake.

The conflict between economic development and environmental protection was especially intense in areas rich in uranium. The Black Hills region—extending over parts of Montana, Wyoming, and North and South Dakota—had enormous uranium resources. The region also was the home of the nation's second-largest concentration of Native Americans, including the Sioux, Shoshones, Arapahos, Crows, and Northern Cheyennes. By the late 1970s, the extraction of uranium by dozens of energy companies had left portions of the Black Hills region contaminated with high levels of radiation and littered with tailings from open-pit mines. The Department of the Interior reported in 1979 that contamination in some areas was "well beyond the safe limit for animals." Opposed to the energy companies was the Black Hills Alliance (BHA), a coalition of Indian and white residents of the region. Among the leaders of the BHA were Winona Laduke (Ojibwa) and Madonna Gilbert (Sioux), first cousin of activist Russell Means. The Black Hills are "not just another mine site with a 'potential' for energy production," Laduke explained. They are "a spiritual center" for the Indian people, "for as long as the old people can remember, there have been prayers and songs to '*Paha Sapa,* our life blood.'"

Following an accident at the Three Mile Island nuclear plant near Harrisburg, Pennsylvania, in March 1979, the market for uranium in the United States declined rapidly. By mid-1982 virtually all domestic uranium production was suspended. Many nuclear plants continued to operate, however, and the Council of Energy Resource Tribes and federal officials began to encourage tribes to open their reservations for use as sites for the storage of nuclear wastes. In 1984 the government began a vigorous campaign to place a major nuclear waste dump on the Yakama and Umatilla reservations in Washington state and on the Nez Perce reservation in northern Idaho. The campaign failed in the face of concerted intertribal opposition organized by Yakama leader Russell Jim. But other tribes welcomed the storage of nuclear wastes on their reservations as a boon to the tribal economy. In 1995 the tribal council of the Mescalero Apaches of southern New Mexico approved the formation of a joint venture for the construction of an above-ground storage facility capable of housing one-quarter of all the high-level spent fuels generated at nuclear power plants in the United States. Some residents of the reservation complained about the potential safety hazards, but tribal leaders emphasized that the storage facility would provide much-needed jobs and revenues. As Mescalero vice-chairman Fred Peso explained, the storage of nuclear waste "would diversify our tribal job base and place one more brick in the structure of economic self-sufficiency."

Controversies over economic development also exacerbated such long-standing tribal rivalries as the Navajo-Hopi land dispute. In 1882 the federal government established a reservation for the Hopis in the middle of the huge Navajo reservation. At the time, fewer than 600 Navajos were living on the newly created Hopi reservation; by the early 1970s, however, the number of Navajos on Hopi land had grown to more than 10,000. Hopi leader Abbott Sekaquaptewa charged that the Navajos had taken both Hopi lands and tribal traditions. "Our shrines have become their shrines," he complained. The Hopi tribal council began legal proceedings to force the Navajos to leave. In 1974 Congress passed the Navajo-Hopi Land Settlement Act to partition the disputed land, and subsequent court orders called for the removal of more than 5,000 Navajos from the Hopi reservation. Among those ordered to leave were the most traditional of Navajos, including many sheepherding families living in isolated enclaves in the Big Mountain area of Black Mesa.

The Navajos who were threatened with removal charged that the real reason for their eviction was the desire of energy corporations and Hopi tribal leaders to develop the millions of tons of coal that lay beneath the surface of Big Mountain. For Navajo traditionalists, Big Mountain was sacred land. "It is the place we go to pray for our livestock," explained one Navajo herder, "and our medicine men go there to get herbs. . . . We need the mountain to live." Pauline White-singer, one of the Navajos ordered to leave, agreed. "In our traditional tongue there is no word for relocation," she said. "To move away means to disappear and never be seen again." In the summer of 1978, Whitesinger joined Indian activists Russell Means and Wallace "Mad Bear" Anderson in the Longest Walk, a demonstration that protested (among other things) the "genocidal" relocation of the Navajos.

The dispute moved toward resolution in the early 1980s when Congress created the Navajo and Hopi Indian Relocation Commission and appropriated $200 million to compensate those who had to be removed. New tribal chairmen were elected by the Hopis and the Navajos in 1982, and the new leaders pledged to cooperate in seeking a compromise solution. "We have to undo all of the hatred that the past leaders have created between the two tribes," said the new Navajo Nation tribal chairman Peterson Zah. Both tribes suspended all law-suits over the issue and formed a joint committee to negotiate future contracts and leases with energy corporations. Several hundred Navajos submitted voluntarily to relocation, but no final solution was reached. By the mid-1990s, at least 250 Navajo families ordered to leave the Hopi reservation remained on lands they had occupied for generations.

Peter MacDonald and other leaders of the Council of Energy Resource Tribes continued to believe that energy development was essential to Indian self-determination, but critics argued that CERT represented the final assault on the reservations by outside forces. Those who opposed the growing role of energy corporations in Indian

PETER MACDONALD
SPEAKS AT WINDOW
ROCK, ARIZONA, CAPI-
TAL OF THE NAVAJO
NATION. FIRST ELECTED
TRIBAL CHAIRMAN IN
1970, MACDONALD
SERVED THREE TERMS
BEFORE BEING CON-
VICTED IN 1990 IN
TRIBAL COURT ON
CHARGES OF BRIBERY
AND ETHICS
VIOLATIONS.

affairs charged that the wealth produced by energy development did not extend far beyond the tribal councils that negotiated the multi-million dollar deals with the corporations. The members of the Navajo tribal council, for instance, received salaries more than twenty times the average income of their fellow tribesmen. Chairman MacDonald, who traveled about in a Lear Jet and Lincoln Continental, was dubbed by his critics "Peter MacDollar." The close relationship between tribal leaders and the corporate elite was made manifest in a festive black-tie dinner in New York City in 1981, attended by several hundred CERT members and corporation executives. Four tribes resigned from CERT, complaining that MacDonald had "sold out to the corporate state."

Charges of corruption and mismanagement of tribal assets increased as millions of dollars flowed into the reservations. The administration of Peter MacDonald was racked by several scandals, including the indictment of the chairman himself for submitting false invoices to a utility company. In 1982 Peterson Zah was elected tribal chairman of the Navajo Nation, but four years later MacDonald returned to office. New charges of bribery, conspiracy, and ethics violations soon were leveled at MacDonald, and in 1989 he was accused of receiving kickbacks from corporations dealing with the tribe. "I knew that the businesses were spending their money to influence me, and I didn't care," MacDonald later acknowledged. "I was not being bribed. I was not selling out." In 1990 MacDonald was convicted in tribal court on more than forty counts and sentenced to nearly six years in prison. Two years later, the former chairman was found guilty in federal court of an additional sixteen charges. Through it all, MacDonald denied any wrongdoing and accused his opponents of engaging in a "concerted effort to undermine tribal sovereignty."

Despite the misfortunes of Peter MacDonald, the acceleration of energy resource development left an enduring legacy in Indian country. As historian Marjane Ambler, author of *Breaking the Iron Bonds: Indian Control of Energy Development* (1990), concluded, the energy tribes of the far west faced the turn of the century "in a much better position than ever before." They were no longer the nation's energy colonies, but had taken an active role in the direction of their own economic affairs. Gaining control over their resources offered the best hope that Indians might yet "break the iron bonds linking them to dependency, paternalism, and exploitation."

THE VARIETIES OF ECONOMIC DEVELOPMENT

The development of energy resources was just one of the many ways that Native Americans pursued greater economic independence in the late twentieth century. As impressive as those resources were, they were concentrated on relatively few reservations. Only 14 percent of the nation's Indian people, in the mid-1980s, lived on reservations that received annual revenues from energy resources equal to $500 or more per resident. Tribes without such resources turned to a wide variety of other economic enterprises.

The Passamaquoddies and Penobscots of New England filed claims in the 1970s in federal court for the return of land—including two-thirds of the state of Maine—that they believed had been illegally taken from them. The tribes argued that various treaties ceding the land had never been approved by Congress and thus were in violation of the Trade and Intercourse Act of 1790. The Supreme Court eventually ruled in favor of the tribes, invalidating the treaties in question, and Congress endorsed a settlement in 1980 providing them with more than $80 million in compensation. The Passamaquoddies wisely used their newfound wealth to purchase land, invest in low-risk securities, and acquire a variety of commercial enterprises. The tribe bought the third largest blueberry farm in Maine and made a handsome profit selling high-quality berries to such buyers as Quaker Oats cereal and Häagen-Dazs ice cream. It also mastered the art of the leveraged buyout, investing $2 million of tribal funds to acquire the state's only cement factory, an asset worth more than $25 million.

Other tribes demonstrated a similar degree of business acumen and financial sophistication. They began to capitalize on their advantages in the marketplace: an abundant labor pool, loan guarantees, tax exemption, and the growing need of federal contractors to work with minority businesses. The Mississippi band of Choctaws used federal grants and a federally guaranteed loan to establish Chahta Enterprises in 1978. This tribally owned corporation then formed a joint venture with a Chicago electronics firm and began manufacturing speakers for Chrysler automobiles. Chahta Enterprises also built and operated a finishing plant for greeting cards, an assembly plant for the making of wire harnesses (used in the electrical systems of cars and trucks), and a 120-bed nursing home. The benefits of economic development were soon apparent. Income levels, housing, education, and health standards among the Choctaws improved, while rates of unemployment, alcoholism, and suicide declined.

The Ak-Chin Community of Tohono O'odhams and Pimas in Arizona experienced similar success with a joint venture in high-tech agribusiness. In 1983 the community negotiated an agreement with the Central Arizona Project for sufficient supplies of water to reclaim thousands of acres of desert land. Using tractors guided by laser beams, the community cultivated high-grade pima cotton to sell to the makers of luxurious bath towels and Brooks Brothers shirts. With farm income at $2 million a year by 1987 and employment at 97 percent, the Tohono O'odhams and Pimas were proud of their achievement.

"A farming venture of our magnitude," boasted the community newspaper, "will take us into the economic mainstream of the nation." Likewise, the Confederated Tribes of the Warm Springs reservation in Oregon achieved remarkable success with a variety of tribally owned enterprises. The Confederated Tribes—Wascos, Warm Springs, and Paiutes—owned and operated their own forest products company, hydroelectric plant, and resort complex. In 1987 the tribes also began assembling clothing and footwear for the Oregon-based Nike and Patagonia corporations. By 1990 the various tribal enterprises were generating $80 million in annual revenue and had become the largest employer in central Oregon.

Perhaps the most visible evidence of the new entrepreneurial spirit among Native Americans was their successful development of tourism. Enticing tourists to Indian country became a big business for many tribes, often in partnership with private non-Indian concerns and aided by government grants or federally guaranteed loans. Some tourist-oriented enterprises were successful, while others languished as conflicts developed with reservation residents who opposed the opening of their homelands to outsiders.

The variety of tourist enterprises was truly remarkable. The eastern band of Cherokees in North Carolina developed a successful charter-bus company to transport tourists into the Great Smoky Mountain National Park. The Mescalero Apaches of New Mexico operated a 230-room luxury retreat called the Inn of the Mountain Gods. In Arizona, the Pimas opened a racetrack along the Gila River, and the White Mountain Apaches developed the state's largest ski resort. The Swinomish people of Washington state built an 800-slip marina and a $15-million resort complex on Padilla Bay. And Indians, Eskimos, and Aleuts of the Far North formed the Alaska Native Tourism Council, offering dozens of expeditions into the interior and encouraging visitors with the slogan "Alaska's Diverse Native Peoples—Visit Them, for a Few Hours or a Few Days."

Typical of the many Native American tourist facilities was the Kah-Nee-Ta Lodge developed by the Confederated Tribes of the Warm Springs reservation in Oregon. Aided by a low-interest loan from the federal government's Economic Development Agency, the tribes invested $750,000 of their own funds to build the 139-room lodge in the late 1960s. The completed facility offered visitors a wide range of activities and amenities, including an eighteen-hole golf course, horseback riding, fishing, and swimming in a pool fed by the reservation's famed warm springs. The resort earned a five-star rating but had difficulty in achieving a high occupancy rate. Kah-Nee-Ta also stimulated intertribal rivalries on the Warm Springs reservation. The Paiutes charged the Wascos with being more interested in promoting tourism than in preserving tribal values. Tourism was speeding assimilation, the Paiutes complained, and undermining traditional culture.

Some of the greatest successes in tourism were in the American Southwest amidst the nation's most spectacular scenic landscape. The Hualapais of Arizona brought visitors to their reservation home on the breathtaking edge of the Grand Canyon and guided hunters on expeditions in pursuit of the desert big horn sheep, charging $18,000 for each sheep bagged. The Navajo tribal government enthusiastically promoted tourism, encouraging visitors to come and see such redrock wonders on the reservation as Monument Valley and Shiprock. The Navajos developed at Chinle a thriving restaurant and hotel complex, the Thunderbird Lodge, for visitors attracted to the ancient ruins and serene beauty of nearby Canyon de Chelly. Beginning in the late 1940s, the Navajos also hosted the nation's largest annual Native American fair. By the mid-1990s, the fair was attracting 150,000 visitors each fall to watch traditional Navajo dancing, attend the all-Indian rodeo, and sample the wares of local weavers and other craftspeople.

The tribal council of the Hopis encouraged tourism by developing the Hopi Cultural Center on Second Mesa, complete with an outstanding museum, comfortable motel, and attractive restaurant. Unfortunately, some visitors abused the Hopis' hospitality. Traditionalists were especially upset by the disrespectful behavior of white visitors who came to witness ceremonial dances. In the summer of 1971, the Snake and Antelope priests of the village of Mishongnovi barred all visitors from witnessing the sacred Snake Ceremony. The following year, the Snake and Antelope Societies in Shongopovi agreed to allow visitors to attend the ceremony, but the village leaders wished to bar them. The controversy attracted the interest of members of the American Indian Movement who appeared at the Shongopovi Snake Ceremony in August 1972 and tried to expel all white visitors from the village.

The challenge for many Native Americans was to maintain a balance between the commercial development of tourism and the preservation of tribal culture. The Iroquois in rural upstate New York generally were not interested in promoting their communities as tourist attractions, yet they welcomed visitors to various tribal museums and cultural centers. The Mohawks in Akwesasne, also known as the town of St. Regis, operated a museum and gift shop that offered tourists an array of traditional black-ash splint baskets and hickory lacrosse sticks. Members of the Hupa tribe in northern California attempted to encourage tourism without commercializing their heritage. The tribe owned the Tsewenaldin Inn, a motel complete with heated pool and spa, and operated a tribal museum displaying items of traditional culture. Hupa guides escorted visitors on raft trips along the Trinity River, stopping at ancient village sites and explaining how the people there once lived. Visitors even were invited to attend the biennial White Deerskin Dance, but were warned not to take photographs, drink alcohol, or engage in loud or boisterous behavior. "When you go to the dance, it's like going to your church," explained Hupa guide Lyle Marshall. "In other words, don't behave like tourists."

As the twentieth century came to a close, the fastest growing and most contentious sector in the Native American economy was legalized gambling. The development of gaming facilities on Indian reservations was just one part of the largest expansion of commercial gambling in U.S. history. By the early 1990s, state-run lotteries were operating in more than three dozen states, whereas thirty years earlier there had been none. State governments discovered that lotteries and other forms of gambling were a relatively painless way to fill depleted coffers without raising taxes. Americans in 1992 spent $330 billion on gambling, $130 billion *more* than what they spent on groceries. The Indian share of this gambling boom was relatively small—less than 5 percent—but its impact on the Native American economy was tremendous.

Gambling in various forms had been a part of Native cultures for thousands of years, but the modern development of commercial gambling began in 1979 when the Seminole tribe in Florida opened a bingo hall. The Seminoles offered prizes of $10,000 or more in defiance of a state law that limited bingo jackpots to $100. When the state attorney general attempted to shut down the Seminoles' bingo hall, the tribe sued in federal court and won. The Seminoles soon opened four new bingo parlors, with seating for 10,000 players, and began netting more than $10 million a year. The next important victory came in California when state authorities tried to close a high-stakes bingo hall operated by the Cabazon band of the Mission Indians. The ensuing legal battle was resolved in 1987 when the U.S. Supreme Court ruled that California could not regulate gambling on the Cabazon reservation. The Court noted that since the state of California operated its own lottery and permitted other forms of legal gambling, it could not prohibit Indians from engaging in similar activities. The Cabazons soon expanded their bingo hall and built a new casino. Gambling revenues allowed the tribe to achieve a degree of economic independence previously unimaginable: Free health care and college scholarships were made available to all tribal members. "We went from having no economic base at all," said Cabazon leader Mark Nichols, "to having a very significant economic base."

At the insistence of state governments, and over the objections of Indian leaders, Congress passed the Indian Gaming Regulatory Act (IGRA) in 1988. The act required tribes and states to negotiate agreements, or "compacts," that established guidelines for tribal gambling operations. If a state refused to negotiate, or if an agreement could not be reached, the tribes could sue the state in federal court. Within five years of the act's passage, more than seventy tribes had successfully negotiated compacts with various states. The Bureau of Indian Affairs encouraged this expansion by assisting in the financing of $64 million worth of tribal casinos and bingo halls. "We believe in economic development," said one BIA official. "If tribes chose this method of economic development, then we support it. They are creating jobs and they are making money." State leaders, who had not expected Indian gambling to grow so rapidly or so large, urged Congress to gut or repeal the IGRA.

The largest and most successful of the new Indian casinos was operated by the Mashantucket Pequot tribe of Connecticut. Their Foxwoods Casino, near the picturesque town of Mystic, had more gaming tables and slot machines than Donald Trump's Taj Mahal, the biggest casino in Atlantic City. Bingo halls the size of airplane hangers soon appeared in the nation's heartland. The Creeks of Oklahoma built three facilities, the largest of which had seating for 1,200 bingo players. In Minnesota, the Mille Lac band of Chippewas built two giant Las Vegas–style casinos on reservation lands near the towns of Garrison and Hinckley. In an arrangement that was typical, the Chippewas contracted with a non-Indian corporation to manage the operation of their casinos.

The rapid growth of gaming enterprises became the source of intense controversy among Native Americans on many reservations. Some Indian leaders argued that gambling was an inherently unstable economic base that provided relatively few jobs for reservation residents. Traditionalists charged that large-scale commercial gambling was having a corrupting influence on tribal members and was incompatible with tribal values. A debate among the Mohawks of New York over gambling erupted into a deadly quarrel that left two Indians dead and thousands intimidated in a wave of vigilantism and gunfire. A militant Mohawk "Warrior Society" championed a multimillion-dollar casino, and a tax-free cigarette and gas smuggling enterprise, over the objections of Mohawk traditionalists. Controversies also developed over the division of the spoils from tribal gambling enterprises. Among the Creeks of Oklahoma, the operators of a tribally owned bingo hall opposed the development of rival halls operated by local tribal communities. The dispute was, in the words of one Indian observer, "an economic war between two groups for the same bingo clients."

The main controversy over Native American gaming pitted individual tribes against various state governments in a high-stakes contest over who would benefit most from America's newfound enthusiasm for gambling. The tribes defended their enterprises on the grounds not only of economic development but also of political sovereignty. The states maintained that they had a right to regulate the kind of economic activity permitted within their borders. State leaders warned that unregulated gambling on the reservations would mean a loss of revenue from state-run lotteries and would also increase the danger of organized crime.

The controversy between the states and the tribes often revolved around the size or type of gaming activities permitted. The state of Arizona, for instance, insisted that Indian gaming be limited to 250 gambling machines per tribe. Several small tribes signed compacts with the state, agreeing to these limits. But three larger tribes—the Tohono O'odhams, Pascua Yaquis, and White Mountain Apaches—sued in federal district court for the right to operate full-service casinos with thousands of gambling machines, dice games, and tables of blackjack or poker. Likewise, Washington state negotiated compacts with several tribes that limited maximum bets to $25, set strict limits on the hours of operation, and absolutely prohibited the use of slot machines. The Colville Confederated Tribes successfully challenged these state-imposed restrictions in 1993 when a federal court declared a portion of the Indian Gaming Regulatory Act unconstitutional since it wrongly compelled states to negotiate with tribes. The following year the Spokane tribe opened its Two Rivers Resort—without benefit of a state-approved compact—and began offering twenty-four-hour, high-stakes gambling, complete with 100 electronic and lever-pull slot machines. When Washington state officials sought an injunction to shut down the casino, Spokane tribal vice chairman John Kieffer was not surprised. "Washington state has always been an Indian fighting state," he observed. "Nothing's changed." Tribal council member Henry Sijohn saw the battle over the casino as part of a larger struggle for sovereignty rights and economic self-reliance. "We're fighting for our sovereignty, we're fighting for our people, we're fighting for our rights to regulate and govern ourselves," he said. "That's what this is all about."

Similar issues were raised in the ongoing fight over Native American gaming in California. The state attempted to limit Indian-run gambling enterprises to low-stakes bingo, poker, and horse-race betting. Republican State Attorney General Dan Lundgren claimed that an enlargement of Indian gambling would be an open invitation to organized crime, leading to an increase in money laundering, bookmaking, and loan sharking. The tribes demanded the right to operate Nevada-style casinos, offering high-stakes bingo and video slot machines, and claimed that the state's real reason for limiting Indian gambling was to protect its own state-run lottery. In 1993 a delegation of California Indian leaders came to the state capital, brandishing a "dream catcher" woven of branches and feathers. They said the dream catcher was a traditional tool used for catching and fulfilling dreams— in this case, the dream of catching sufficient gambling profits to achieve tribal self-sufficiency. "Our dream is to ensure the survival of our people and our culture," said Marshall McKay (Wintun), chairman of the California-Nevada Indian Gambling Association. "Gambling is the most effective way to accomplish tribal sovereignty. Indian gambling in the last ten years has had a more significant impact on Indian people than the last 150 years of government support."

Among those who rejected gaming as a means of economic advancement were the nation's largest tribe, the Navajo, and their Hopi neighbors. Navajo voters defeated a referendum in 1994 to allow casino gambling on their reservation, and the newly elected tribal president, Albert Hale, agreed to honor the decision and not attempt to have the issue considered again. Typical of the anti-gaming sentiment was a resolution passed by one of the reservation's units of local government: "Gambling causes loss of family and properties, respect of oneself, and countless other negative effects." The following year, Hopi voters rejected a similar proposal to build a casino on their reservation. The tribe's Cultural Preservation Office circulated flyers opposing gambling as an assault on tradition. "It was a loud and clear message," said tribal chairman Ferrell Secakuku, "that culture is more important and more valuable than the money."

The issue of Indian gaming remained unresolved as federal, state, and tribal officials engaged in dozens of legal skirmishes. Democratic President Bill Clinton met with tribal leaders in April 1994 and assured them of his support in their struggle to achieve greater economic self-sufficiency. "As a former governor, I understand some of the concerns that the governors have raised about gambling," Clinton said. "But as president, I know that gaming gives you a competitive edge. My goal is this: I want the tribes to continue to benefit from gaming." Opposing the president were members of Congress from several western states who introduced legislation in 1995 to place a two-year moratorium on the opening of new Indian casinos.

Journalist Robert H. White, author of *Tribal Assets: The Rebirth of Native America* (1990), described the development of the vast array of Native American commercial enterprises in the late twentieth century as "a quiet economic revolution, which has the potential for reestablishing a Native American independence based on economic sovereignty." Although the results of this revolution were limited—only about 10 percent of the nation's Indian communities had truly gained control over their economic destiny—it was producing a new sense of pride and self-confidence throughout Indian America. The new enterprises had an enormous advantage over earlier forms of economic development: They were initiated and directed by the Indian people themselves. After decades of dependence, this was an exhilarating experience. Many Native Americans could agree with the conclusion of Cherokee Chief Wilma Mankiller: "The best solutions to our problems are within our own communities."

RENEWED TENSIONS

While issues of economic development tended to dominate Native American affairs in the years after Wounded Knee, the political struggle for greater independence also continued. Tribal leaders and others defended the gains of the recent past and worked diligently to gain additional rights for Native people.

The more radical movement to win recognition of full tribal sovereignty shifted to the international arena where it achieved only limited and largely symbolic success. Native American traditionalists and activists formed the International Indian Treaty Council in 1974 at a meeting held near the grave of Sitting Bull on the Standing Rock Sioux reservation in South Dakota. Attending the meeting were representatives of nearly 100 tribes. The council decided to take the fight for sovereignty over the heads of national leaders and appeal directly to the United Nations and other international agencies. In spite of opposition by the United States, the UN granted the council official recognition as a nongovernmental organization. Council representatives attending UN-sponsored conferences in New York, Geneva, and Rotterdam spoke movingly about the struggle of Indian people "against colonialism and for human rights and sovereignty." In 1982 the Movement of Non-Aligned Nations accorded the council full observer status at its triennial meeting in Baghdad, Iraq.

Meanwhile, closer to home, Native Americans scored more meaningful victories by gaining from the federal government either the restoration or acknowledgment of their tribal status. Following the passage of the Menominee Restoration Act in 1973, additional tribes appealed to the federal government for the restoration of federal recognition and federal benefits. The Siletz tribe of western Oregon, terminated in 1954, spent twenty years petitioning federal officials for the restoration of their tribal status. Tribal members complained that their loss of recognition had left them in "a state of limbo, unrecognized as equals by members of the white community, and looked down upon by other Indian people as well." Finally, in 1977 Congress passed legislation restoring the tribal status of the Siletz and other tribes in western Oregon. Similar struggles culminated in restoration of the Modocs, Ottawas, Peorias, and Wyandots in 1978 and the Paiutes in 1980.

Native Americans won a major victory in 1978 when Congress created the Acknowledgment Project, a program directed by the Bureau of Indian Affairs to evaluate the claims of Native groups never before recognized by the United States as tribes. The federal government officially recognized 283 tribes in 1981; by 1995, the number of federally recognized tribes had increased to more than 550, including 200 village groups in Alaska. Even so, the procedure for obtaining federal recognition could be—and often was—agonizingly slow. The BIA required the compilation of detailed histories of each tribe seeking recognition, a process that took years to complete. Kurt Blue Dog (Sioux), a lawyer for the Native American Rights Fund, testified before the Senate that such delays were unconscionable. He argued that the continued existence of such groups as the Traditional Kickapoo Tribe of Texas, a band of 600 people desperately seeking federal acknowledgment and the infusion of federal aid, depended upon the streamlining of the process.

Among the tribes that successfully completed the acknowledgment process were the Cow Creek Band of the Oregon Umpquas and the Narragansetts of Rhode Island. The Cow Creek Band won federal recognition in 1982 after years of lobbying by tribal leaders and members of the Native American Rights Fund. The Narragansetts achieved a remarkable comeback from near extinction in the nineteenth century to gain federal acknowledgment in 1984 and the return of portions of their traditional land. Perhaps equally important, recent archaeological discoveries and the revival of traditional ceremonies gave the Narragansetts a renewed sense of cultural identity. Ten years later, the struggle for recognition by the Ohlone-Muwekma tribe of California was celebrated at the American Indian Music and Cultural Festival, held on former tribal lands on the San Francisco Presidio.

To safeguard the status of existing tribes, tribal leaders supported legislation in the early 1990s to abolish a newly adopted policy by the Bureau of Indian Affairs that distinguished between historic tribes and those deemed "nonhistoric" or "created." The so-called nonhistoric tribes included those that had been formed out of the remnants of tribes decimated in the nineteenth century by war and disease. Allogan Slagle (Cherokee), a lawyer who specialized in sovereignty issues, estimated that 230 tribes around the nation were at risk as nonhistoric. If a tribe were declared to be nonhistoric, it could lose its right to substantial federal aid. Congress considered legislation in 1994 to protect such tribes, prohibiting government officials and agencies from changing the privileges and powers of any federally recognized tribe.

In the midst of (and largely *because* of) these impressive victories, Native American leaders had to contend with a growing anti-Indian backlash. The strengthening of tribal governments, following the passage of the Indian Self-Determination and Education Assistance Act of 1975, led some European Americans to conclude that Native Americans were gaining too much power. Conflicts over hunting and fishing rights were the catalyst for what came to be called the "antisovereignty" movement among whites who lived on or near reservations. In 1978 a commercial fisherman in Washington state published a manifesto denouncing the attempt by tribal governments to regulate the activities of non-Indian hunters and fishermen. "Uncle Sam is giving America back to the Indians," the manifesto complained. It denounced federal Indian policy as "a nationwide, sinister juggernaut, exacting from Americans sacrifices of property, money, rights, and identity."

As tribal governments broadened their authority over reservation resources, local whites complained that they now were the victims of discrimination. An outspoken leader of the antisovereignty forces was Delbert Palmer, a white resident of the Flathead reservation in Montana, arrested for hunting on his land without a permit from the tribal government. "No Indian government is going to tell me what I can do on my own land or anywhere else," he said. "I don't recognize that government's authority at all." The Citizens Equal Rights Alliance (CERA), an umbrella organization for the national antisovereignty movement, claimed to have more than 500,000 supporters. Its ranks swelled following a dramatic confrontation in 1981 on the Crow reservation in Montana. Crow tribesmen barricaded a highway bridge over the Bighorn River to prevent non-Indians from fishing the river as it flowed through the reservation. Members of CERA raised defense funds, filed lawsuits, and drafted legislation aimed at curbing the power of tribal governments. Its supporters included real estate interests, agribusinesses, and mining companies threatened by the tribes' growing control over their resources.

Native American leaders believed that racism and jealousy were the root causes of the white backlash against tribal governments. "You're going to see more of this," said Henry Stockbeson of the Native American Rights Fund. "As long as the Indians are downtrodden, racism is at a simmer point. But as soon as Indians successfully assert their rights, these people are screaming, 'Why should they have something I can't have?'" Lucille Otter, an elder of the Salish tribe, agreed. Speaking of the antisovereignty forces, she said: "They were comfortable thinking of the poor half-wit Indian. Now that we're taking control of our assets they are just in shock." And journalist Margaret L. Knox summed up the backlash succinctly: "Lots of whites are just plain jealous."

Tensions also increased as the Pacific Northwest fishing rights controversy was rekindled in the 1980s and 1990s. The decision by U.S. District Court Judge George H. Boldt in 1974 had acknowledged the right of Native Americans to half the harvestable salmon from the waters of Washington state. Tribal leaders then began to push for an expansion of the decision to include the gathering of half the available shellfish as well. They argued that their people had been digging clams and picking oysters from the tidelands of the Northwest for centuries and that these activities were also protected by the treaties signed in the 1850s. "Historically, shellfish are equally as important as salmon," said one Native leader. The issue raised passionate opposition from property owners who feared that Indians would be permitted to gather shellfish on privately owned tidelands. "It's private property," said one outraged white property owner who lived near the Suquamish reservation in Washington state. "I don't believe anyone would want people crossing their land." After years of unsuccessful efforts to resolve the issue through negotiation, sixteen tribes sued the state of Washington in 1994 for access to half the annual harvest of shellfish.

The tribes of the Pacific Northwest were also in the forefront of renewed controversies over environmental protection. In the early 1990s the Shoalwater Bay Tribe in southwestern Washington state suffered from an unusually high rate of miscarriages, stillbirths, and infant deaths. "We're losing a whole generation of people and it's hard to take," said tribal chairman Herb Whitish. The suspected causes of the tribe's problems were herbicides dumped on surrounding forest lands and insecticides sprayed on nearby cranberry bogs that contaminated the tidelands where tribal members gathered shellfish. Tribal leaders demanded stricter controls on local polluters and pesticide users. In 1992 the Environmental Protection Agency concluded that contamination of inland and coastal waters in the Northwest exposed Indian people to greater risks of cancer because of their high levels of fish consumption. Subsequent federal legislation authorized tribal governments to regulate water quality not only on reservation land but also on upstream sources that affected it. Armed with this new authority, several Northwest tribes in 1993 sought to impose costly, tough pollution standards on major industries operating near their reservations. Meanwhile, a study of the children of the Coeur d'Alene tribe in northwestern Idaho found that one-fifth had elevated levels of lead in their blood. Tribal chairman Ernest Stensgar called upon the federal government to help clean up the local water supply poisoned by lead, zinc, and arsenic left over from decades of hardrock mining.

Another flash point of conflict between Native Americans and European Americans was the attempt by tribal governments to increase the rents of whites living on reservation land. In upstate New York, the town of Salamanca was built entirely on land belonging to the

Seneca Nation. The Senecas had signed a ninety-nine-year lease with the town in 1892, agreeing to accept payment of $17,000 a year. When the lease came up for renewal in the early 1990s, townspeople feared the tribe would evict them all and reclaim the land. Tensions steadily increased and some families even obtained permits to dynamite their homes rather than turn them over to the Senecas. After a burst of national media attention, the issue was quietly resolved when the tribe and town signed a new forty-year lease, with the town agreeing to pay the Senecas $60 million in rent each year. A similar conflict erupted along the shores of Lake Havasu in southern California. The Chemehuevi tribal government raised the annual rents of white residents on tribal land from a few hundred dollars to $5,000 a year. When some of the whites refused to pay, the tribe won the support of the Bureau of Indian Affairs to evict them. Tribal chairman Matthew Leivas hoped to use the disputed land to build a casino. "It's the tribe standing on its own ground," he explained, "saying we want to do economic development for our people."

Even more contentious was the attempt by Native Americans to protect sacred sites from desecration by unwanted development. One of the longest-running controversies, movingly chronicled in Peter Matthiessen's *Indian Country* (1984), centered on the proposed construction of a $25 million all-weather road through the high country of the Siskiyou Mountains of northern California. The road would traverse several mountain ridges and connect the remote villages of Gasquet and Orleans, thus it was known as the Gasquet-Orleans Road, or G-O Road. The road would open a large area in the Six Rivers National Forest to expanded logging operations and also provide public access to sites sacred to local Native Americans. For centuries, the Yuroks and their neighbors—the Karuks, Tolowas, and Hupas—ascended a network of old paths into the high country. Women went there for medicine training and men went on vision quests seeking spiritual power. When the G-O Road was first proposed in the 1960s, local Indian people voiced strong opposition. They were joined in 1974 by the Sierra Club and other environmental organizations that filed suit to halt construction. Yurok medicine man Calvin Rube was among those who testified that the high country should be left as it was, a "good place" where Indians could go to be restored.

The G-O Road controversy continued throughout the 1980s. Congress passed the California Wilderness Act in 1980, providing considerable protection for the Siskiyous, and the following year the Forest

Service acknowledged that the area contained valid Indian religious sites. A federal court issued an injunction in 1983 prohibiting construction of the road along any route "which would traverse the high country." Basing its decision on the religious freedom provision of the First Amendment, the court ruled that the G-O Road must be stopped to protect ground sacred to the Indian people of the area. Proponents of the road, however, continued to push for its completion and in 1988 the lower court's ruling was overturned by the U.S. Supreme Court. "Even if we assume [the G-O Road] will virtually destroy the Indians' ability to practice their religion," wrote Justice Sandra Day O'Connor, "the Constitution simply does not provide a principle that would justify upholding [the Indians'] legal claims." Justice William J. Brennan dissented from the majority opinion, saying that the ruling reduced the Indians' religious freedom to "nothing more than the right to believe that their religion will be destroyed."

The ability of Native Americans to defend sacred sites was strengthened in 1978 with the passage of the American Indian Religious Freedom Act, but unfortunately the act often went unenforced. Signed by President Jimmy Carter, the act announced that it was the policy of the United States to protect the "inherent right" of American Indians to practice their traditional religions, including access to sacred sites. The new policy was adopted in the midst of a controversy over the construction of a huge liquified natural gas (LNG) terminal at Point Conception along the southern California coast. The $600 million terminal was proposed by a consortium of utility companies that maintained the facility was essential for the importation of much-needed supplies of natural gas from Indonesia. To the local Chumash Indians, Point Conception was known as *Humqaq* or *Tolakwe*, the "Western Gate," through which all new life came into the world and the spirits of the dead departed. They objected to the construction of the LNG facility on what they believed was one of the most hallowed sites in all of California. The utility companies denied that the newly enacted American Indian Religious Freedom Act applied to Point Conception and proceeded with preliminary excavation. Twenty-five Indian activists occupied the construction site and announced that they would lie in the path of the bulldozers rather than allow any further desecration of this holy ground. "If that place were destroyed tomorrow," said Chumash spiritual leader Kote Lotah, "I feel so strongly about it, I would want to die today so that I could pass through the Western Gate."

The applicability of the American Indian Religious Freedom Act to the Point Conception site was never fully resolved, but the battle over construction of the LNG facility was a victory nonetheless for Native Americans. Protests by the Chumash and their allies from around the country delayed the project sufficiently so that when gas prices were deregulated in 1980 building the facility no longer made economic sense. (Deregulation led to the profitable domestic production of natural gas and thus made its importation less imperative.) Various regulatory commissions and the utilities themselves eventually withdrew support for the project. Native leaders congratulated themselves on successfully defending the Western Gate. "We formed a confederation to offer protection of our holy lands," said Lakota medicine man Archie Fire Lame Deer. "If we can't count on the government to protect our religious rights, then we are willing to protect Mother Earth ourselves from further desecration."

Similar battles over the protection of sacred sites continued to be waged by Native Americans throughout the 1980s and 1990s. Both the Hopi and Navajo tribal councils fought to halt the proposed expansion of skiing facilities on the San Francisco Peaks in the Coconino National Forest in Arizona. The peaks were believed to be the home of the *Kachinas,* the mighty rain beings on whom all life in the parched Southwest depended. If the mountains were desecrated by further development, the Navajo council warned, there would be a terrible disaster: "The rain and snow will cease to fall; the Navajo people will be unprotected from the forces of destruction; our traditions will die." A decade later a coalition of Native people battled a southern California developer's plans to bulldoze a burial mound and put up a parking lot for a Wal-Mart discount store. The developer contended that the mound had to be leveled so that the store would be clearly visible from a nearby freeway; the Indians said the burial ground was as sacred as a church or a synagogue and therefore must be preserved. "They are destroying our people," complained Pilulaw Khus, a traditional Chumash elder and healer. "They're willing to destroy this sacred burial ground for the sake of advertising."

In some instances the conflict over sacred sites involved conflicting religious traditions. Bear Butte, a 4,000-foot landmark in South Dakota, became a magnet for followers of a non-Indian New Age sect in the early 1990s. New Agers climbed to the top of the butte for weekends of male-bonding and ceremonies involving crystals and ersatz shamanism. The butte was popular among New Agers because it had been used for centuries as a traditional vision-quest site by Northern Plains tribes, including Cheyennes, Arapahos, and Sioux. Native leaders charged the New Agers with desecrating the site. Bill Miller, of the Cheyenne River Sioux, likened the New Agers' holding ceremonies on Bear Butte to someone coming into the sanctuary of a Christian church to conduct pagan rituals and worship false idols. "This is a problem that's happening to Indian people all over the country," said John LaVelle, a Santee Sioux lawyer. He called the situation at Bear Butte "an outrage" and an instance of "spiritual genocide."

REPATRIATION

The issue that captured the greatest public attention in the late twentieth century was what came to be called *repatriation*—the return of skeletal remains, religious artifacts, and other items of material culture to Native Americans. Physical anthropologists, archaeologists, and museum curators had been collecting and studying such objects for decades. Beginning in the early 1970s, a growing number of Indian people began to question the wisdom of allowing the evidence of their past to be removed, cataloged, and displayed in distant institutions. Indians began to demand that the bones of their ancestors be returned to them for reburial and that other objects be removed from public display.

Of special concern to both sides were the skeletal remains of the more than 500,000 Indians that were held in the nation's universities and museums. Archaeologists used the bones to learn about such things as diet, customs, and mortuary practices; physical anthropologists analyzed them to determine the age, sex, stature, and general health of individuals. Indians believed the spirits of the dead should be respected and their remains left in peace in the earth; attorney Walter Echo-Hawk called repatriation "the paramount human rights problem for Indians today." Scientists were accustomed to seeing themselves as benefiting the cultures they studied, by unearthing and preserving objects from the past that otherwise would have been lost. They were dismayed when Indians denounced their work as simply another form of exploitation.

The issue was dramatized in the early 1970s when Indian activists challenged several archaeological digs and museum collections. Members of the American Indian Movement raided a Minnesota excavation site in 1973 and confiscated tools, filled in trenches, and burned research notes. One archaeology graduate student, who witnessed the action, was shocked. "We were trying to preserve their culture," he said, "not destroy it." The activists responded with the ironic rejoinder that archaeologists seemed to think the only real Indians were dead ones. Indian activists also staged occupations and protests at the Field Museum in Chicago and the Southwest Museum in Los Angeles, charging that their exhibits failed to show proper respect for Native cultures.

An early first step in resolving the repatriation issue came in 1976 when—at the urging of David Risling (Hupa/Yurok) and other outspoken Indian leaders—the California legislature created the Native American Heritage Commission (NAHC). Consisting of nine Native members, the commission was to be informed whenever an Indian burial site was discovered. The NAHC was charged with identifying the "persons most likely descended" from the deceased and informing them of the discovery. The descendants then were authorized to monitor the excavation and claim the remains for reburial. Tribal leaders applauded the new policy, but some anthropologists denounced it as "political interference." Under the leadership of such energetic executive directors as Steven Rios (Juaneño) and Larry Myers (Pomo), the NAHC became a powerful force for cultural resource protection. It filed suit to halt the development of a sacred site (*Puvungna*) on the campus of the state university at Long Beach and negotiated successfully with the mission at San Diego to end the desecration of an Indian cemetery. Seventeen other states followed the lead of California and adopted similar laws governing the handling of Indian remains, but none created a commission comparable to the NAHC.

Left unresolved was the question of what to do with the hundreds of thousands of Native American skeletal remains and other objects held in existing collections. The largest single collection of bones (18,000 individuals) was at the Smithsonian Institution in Washington, D.C. In 1989 Congress approved legislation requiring the Smithsonian to begin returning most of its skeletal remains and associated funerary objects to their modern descendants. Called the "Bridge of Respect Law," the legislation won the enthusiastic support of Native American tribal and spiritual leaders. The American Committee for the Preservation of Archeological Collections (ACPAC), an organization of physical anthropologists and others, denounced the new law:

Once again the public is sacrificed to small pressure groups. Once again the religious claims of 'traditional Indians' are more important than any other consideration. . . . Once again the proposed rules simply fail to recognize that there is a difference between a recent cemetery and an archeological find thousands of years old.

Several private and public universities also acceded to the demands of Native Americans for the repatriation of skeletal remains and other objects. Stanford University had in its collection more than 500 skeletal remains when local tribal leaders began pressing for their return in the mid-1980s. Over the strenuous opposition of an anthropologist who had spent forty years collecting the bones, the university administration agreed in 1989 to their return. Larry Myers, of the Native American Heritage Commission, helped to coordinate the transfer, and Rosemary Cambra, an Ohlone activist, was one of the many Native people who participated in the reburial ceremony on a hill overlooking San Francisco Bay. "We were helped by the Great Spirit, through the prayers of women and men who have a healthy relationship with each other," said Cambra. "Our old ones gave life to us. Now we gave a final life to them by putting them to rest back where they belonged." San Jose State University also agreed, over the objections of members of its anthropology department, to return more than 200 skeletal remains to the Ohlones. In 1989 the University of Minnesota agreed to repatriate 1,000 Indian remains taken from burial mounds, and the University of Nebraska agreed to return 100 Omaha skeletons to tribal authorities. In 1990 Harvard University's Peabody Museum also repatriated about 280 sacred Omaha artifacts to the tribe.

The most important resolution of the issue came in 1990 when Congress passed the Native American Grave Protection and Repatriation Act. The law required all institutions receiving federal funds— which included virtually every museum and university in the country— to inventory fully their collections of Indian bones and other artifacts, share this information with existing tribes, and return to the tribes whatever items they requested. The law fulfilled precisely what Rosemary Cambra and other Indian leaders had been saying for years: "We have to respect the remains of our ancestors."

The repatriation law provoked a mixed reaction from museum officials and scientists. Frank Norick, a principal researcher at the University of California's museum of anthropology in Berkeley, labeled the new law "disastrous." He was determined to keep intact the museum's collection of the bones of about 10,000 individuals. "I don't think science should be sacrificed on the altar of religious beliefs," Norick said. "Some Native Americans claim they believe in spirits and that's why they want the bones back. But to me, that just isn't good enough. That kind of thinking disappeared in the Dark Ages." Other museum officials accepted the new national policy with equanimity. Barbara O'Connell, a professor of anthropology at Hamline University in Minnesota, urged her fellow scientists to cooperate fully with the new policy on repatriation. To resist would only further alienate Native Americans. "Science always operates under limits," she reminded her colleagues. "If we resist this movement, the field may be stopped a lot quicker than if we work together on this issue." Many cultural anthropologists also supported the new policy; they agreed with the proponents of repatriation that respecting the sensitivities of living Indians outweighed scientific values.

Implementation of the new repatriation policy posed some unexpected problems for Native Americans. Tribal governments were inundated with inventory lists from universities and museums around the country that detailed the human remains, burial items, rugs, jewelry, and other items held in their collections. The Navajos alone received more than 300 inventories listing thousands of items that could be returned. "We want to get the items returned, but we don't have the staff or the money to take care of all of [them]," explained the director of the Navajo Historical Preservation Office. The Navajos completed a new cultural center in 1994, but even it did not have enough space for all the incoming items. Daniel Deschinny, leader of an organization of Navajo medicine men, was especially concerned with getting back the hundreds of medicine bundles due to be returned to the tribe. The bundles were among the most sacred of ceremonial objects and contained such items as eagle feathers, corn pollen, and ritual stones. Deschinny said that once the bundles were repatriated, their contents would be removed by medicine men and "returned to the earth."

Typical of the careful treatment accorded repatriated human remains was the burial in Montana of the skeletons of eighteen Northern Cheyenne men, women, and children. Soldiers had killed the Indians in 1879 as they were trying to escape from the disease and starvation of a reservation in Oklahoma. Their remains were collected as objects of scientific curiosity by the Army medical examiner and held in Washington, D.C., for more than a century. In the early 1990s, tribal leaders requested the remains be returned under terms of the repatriation act. Once the bones were returned, a group of 200 Northern Cheyennes gathered for a traditional tribal burial on a crisp Saturday morning in the fall of 1993. "They've been held in captivity for too long," said tribal chairman Llevando Fisher. "All we wanted to do was to bring them home and bury them." For these Northern Cheyennes, brought home after an exile of 114 years, their struggle at last was over.

SOURCES AND SUGGESTIONS FOR FURTHER READING

The most important source for the discussion of recent economic developments is Robert H. White, *Tribal Assets: The Rebirth of Native America* (1990). Also extremely useful are Peter Matthiessen, *Indian Country* (1984); Marjane Ambler, *Breaking the Bonds: Indian Control of Energy Development* (1990); Peter Nabokov, *Native American Testimony: A Chronicle of Indian-White Relations from Prophecy to the Present, 1492–1992* (1991); and Ward Churchill, *Struggle for the Land: Indigenous Resistance to Genocide, Ecocide, and Expropriation in Contemporary North America* (1993). See also Sar A. Levitan and Barbara Hetrick, *Big Brother's Indian Programs—With Reservations* (1971); John H. Moore, ed., *The Political Economy of North American Indians* (1993); Lloyd Burton, *American Indian Water Rights and the Limits of Law* (1991); and the summaries in Arlene Hirschfelder and Martha Kreipe de Montaño, *The Native American Almanac: A Portrait of Native America Today* (1993) and Duane Champagne, ed., *The Native North American Almanac* (1994).

Of the works previously cited, two are particularly important for this chapter: James S. Olson and Raymond Wilson, *Native Americans in the Twentieth Century* (1984) and Alvin M. Josephy, Jr., *Now That the Buffalo's Gone: A Study of Today's American Indians* (1982).

On the recent economic activities of the Navajos, see Robert H. Young, *A Political History of the Navajo Tribe* (1978) and Peter Iverson, *The Navajos* (1990). The triumphs and travails of the Navajo tribal chairman are described in Peter MacDonald and Ted Schwarz, *The Last Warrior: Peter MacDonald and the Navajo Nation* (1994) and Peter Iverson, "Peter MacDonald," in R. David Edmunds, ed., *American Indian Leaders* (1980). For an account of Hopi economic activities, see Harry C. James, *Pages from Hopi History* (1990). The definitive work on the land dispute between the Navajos and the Hopis is Emily Benedek, *The Wind Won't Know Me: A History of the Navajo-Hopi Land Dispute* (1993). An excellent introduction to the gambling issue is provided in several articles published in the *Seattle Post-Intelligencer* (July 26, 1993). For the larger picture, see David Johnston, *Temples of Chance* (1993).

Peter Matthiessen's *Indian Country* is also the main source for the account of recent political issues, including the G-O Road and Point Conception controversies in California. The account of the anti-Indian backlash is based largely on Margaret L. Knox's "The New Indian Wars," an article first published in the *Los Angeles Times Magazine* and reprinted in the *San Francisco Chronicle*, November 28, 1993. See also Donald L. Parman's discussion of the backlash in his *Indians and the American West in the Twentieth Century* (1994). Two excellent accounts of the repatriation issue are Steve Heimoff, "Angle of Repose," *The East Bay Express* (July 21, 1989) and Chris Raymond, "Reburial of Indian Remains Stimulates Studies, Friction among Scholars," *The Chronicle of Higher Education* (October 3, 1990). For a complete story, see Roger C. Echo-Hawk and Walter R. Echo-Hawk, *Battlefields and Burial Grounds* (1994).

Other sources for this chapter include articles in the *New York Times, Washington Post, Arizona Republic, Seattle Times, Santa Rosa Press-Democrat, San Francisco Chronicle, San Francisco Examiner, Business Week, Forbes, Time, Newsweek, News from Native California* and *Native Peoples Magazine*.

7

BETWEEN
TWO WORLDS

→ → → → → → →

 ESSENTIAL TO THE NATIVE American struggle for self-determination in the late twentieth century was the preservation and revival of traditional Indian cultures. Underlying the battles over economic development and political power was a deep and abiding concern about the survival of traditional religions, languages, and aspects of material culture. Individual tribes and pan-Indian organizations developed a variety of new and creative ways to live successfully in the modern world while also keeping the old ways alive. Native artists produced works that balanced tradition and innovation in a fine arts movement that won widespread critical acclaim.

NATIVE AMERICAN RELIGIONS

Concern about preserving traditional cultures—and traditional religions in particular—was one of the bonds that united young activists and tribal elders in the 1960s and 1970s. This concern led to the historic meeting in Santa Fe between Native American college students and tribal elders in 1954 and to the moving encounter eighteen years later between leaders of the American Indian Movement (AIM) and Sioux elders at the Sun Dance on the Rosebud reservation in South Dakota (see chapter 5). "No one had dreamed," observed Sioux historian Vine Deloria, Jr., "that the offshoot of activism [would be] to revive the inherent strengths of basic tribal beliefs." Elders

171

and spiritual leaders from many tribes gathered in 1970 on the Crow reservation in Montana to form the North American Indian Ecumenical Movement. The delegates professed the sacredness of "Mother Earth," the centrality of Indian prophecy, and the importance of spiritual powers possessed by ritual specialists. Activists in the mid-1970s began to emphasize the more personal religious side of their message of Indian empowerment; Tuscarora firebrand Wallace "Mad Bear" Anderson toured the country lecturing on Indian spirituality.

Passage of the American Indian Religious Freedom Act in 1978 encouraged further the revival of traditional religions. The act directed federal agencies to eliminate regulations that prevented Native Americans from performing traditional ceremonies or deprived them of access to sacred places on government land. Access thus was guaranteed to places such as the Medicine Wheel, a circle of stones located on national forest land high in the Big Horn Mountains of northern Wyoming. Spiritual leaders from the Crow, Northern Cheyenne, and Arapaho tribes once again conducted religious ceremonies there, just as their ancestors had centuries ago. "The Medicine Wheel is our church," explained Crow elder John Hill. "We have worshiped here since before the birth of Christ." When his tribe was deeply divided in the late 1980s, Hill fasted and prayed at the Medicine Wheel for four days, seeking guidance from the Creator God *Akbaatatdia*. Following Operation Desert Storm, tribal members gathered at the Medicine Wheel to give thanks for the safe homecoming of loved ones. Crow elder Art Bigman expressed the view of many of his fellow tribesmen, "I hope and pray that the Medicine Wheel will remain a sacred place for my grandchildren and their children."

The religious revival among Native people had been prophesied many years earlier by Indian spiritual leaders. Following the massacre at Wounded Knee in 1890, a Sioux medicine man had a vision that the Dark Night of the Lakota would last 100 years. The Sacred Hoop, symbol of the Sioux nation's wholeness, would be mended in the seventh generation. Evidence of the predicted "mending" began to accumulate in the 1970s and 1980s as a new spiritual fervor spread among the Lakota. Only a few hundred of the 8,000 residents on the Cheyenne River reservation still practiced traditional Lakota religion in earlier decades, but by 1990 one out of four openly worshiped the Great Spirit and sought the services of Lakota spiritual leaders. On the centennial of the Wounded Knee massacre, 350 Sioux horsemen gathered at the site and celebrated a rite of deliverance called Wiping the

Tears of the Seventh Generation. "*Wolakota,* the peace and harmony of the world of our fathers, is coming back," said Arvol Looking Horse, a Lakota medicine man. "The Sacred Hoop is mending." Looking Horse believed that it was the unique task of his generation to restore the old values and beliefs. His own services as a spiritual leader were much in demand to conduct weddings, funerals, and naming rites; to preside at healing and house-blessing ceremonies; and to offer counseling for marital, family, and substance-abuse problems.

The strength of Native American religious beliefs and practices was also evident among the thousands of assimilated Indians who were members of assorted Christian denominations. Throughout the Northeast and Pacific Northwest, where French priests had once proselytized, and in the Southwest, where Spanish missionaries had been active for centuries, tribes such as the Flatheads and the various Pueblos were largely Roman Catholic. Flourishing Indian congregations of the Church of Jesus Christ of Latter-day Saints (the Mormon Church) could be found in most western cities. Native American Baptists, Episcopalians, Methodists, and Presbyterians also held their own worship services on many reservations and in major cities. The largest and most active Native American church in the Los Angeles area was the Assembly of God's Indian Revival Center in Bell Gardens.

Many Native Americans successfully blended Christianity with traditional religions to produce a unique variety of new spiritual practices. The White Mountain Apaches of Arizona combined their fervent Roman Catholicism with such traditional Apache rituals as the Sunrise Ceremonial for adolescent girls. At the Sunrise Ceremonial for eleven-year-old Carla Goseyun in 1990, a local Catholic priest blessed the service with a special mass while an Apache medicine man officiated at four days of traditional dancing, singing, and praying. Prayers were offered to the Creator, *Usen,* and sacred dances were dedicated to the Blessed Virgin Mary. At the Old Pascua Village, near Tucson, the predominantly Catholic Yaquis still practiced the ancient Deer Dance, invoking the spirit of *Maaso.* The dance was performed on village feast days and at house blessings, as well as on Palm Sunday and Easter. "Our elders performed the Deer Dance long before the Spaniards came here in the early 1600s," explained one young Yaqui dancer in 1993. "The Spaniards brought Christian beliefs to us that we blended with our own traditions." On the Pine Ridge reservation in South Dakota, Our Lady of the Sioux Catholic Church placed traditional images of the peace pipe and the thunderbird next to its statues of

Jesus Christ and Christian saints; it also substituted the sacred pipe for the wine and wafer during celebration of the Holy Eucharist.

The best-known example of Indian syncretism was the Native American Church, whose tens of thousands of adherents blended Christian symbols and beliefs with peyote-produced visions. Peyote "beans," derived from a cactus found throughout northern Mexico, contained the drug mescaline, a narcotic capable of producing mild hallucinations. Peyote users claimed that mescaline induced visions of unity with God and the universe, and a sense of closeness with fellow peyotists. The ritual use of peyote began in northern Mexico and spread rapidly to dozens of tribes in the United States in the late nineteenth and early twentieth centuries. In 1918 the Native American Church was formally established, a loose collection of peyote groups whose members adhered to an ethical code promoting brotherly love, honesty, diligence, family responsibility, and abstention from the use of alcohol.

State and federal officials, and also many Native Americans, op-posed the use of peyote. By 1923 fourteen states had outlawed the use of peyote as a dangerous drug, and the Bureau of Indian Affairs (BIA) was asking Congress to ban peyote nationwide. Full-bloods and tra-ditionalists in many tribes opposed peyote because they believed it tended to undermine established tribal religions, and Christian Indians denounced its use by the Native American Church as sacrilegious and blasphemous. In 1940 the Navajo Nation tribal council, led by Chris-tians, prohibited the importation, possession, and use of the drug any-where on the reservation. The Native American Church responded by suing the tribal government, claiming a violation of its constitutional right to the free exercise of religion. In 1959 a circuit court denied the church's claim and affirmed the tribe's right to prohibit the drug.

In spite of such opposition, the use of peyote continued to spread among Native Americans. By 1960 members of more than eighty tribes were practicing some form of peyotism. Opposition to peyote diminished somewhat in the aftermath of a celebrated decision by the California Supreme Court, *People v. Woody* (1964). John Woody was among a group of Navajos who had been arrested near Needles, Cali-fornia, while participating in a peyote ceremony. Woody was convicted of possessing a controlled substance, but the state supreme court over-turned his conviction and held that the state could not prohibit the use of peyote when it was taken as a sacrament similar to the eucharistic wine used in many Christian churches. Leaders of the Native American

Church praised the decision as a major victory in the movement for cultural self-determination. They also welcomed the passage of the American Indian Religious Freedom Act in 1978 but soon were disappointed to learn that its provisions did not extend to the use of peyote.

The greatest setback for the peyotists came in the widely criticized case of *Employment Division of Oregon v. Smith* (1990). Alfred Smith and another member of the Native American Church had been fired as alcohol and drug counselors by the state of Oregon for taking small amounts of peyote at church. The U.S. Supreme Court upheld their dismissal and ruled that states may ban even the religious use of peyote without violating the constitutional right of free religious exercise. The Court acknowledged that its decision would "place at a relative disadvantage those religious practices that are not widely engaged in." Fearing that the decision threatened the religious liberties of all Americans, groups such as the National Association of Evangelicals, the National Council of Churches, and the American Jewish Committee joined with Native American spiritual leaders to ask the Court to reconsider the case.

The remarkable resiliency of Native American religions was recognized in 1993 at a joyous celebration of the Parliament of World Religions. Meeting in Chicago, 6,000 delegates from more than sixty countries greeted a contingent of Indian spiritual leaders with an overwhelming ovation. A Navajo medicine woman told the other delegates that the religion of her people long had been misunderstood. "We speak of animals as our brothers," Jennie Joe explained. "We point to sacred places as having special meaning to us because our deities live there." She recalled that many of her people once had been ashamed of their beliefs, but Native American spiritual traditions were now flourishing again. To be accepted as equals among the world's faiths, she said, was an important victory for all Native people.

TRADITIONAL LANGUAGES AND MATERIAL CULTURE

Paralleling the revival of Native American religions was a resurgence of interest in the preservation of traditional Indian languages. The challenge was an enormous one because many of the several hundred languages once spoken in North America were extinct, or nearly so.

(The exact number of indigenous languages is impossible to determine because linguists disagree about what comprises a separate language rather than a dialect.) By the mid-twentieth century, most Native languages were spoken only by the older generation; few children were interested in mastering the complex vocabulary and grammar of the language of their ancestors. Michael Krauss, a linguist at the University of Alaska, estimated in 1993 that children were learning only thirty-eight of the 187 remaining Native languages in the United States. According to the 1990 census, the American Indian language with the most speakers was Navajo (148,539). There also were thousands of speakers of the Algonquian languages (Delawares, Cheyennes, Kicka-poos, Blackfeet, Shawnees); the Iroquoian languages (Wyandots, Oneidas, Mohawks, Senecas, Cherokees); and several other major language groups. Typical of many tribes, however, were the Mandans and the Osages who had only a handful of Native speakers left.

One of the major causes of the decline of Native languages was the policy of enforced acculturation pursued by the federal government in the late nineteenth and early twentieth centuries. Prior to the administration of Indian Commissioner John Collier in the 1930s, Indian languages were brutally suppressed on reservations and at off-reservation boarding schools. In 1868 a federal commission on Indian affairs recommended that the Indians' "barbarous dialects be blotted out and the English language substituted." Pomo elder Elsie Allen recalled being beaten with a leather strap for speaking her Native language at a boarding school in California in 1910: "I'd lay awake and think . . . 'I'll never teach my children the language.' I didn't want my children to be treated like they treated me."

In the later decades of the twentieth century, more subtle pressures diminished the transmission of Native languages from one generation to the next. The advent of instant communications and mass media took a heavy toll on the number of Native language speakers. As linguist James Crawford observed in 1993, "Nowadays it hardly matters that Bureau of Indian Affairs schools have stopped suppressing Indian vernaculars because students often prefer the language of Teen-Age Mutant Ninja Turtles to that of their ancestors."

The resurgence of interest in Native American languages began in the mid-1960s and grew stronger in later decades. On reservations across the country, the younger generation of Indians came to realize that an essential part of their cultural heritage was about to disappear. If they failed to learn the language of their parents and grandparents part of their own identity would be lost. Dozens of community-based programs and initiatives were begun to revitalize languages that were on the brink of extinction. David Francis (Passamaquoddy) worked with a linguist from the Massachusetts Institute of Technology in 1973 to compose a dictionary of his people's language. He and others developed a collection of Passamaquoddy learning aids, including bilingual textbooks and language-lab tapes. They offered language classes at the tribal museum and placed ads in the tribal newspaper. Their message was simple and direct: "You adults are not too old to learn to read what you speak; young folks . . . if we don't use it we'll lose it. . . . Come and be a part of the renaissance of our language." Similar programs were developed in the 1980s by the Confederated Tribes of the Warm Springs reservation in Oregon. The Warm Springs Culture and Heritage Office published training materials for teachers of the Warm Springs and Wasco languages and developed bilingual preschool curricula. "The languages damn near died out," observed tribal leader Jeff Sanders, "but they're still spoken here, and we're working with elders to rebuild them."

The federal government encouraged the revival of Native languages with the passage of important (if largely symbolic) legislation in the early 1990s. A report issued by the U.S. Senate Select Committee on Indian Affairs in 1990 formally denounced the historic policy of suppressing Native languages. That policy, the report said, made children "feel like foreigners in their classrooms and homelands." Also in 1990 Congress passed the Native American Languages Act, declaring that the federal government should "preserve, protect and promote the rights and freedom of Native Americans to use, practice and develop Native American Languages." Two years later, additional legislation was approved authorizing federal grants to revitalize Native languages through classroom instruction and the recording of oral histories.

The situation was especially critical in California, where about half of the state's nearly 100 indigenous languages had completely disappeared by 1990. Most of the languages still in use were spoken fluently by only a handful of elders. All along the central California coast, from San Francisco to Los Angeles, there were no longer any fluent speakers of the languages of the Ohlones, Esselens, Salinans, and Chumash. University of California linguist Leanne Hinton and anthropologist Yolanda Montijo (Chemehuevi) reported in 1994 that "not a single California Indian language is being learned by children as the primary language of the household."

California also was the home of some of the nation's most innovative and successful programs to revive Native languages. A statewide activist group called Advocates for Indigenous California Language Survival (AICLS) set up two-member teams specializing in the Mohave, Yurok, Wintu, Hupa, and Yowlumni languages. Younger tribal members were matched with elders who were fluent in the language. This program of "master-apprentice" instruction was remarkably successful in increasing the number of speakers of endangered languages. Matt Vera (Yowlumni) was matched with a closely related "master"— his mother Agnes—on the Tule River reservation in California's San Joaquin Valley. Matt had grown up with English as his primary language. "I guess we took it for granted," he said. "It was an era of not being into cultural preservation of any kind." But then, when he was in his mid-thirties, he developed a passionate interest in learning more about his cultural and religious heritage. After studying with his mother in an intensive AICLS-sponsored workshop, Matt Vera became proficient in Yowlumni and experienced a new sense of fulfillment. "To me, the sound of my language was like a beautiful song filling the air." Additional teams, sponsored by the University of California's Master Apprenticeship Language Learning Program, targeted speakers of the Hupa, Karuk, Washo, Chemehuevi, and Tubatulabal languages.

Community-based programs flourished throughout the state. When Loren Bommelyn (Tolowa) realized that the language of his people was being spoken only by a few elders, he taught himself the language and then began offering classes in Tolowa at a local high school in Crescent City. In the northern Sacramento Valley, Mary Jones (Konkow) tape-recorded lessons in the phonetics of her language for linguist Brian Bibby who was developing an interactive computer program for teaching California Native languages. Along the north coast, the Karuk tribe ran a weekly transportation service to bring together its few remaining fluent elders. Nancy Richardson Riley, a semifluent Karuk speaker, worked with elders to preserve their language and make it available for younger tribal members. "Our languages define our whole world views," she explained. "We're trying to make our traditional ways fit into a modern and changing world. The only way we'll stay alive as a people is if we practice and live our culture."

The continuing vibrancy of "traditional ways" was also evident in the revival of various aspects of material culture. Traditional boat-building skills, for instance, were revitalized among Native peoples all along the Northwest coast. Aleuts rediscovered the technological secrets of their ancestors who for 5,000 years had built kayaks, or *baidarkas*, of animal skins and bone. Around the shores of Puget Sound, young members of twenty different tribes mastered the ancient art of carving dugout cedar canoes so that they might participate in a flotilla set to sail on the centennial of Washington statehood in 1989. The coordinator of the event was Emmett Oliver (Quinault), an educator who was determined to recreate a cherished feature of Northwest culture. He challenged his fellow Native Americans: "As important as the canoe is to the native lore and way of life, can you tolerate that it may be lost forever?" With special permission from the Forest Service, Indians felled 600-year-old cedars to carve their canoes. As the trees were cut, drumming and singing accompanied the work of the woodsmen. "I could see the old people again," mused Marya Moses (Tulalip). "I don't want to dwell on it. It is too moving for me." Using traditional methods, the Native craftsmen carved, painted, and outfitted their canoes. More than 700 Northwest Indians were on hand for the launching of the flotilla amidst a ceremonial potlatch of singing and dancing. One of the tribal leaders saw the larger significance of their accomplishment: "To lose a ceremony is to lose the past; to create a ceremony is to create the future."

Totem-pole carving also experienced something of a renaissance among Native artisans in the 1980s and 1990s. Master carver Norman Tait (Nisga'a) taught younger members of his tribe how to design and carve a forty-two-foot ceremonial doorway pole. By sharing his skill with the next generation, Tait also was able to teach them other lessons about traditional culture. "We're learning a little bit of everything on this pole," Tate's son observed in 1985. "It's all one big lesson!" When Tate's nephew succeeded in carving his own special part of the pole—the Whale's fin—he exclaimed, "Wow, I really *am* an Indian, I really *am* a Nisga'a." Likewise, a Tsimshian carver living near Kingston, Washington, taught his son the many steps involved in totem-pole making. "As I listen to the chanted songs and move to the ancient music of my ancestors, I am proud," the son remarked in 1990. "I am proud to have a father who can transform a straight cedar log into a magnificent totem pole. . . . I am proud of my people."

Even the diet of Native Americans showed evidence of the resurgence of interest in traditional cultures. While most Indian people in the late twentieth century consumed foods that were no different from those of their non-Indian neighbors—and used such modern food preparation processes as blenders and microwave ovens—many also enjoyed traditional food items. In 1990 nutritionists among the Pimas of Arizona urged tribal members to return to traditional plant foods as a way of reducing the world's highest incidence of diabetes. Among the Walker River Paiutes of western Nevada, the gathering and eating of pine nuts gained popularity in the early 1990s. Anita Whitefeather Collins, the chairwoman of the Walker River tribe, encouraged local families to go into the pine forests of the high country to gather this traditional food staple. Collecting pine nuts, she believed, was a good way for her people to keep the old ways alive. "It's all part of holding our community together and keeping us in touch with our ancestors." In the far north, Ellen Paneok (Inupiat) was an Alaskan bush pilot and accomplished scrimshaw artist who still enjoyed the taste of traditional food items. "There is nothing better tasting than walrus flipper," she commented in 1991. "On second thought, bear paw is better. The meat is so tender when boiled."

One of the most ambitious efforts to revive Native American material culture was the rebuilding of the buffalo (or bison) herds of the Great Plains. Twenty-seven tribes joined forces in the early 1990s to form the Inter Tribal Bison Cooperative (ITBC) to bring the buffalo back to the nation's Indian reservations. Whereas sixty million buffalo once had roamed the plains, by the early 1900s only twenty individuals were known to be alive. Protected by federal law, these few survivors were the ancestors of the large herds now found in several state and national parks. "The story of the buffalo is also the story of the Cheyenne," observed Ernie Robinson (Northern Cheyenne), vice president of the ITBC. "They were almost extinct, but now they're coming back strong. They're survivors—just like us." The return of the buffalo to the reservations spurred a revival of such traditional arts as the fashioning of buffalo robes and rattles. Buffalo meat—leaner and more protein-rich than beef—grew in popularity as a food item. Lakota spiritual leader Lester Ducheneaux looked forward to a renewal of the ceremonial life associated with the buffalo. "I want to recreate the spiritual relationship we had with the buffalo," he said. "Then, all things are possible. Then we can become a great and powerful nation again."

The renewed interest in preserving traditional Native cultures spawned a wide range of successful activities and programs. Many individual tribes established offices of cultural preservation to work with elders who could contribute to an accurate understanding of tribal culture. Pomo leaders in Sonoma County, California, founded the Ya-Ka-Ama Center, hosting an annual springtime festival of traditional dances, games, and foods. Farther south, on the Morongo reservation in Riverside County, Katherine Saubel and other tribal leaders established the Malki Museum as a repository for Cahuilla artifacts and ethnographic information. In 1988 the Nez Perce tribe formed a Cultural Resources Program to preserve its unique language, history, and arts. Chris Webb, the director of the program, fostered the revival of Nez Perce beadwork, painting, buckskin tanning, and the weaving of cornhusk baskets. He also began work on a language curriculum and audiovisual program for Nez Perce schoolchildren. "We have a real problem here as far as our culture dying out," said Diane Miles (Nez Perce/Paiute/Shoshone), a ranger at the Nez Perce National Historic Park in Spalding, Idaho. "But my kids want to know more about the culture. They want to know the language. They want to know what things meant." Likewise, the Hopi tribe established a Cultural Preservation Office and began working closely with archaeologists from Arizona State University to help preserve and interpret local archaeological sites. The director of the office, Leigh Jenkins, brought together tribal elders and university experts in a unique joint venture for the study of Hopi artifacts and oral traditions.

Native Americans also helped preserve traditional cultures by working closely with local museums. In Oregon, members of the Confederated Tribes of the Siletz and Grand Ronde cooperated with the Tillamook County Museum to mount an exhibit in 1994 on the culture of the Tillamook and Nehalem people. Tribal members welcomed the exhibit as a way of bringing together the fragmentary evidence of the ways of their ancestors. Joe Scovell (Tillamook) helped identify the origin and function of many items on display, bringing back memories of a way of life that many had forgotten. "We lost some culture to assimilation," he said with regret. "The word 'assimilation' is kind of a bad word among people who cling to close cultural ties." A far more ambitious program at the Heard Museum in Phoenix, Arizona, brought together Native American high-school students from various tribes to learn about and to share their ancestors' traditions. Coordinator Roger McKinney (Kickapoo) developed the program as a way to encourage youngsters to appreciate their heritage and also to give museum-goers a more authentic experience. Once the teens completed their training, they became student guides at the museum. Tara Kisto (Pima), a seventeen-year-old high-school junior, said that becoming a student guide gave her a new sense of pride and self-confidence. "It has made me outspoken. Before, I couldn't talk to anybody."

In addition to the efforts of individual tribes, pan-Indian activities also contributed to the preservation and revival of Native American cultures. Especially popular were powwows—extended periods of intertribal singing, dancing, drumming, feasting, and socializing—that came into vogue in the mid-twentieth century. In earlier decades, tribal differences and rivalries had made such large gatherings impractical. But urbanization, intermarriage, and increased mobility led many Native people to seek out new ways to celebrate their pan-Indian identity. By the early 1970s, powwows were widely accepted as useful tools for building cultural awareness and political power. Twenty years later a published guide listed 930 major powwows and dozens of smaller get-togethers. One of the most popular intertribal gatherings was held each spring, since 1971, on the campus of Stanford University. "The main thrust for the powwow is the strengthening of our cultures and building solidarity between the tribes," explained Stanford coordinator Dennis Woodward (Mescalero Apache).

Non-Indian visitors at powwows sometimes were disappointed to see the dancers, arrayed in their feathers and beaded buckskins, using tape recorders and other items of modern technology. This somehow spoiled the illusion that the visitor was witnessing an untainted ancient ceremonial. Such was the experience of Michael Parfit, a journalist who traveled the "powwow highway" doing research for an article for *National Geographic* in 1994. But at the great Crow Fair powwow, Parfit came to understand what he was truly seeing. "I realize that these Indians are not playing games about how it was. They're trying to carry a long heritage right into the future. This is not how it *was*. This is how it *is*."

Attending powwows was just one of the many ways that Native people living in urban areas were able to maintain their sense of ethnic identity in an alien and often hostile environment. The nation's largest urban Indian community was in Los Angeles, home to nearly 75,000 Native Americans by 1990. Although there were no distinct Indian neighborhoods in the city, a network of social, educational, recreational, religious, political, and economic institutions provided the Native people of Los Angeles with feelings of tradition and community. The Concerned Community Indian Movement of Los Angeles supported weekly powwows that provided a regular venue for various drum and dance groups. The Iroquois Social Dance Group dedicated its efforts to preserving elements of Iroquois culture, while the Native American Fine Arts Society encouraged traditional handicrafts. The most important Native institution in Los Angeles—as in most American cities—was the local Indian Center. It coordinated citywide events and published a monthly newspaper, *Talking Leaf,* that reported the institutional and ceremonial activities of the Indian community.

Schools also played a crucial role in helping young Native Americans in the city keep in touch with their traditional cultures. Encouraged by the passage of the Indian Self-Determination and Education Assistance Act, parents and educators developed dozens of innovative ways to teach traditional cultures. In St. Paul, Minnesota, the American Indian Magnet School offered a fully integrated curriculum of Native studies from kindergarten to the eighth grade. Elders were invited to share traditional stories, and local drum groups taught traditional songs and dances. The school succeeded in motivating hundreds of Native American children who had been "at risk" in their neighborhood schools. "Our students achieve because Native American sports, games, music, and crafts are incorporated across the curriculum," explained the magnet school's principal, Cornel Pewewardy (Comanche/Kiowa). Similar success was achieved at the American Indian Heritage School, founded in Seattle, Washington, in 1974.

In Berkeley, California, a local high school established an interdisciplinary student-exchange program with a school in the northern part of the state where 60 percent of the students were Yurok, Hupa, and Karuk Indians. While in Berkeley, the students studied Native American myths, analyzed tribal constitutions, and compared Yurok culture with urban life. Eighteen-year-old J. R. Bowen (Yurok) was revitalized by the experience. "I want to start doing our sweats," he said. "I want to go to more tribal meetings with my aunt." At a suburban school near Washington, D.C., Rose Ann Abrahamson (Shoshone-Bannock), introduced students to the realities of Indian life and culture as a way of dispelling common misconceptions and stereotypes. Although the students were primarily non-Indians, Abrahamson saw her work as part of the larger movement to preserve the traditional cultures of American Indians. "We're interested in cultural preservation," she explained. "Educating the larger culture is a way to do it."

Providing vital resources for the preservation and revival of Native American traditional cultures was a goal of the Smithsonian Institution's American Indian Program. Created in 1987, the program brought Native scholars to the Smithsonian to conduct research in collections relevant to their tribal heritage. Surveying the many instances of cultural revival flourishing across the nation, program director JoAllyn Archambault (Standing Rock Sioux) offered an upbeat assessment in 1992:

> To say that there has been an American Indian cultural renaissance over the last thirty years is a pale statement of the obvious. American Indians, young and old, are reinvesting their tribal cultures with a commitment and energy that is inspiring. Young people are flocking to cultural activities of all sorts, clamoring to participate, while in previous years older generations had despaired of being able to preserve certain traditions. Now, there is no need to worry about the future of Indian cultures.

THE NATIVE AMERICAN FINE ARTS MOVEMENT

One of the most promising signs of an Indian cultural renaissance was the flourishing of what came to be called the Native American fine arts movement. Contemporary Indian artists, sculptors, jewelers, and ceramicists produced works of art in the late twentieth century that won worldwide acclaim for their technical excellence and artistic merit. At the heart of the movement was an attempt by Native American artists to maintain a balance between tradition and innovation. While many Indian artists were committed to remaining true to traditional values, they also were eager to experiment with new techniques and styles of expression. Their works often mirrored the evolution of twentieth-century Indian life, conveying a nostalgia for the old world of lost freedoms while commenting bitterly on the new world of dislocation and impoverishment. Native artists strove mightily to achieve an "authenticity" in their work, a true and honest expression of what it meant to be an Indian and an artist in contemporary American society.

The roots of the twentieth-century Native American fine arts movement lay deep in the cultural achievements and aesthetic values of earlier generations. In a time beyond memory, the "ancient ones" of the American Southwest—the so-called Anasazi and Hohokam people—created ceramics of incredible beauty and variety; woodcarvers in the forested Northeast fashioned ceremonial masks, adorned with natural pigments and festooned with strips of fur; and throughout prehistoric North America elaborate pictographs and petroglyphs were executed on rock outcroppings and the walls of caves. With the coming of Europeans, the evolution of Native arts and crafts accelerated. From the wool of sheep introduced by the Spanish, Navajo weavers produced blankets and rugs in a dazzling array of colors and styles. Navajo, Zuni, and Hopi craftsmen hammered silver coins into necklaces and bracelets, decorated with bits of turquoise, coral, and jet. Artisans everywhere ornamented clothing with woven, embroidered, or beaded patterns; they painted designs on ceremonial rattles, flutes, and drums; and they carved sacred objects such as stone fetishes, effigy jars, and *Kachina* dolls.

Yet the creators of such traditional Native American arts did not generally consider themselves "artists," persons of special talents and status set apart from the rest of the community. Artistic creation was more often a communal activity, something shared by the people as a whole. This was one way in which the twentieth-century Native American fine arts movement diverged from earlier traditions. As Patricia Janis Broder, author of *American Indian Painting and Sculpture* (1981), observed, "Contemporary Indian painters and sculptors differ from their ancestors in that they recognize artistic creation as an independent activity and have a sense of individual identity as artists."

One of the early centers of twentieth-century Native American art was San Ildefonso, a small Pueblo village just north of Santa Fe. The people of San Ildefonso were among the first to accept the benefits— commercial and otherwise—of producing works for the national art market. Encouraged by the staff of the San Ildefonso Day School, young Pueblo artists in the first decade of the twentieth century produced sketches and paintings that were exhibited internationally. Julian Martinez, one of the most talented of these young artists, was commissioned by local archaeologists to produce a series of paintings of ancient Pueblo ceremonies.

When Julian Martinez and his wife Maria showed a special interest in the pottery shards that were being uncovered near San Ildefonso, the archaeologists encouraged them to reproduce as precisely as they could the polychrome style of pottery made in the area centuries before. It soon became apparent that the vessels produced by Julian and Maria Martinez were more than mere reproductions, they were an exciting new art form. Maria went on to perfect her own unique matte-black-on-polished-black ware that won her recognition as the nation's foremost ceramicist. Her works were widely exhibited and sold throughout the 1920s; in 1934 Maria and Julian Martinez were invited to attend the Chicago World's Fair where they were presented with several national commendations and awards.

PUEBLO ARTIST MARIA MARTINEZ DISPLAYS SOME OF HER CREATIONS AT THE VILLAGE OF SAN ILDEFONSO NEAR SANTA FE, NEW MEXICO. HER OUTSTANDING WORK WON HER RECOGNITION AS THE NATION'S FOREMOST CERAMICIST.

The New Deal era of the 1930s was a time of major change in the development of Native American art. With Franklin Roosevelt in the White House and John Collier at the Bureau of Indian Affairs, official attitudes toward Indian artists and their work shifted dramatically. In 1933 federal officials for the first time sanctioned the painting of traditional Indian subjects in government schools, and two years later Congress created the Indian Arts and Crafts Board to assist in the production and marketing of Indian works. Also in 1935 one of the nation's first college-level Native American art programs was established at Bacone Junior College in Muskogee, Oklahoma. Under the direction of founder Acee Blue Eagle (Creek/Pawnee) and his successors Woodrow Wilson Crumbo (Creek/Potawatomi) and W. Richard West (Cheyenne), students at Bacone were taught to incorporate complex design elements in paintings that "romanced" the past and presented the mythology of the Plains cultures with a sense of drama and mystery. The Bacone faculty emphasized the importance of firsthand knowledge of tribal traditions and customs. "There will always be Indian art because of the color of skin," W. Richard West observed. "But without exposure to the old culture, it's like a non-Indian trying to paint Indian."

Another milestone in the history of Native American art was the founding of The Studio at the Santa Fe Indian School in 1932 by artist and educator Dorothy Dunn. Attracting students from tribes throughout the country, The Studio became the premier training ground for an entire generation of Indian artists. Dunn encouraged her students to draw inspiration from the traditional ceremonies and daily life of their people, emphasizing particular animal and plant forms as the basic ingredients of Indian art. She taught her students to paint in a flat, two-dimensional style, with figures rendered in opaque colors and even contours. This so-called Studio style was soon adopted by instructors elsewhere, defining the acceptable canon of Indian art for the next several decades.

One of the finest practitioners of the Studio style was Fred Kabotie (Hopi) whose paintings depicted tribal dancers and other figures "floating" in the picture plane, lacking either foreground or background. Kabotie's works brought Indian painting into a golden age of appreciation and respect in the late 1930s and 1940s. Another of the most successful Studio painters was Harrison Begay (Navajo), whose works often depict tribal scenes with compassion and a delicate humor. His stylized figures are painted with flat areas filled with radiant colors, appearing more as collections of generic types than individual portraits. Pablita Velarde (Santa Clara Pueblo) mastered the Studio style while studying with Dorothy Dunn in the 1930s. Among her most renowned paintings are a series of murals containing composite images of the daily life and culture of the Rio Grande Pueblos. Dozens of other artists, with varying degrees of skill, produced hundreds of paintings and drawings in the easily recognizable style of The Studio.

In the years after World War II, Native American artists became increasingly restive within the narrow limits of what was acceptable as Indian art. Wealthy patrons, government agencies, and private galleries had come to prefer art produced in the Studio style almost to the exclusion of any other forms of Native American expression. Many Indian artists complained that those who were painting in the accepted style were becoming imitative and repetitive; they challenged their fellow artists to break new ground and regain the dynamism of experimentation that is essential for great art. Bob Haozous (Chiricahua Apache), an outspoken Native American critic and sculptor, denounced contemporary Indian art as:

> A bundle of safe, decorative ideas and motifs that have been repeated so doggedly they have lost all ability to communicate or awaken our aesthetic senses. It's become a prop for the interior decorator. It is a safe niche. It is a place where Indians can hide when they do not want to compete with the great artists of the non-Indian world.

Two of the first postwar artists to challenge the canon of Studio art were Joe Herrera (Cochiti Pueblo) and Oscar Howe (Yanktonai Sioux). Both Herrera and Howe had received formal training at The Studio, and their early works reflect the influence of Dorothy Dunn and her successors. By the mid-twentieth century, however, both artists had become convinced that a synthesis of European-American modernism and Indian traditionalism was not only possible but also necessary. A critical juncture in Herrera's career came in the early 1950s when he studied with modernist Raymond Jonson at the University of New Mexico and was introduced to the cubism of Picasso, the abstract expressionism of Kandinsky, and the primitivism of Paul Klee. "We were taught at the Santa Fe Indian School what traditional Indian art was supposed to be," Herrera later recalled, "but Jonson exposed me to world art." Jonson also encouraged Herrera to study Anasazi rock art, traditional kiva murals, and Pueblo pottery and textile designs. From these varied influences, Herrera developed his own style of "Pueblo modernism" where images from ancient petroglyphs and other traditional sources were integrated in paintings that were highly abstract. As Rennard Strickland and Margaret Archuleta, authors of *Shared Visions: Native American Painting and Sculpture in the Twentieth Century* (1991), observed, Herrera's work is especially interesting because it illustrates so well the cross-fertilization of modern art: Primitivists like Klee and modernists like Jonson (who influenced Herrera) had themselves been influenced by so-called aboriginal art.

Oscar Howe also chose the difficult path of trying to fuse elements of traditional Indian culture with the techniques of modern art. "My reason for painting is to record visually and artistically the culture of the American Indian, particularly the Dakota Indian," he once explained. Howe was convinced that cubism and surrealism were the best means of recording the complexity and mystery of that culture. Thus, his paintings bear such titles as *Medicine Man, Head Dancer,* and *War Dancer,* yet in appearance they are abstract compositions of intersecting lines and bold planes of color. Like the work of Joe Herrera, Howe's paintings are examples of what critics have called "double cross-pollenization." Viewing one of Howe's paintings "is like peering into a series of mirrors where modernism reflects primitivism which reflects modernism and on and on."

Both Herrera and Howe encountered stiff resistance from those who criticized their works as "non-Indian." In 1959 one of Howe's cubist paintings was rejected from an exhibition of Native American works because of its "non-traditional Indian style." He responded with an eloquent statement in defense of the freedom of the Indian artist:

> Are we to be held back forever with one phase of Indian painting, with no right for individualism, dictated to as the Indian always has been, put on reservations and treated like a child, and only the White Man knows what is best for him? Now, even in Art, "You little child do what we think is best for you, nothing different." Well, I am not going to stand for it. Indian Art can compete with any Art in the world, but not as a suppressed Art.

Reminding his critics that Indian art has always been evolving and adapting, Herrera concluded that "Whoever said that my paintings are not in the traditional Indian style has poor knowledge of Indian art indeed."

The discontent among avant-garde Native American artists was fully expressed at a conference on "Directions in Indian Art," sponsored by the Rockefeller Foundation in 1959 at the University of Arizona. Artists, educators, administrators, and traders gathered to discuss ways to expand the definition of Indian art and to devise new strategies for marketing it. From the conference emerged a consensus that the current standards of acceptable Indian art were based on an arbitrary ideal, and a break with those standards was essential if Indian art was to remain vital. "The future of Indian art lies in the future, not the past," proclaimed one conferee. "Let's stop looking backward for our standards of Indian art production." Yet the conference also acknowledged the dilemma of promoting further innovation by Native American artists while maintaining a sense of tradition: Innovation without tradition might render Indian art indistinguishable from that produced by non-Indians, yet tradition without innovation yielded art that was stereotyped and trivialized by endless repetitions.

The Rockefeller Foundation conference led directly to the establishment of the University of Arizona's Southwest Indian Art Project, held during the summers of 1960–1962. The stated goal of the project was to help the Native American artist "develop an individual creative consciousness, and to develop to the fullest his talent in art without the loss of pride in himself as an Indian." Indian artists participating in the project were introduced to major trends in modern art through seminars, workshops, lectures, and films. Project director Lloyd New, who encouraged participants to develop their own unique styles of expression, was convinced that the new generation of Indian artists must be freed from the "hopeless prospect of mere remanipulation of the past."

The single most important event in the revitalization of Native American art was the establishment of the Institute of American Indian Arts (IAIA) in 1962. Founded by the Bureau of Indian Affairs on the grounds of the old Santa Fe Indian School, the institute was committed to dispelling all stereotypical expectations about the nature of Indian art. Its curriculum was strongly bicultural: Courses in traditional techniques taught students the use of sinew, hide, beads, and shells; while courses in art history introduced them to the latest examples of abstract expressionism and pop art. Students in studio classes were encouraged to convey only the "essence" of their Indianness in works that were innovative in style, technique, and media. A major touring exhibition of IAIA artists, in 1966 to 1968, included works that were invariably experimental yet suggestive of some traditional source. The exhibition drew large crowds on four continents, winning high praise at major art festivals in Berlin, Edinburgh, and Mexico City.

Teaching at the Institute of American Indian Arts were several of the most important Native American artists of the twentieth century, including Charles Loloma (Hopi), Fritz Scholder (Luiseño), and Allan Houser (Chiricahua Apache). Loloma was the acknowledged grand master of contemporary jewelry art, creating works that joined abstract modern forms with ancient Hopi myth. Typical of his creations is a sculpted bracelet made of loosely strung turquoise discs that fall gently upon one another when the bracelet is moved. The piece bears little resemblance to the Indian jewelry sought eagerly by tourists traveling through the Southwest, but it is deeply rooted in the traditional world of the Hopi. Loloma's inspiration for the bracelet was the Hopi mystical concept of turquoise as water, thus the softly clinking stone discs are reminiscent of the waters of *Huruing Wahi,* the Ancient Earth Mother. Like many other Indian innovators, Loloma's work was

INDIAN (1976), AN ACRYLIC ON CANVAS BY LUISEÑO ARTIST FRITZ SCHOLDER. SCHOLDER BECAME AN INSTRUCTOR AT THE INSTITUTE OF AMERICAN INDIAN ART (IAIA) IN 1962 AND DIRECTED A NEW GENERATION OF NATIVE AMERICAN ARTISTS TOWARD GREATER EXPERIMENTATION IN THEIR WORK.

rejected at first as not being "legitimately Indian" because it did not conform to the accepted criteria of Indian art. But at the IAIA, Loloma found validation and acceptance. Reminiscing about the early days of the Institute, where he began teaching in 1962, he recalled with pleasure the shared outlook of the faculty: "The original idea was to use our backgrounds as stepping-stones to project beyond all Indianisms, to blend a traditional point of view with contemporary expression for talented young Indians. My 'style' fit right in."

Mixed-blood artist Fritz Scholder joined the staff of the Institute of American Indian Arts in the early 1960s and soon became the most widely known contemporary Native American painter. Calling himself "a non-Indian Indian artist," Scholder combined his own version of pop art and abstract expressionism to create what has been called "Native American postmodernism." Typical of other postmodernists, Scholder's goal was to deconstruct fixed images and accepted orthodoxies wherever he might find them. In such paintings as *Indian with a Beer Can* (1969) and *Indian* (1976), he took on the fixed identity of the Indian in popular culture. "The subject of the American Indian is a visual cliché," Scholder explained. "For decades, this loaded subject has been romanticized and stylized by the non-Indian painter and Indian painter alike. Therefore, my aim is to create a new visual experience and to extend my viewer's frame of reference." His series of paintings known as *Super Indians* projected a powerful vision of a grotesque, distorted world—the world of contemporary Indian America. Early exhibitions of his paintings were picketed by those who found them offensive, but eventually Scholder gained widespread critical acclaim and his works were copied by other Indian artists. As Scholder acknowledged:

> In a way, I am a paradox. I have changed the direction of so-called Indian painting but I don't consider myself an Indian painter. Although I am extremely proud of being one-quarter Luiseño Indian from Southern California, one cannot be any more or less than what he is.

Known as the "Patriarch of American Indian Sculptors," Allan Houser taught for fifteen years at the Institute of American Indian Arts. Houser's early works reflected his training at The Studio and often were based on the stories of his Apache ancestors that he had learned from his father. As he matured, Houser became increasingly experimental. His works moved toward greater abstraction, yet always remained tethered to traditional Indian sources. His *Offering the Pipe* (1978) consists of elongated planes of textured bronze surmounted by the head of a tribal elder lifting his pipe skyward. Images from the cosmology of the Native American Church also figure prominently in Houser's work. *Water Bird* (1980), a sleek bronze sculpture of a major peyote figure, illustrates his belief that "even if I use an abstract approach, the finished piece has a relation to the Indian." Likewise, his *Eagle Dancer* (1981), a stylized rendering in black marble, suggests another familiar, other-worldly aspect of traditional culture. Its soaring strength reaffirms Houser's creed: "Nothing will hold me back. I'm thinking of steel, I'm thinking of concrete. I'm reaching for the stars."

During the final quarter of the twentieth century, Native American art became increasingly diverse. By the 1970s, art critics generally referred to works produced in the Studio style as "traditional" Indian art, but even within this tradition there were signs of innovation. In 1973 several Hopi artists formed what they called the *Artists Hopid* to express their tribe's aesthetic values through (in the words of Patricia

Broder) "a synthesis of past and present, tradition and innovation." Hopi artists Mike Kabotie, Delbridge Honanie, and Neil David—all born in the 1940s—produced original works based on traditional Hopi myths, petroglyphs, and kiva murals. One of the most talented of the *Artists Hopid* group was Millard Dawa Lomakema, who described his work as "abstract design in traditional style." In his *Two Horn Priest with Maiden* (1978), fertility images form the background of a portrait of a priest and a young woman exchanging loaves of sacred blue *piki* bread. In this and his other works, Lomakema successfully conveys the spiritual and symbolic elements of Hopi tribal life.

Art historians Edwin L. Wade and Rennard Strickland, authors of *Magic Images: Contemporary Native American Art* (1981), have divided the works of "nontraditional" Native American artists into two broad categories: modernism and individualism. Modernist works are those that freely experiment with such mainstream contemporary styles as cubism, surrealism, and photorealism, yet remain visually identifiable as Native American art because they include Indian motifs and themes. Individualist works, on the other hand, are virtually "indistinguishable from mainstream contemporary art." They were created by Native artists but the works themselves have few or no identifying "Indian" characteristics. Wade and Strickland acknowledge that many contemporary artists produce works in various styles, thus their scheme of classification applies to objects, not artists.

Included in the modernist category are the works of R. C. Gorman (Navajo), the most commercially successful Indian artist of all time. Son of a World War II code talker, Gorman received a Navajo tribal scholarship to study art in Mexico City. There he was powerfully influenced by the works of the great Mexican muralists Diego Rivera and José Clemente Orozco. Gorman's own paintings and drawings often portray Native women in ways that convey the tranquility, solemnity, and timelessness of their lives. Yet Gorman carefully distinguished his works from those done in the traditional style of The Studio. Contemporary Indian artists, he maintained, must "leave traditional Indian painting to those who brought it to full bloom . . . today is another day and we have to learn to paint in terms of ourselves." Like Fritz Scholder, Gorman was reluctant to place too much emphasis on his own Indianness. "I don't think about being Indian or not being Indian. I'm an Indian and I paint and that's all there is to it. I'd rather be considered a painter who is Indian than an Indian who paints."

The works of two California-born Native American artists reveal further the varied currents and possibilities within modernism. Frank LaPena (Wintu/Nomtipom), born in San Francisco in 1937, produced abstract paintings of flowing lines and dynamic colors that are rooted in the mystical traditions of Indian life and art. His *Deer Rattle-Deer Dancer* (1981) evokes a mystical apparition of a ghostlike skull with eyes that are empty yet piercing; its skull-crested dancer has been described as "one of the strongest figures evoked in a modern Indian painting." The beaming and red-capped figure in *Earth Mother* (1990) illustrates LaPena's conviction that "art and life are reflections of the spirit."

A nascent spirituality also is present in the works of mixed-blood artist Harry Fonseca (Maidu/Portuguese/Hawaiian). Born in Sacramento in 1946, Fonseca was influenced by styles as diverse as funk art, pop art, and traditional Indian painting. His *Coyote* series, including such paintings as *When Coyote Leaves the Res* (1980) and *Coyote in the Mission* (1989), are variations on a single theme: the traditional trickster figure of Indian mythology transported to strange new times and places. "I believe my *Coyote* paintings to be the most contemporary statement I have painted in regard to traditional belief and contemporary reality," Fonseca observed. "I have taken a universal Indian image, Coyote, and have placed him in a contemporary setting." In the late 1980s and 1990s, Fonseca produced a series called *Stone Poems* in which designs from ancient petroglyphs form the basis for abstract compositions. Like other Indian modernists, Fonseca saw his works bridging two worlds: "In the *Stone Poems* I am using Native American rock art images to make new paintings, not historical or traditional pieces."

Among the Native American practitioners of the plastic arts were several notable modernists who also combined innovation and tradition to produce works of remarkable beauty. Tony Da (Pueblo), the grandson of ceramicist Maria Martinez, continued the family tradition of making fine pottery. His ceramic sculptures during the late 1970s and 1980s became steadily more abstract in design and were the first to incorporate the use of turquoise and incised patterns. Tony Da credited the works of Sioux artist Oscar Howe with first introducing him to the realm of abstract art. "I find abstraction particularly challenging," Da explained, "because of its infinite possibilities." Ben Nighthorse Campbell (Northern Cheyenne) was likewise inspired to develop his own unique style of jewelry by the innovative designs of

Hopi jeweler Charles Loloma. Using modern inlaying and laminating techniques to combine gold, silver, copper, and brass, Campbell decorated rings, bracelets, and belts with patterns taken from the ancient ceremonial art of sandpainting. "I believe it is the first really new style of Indian jewelry in more than two decades," he said in 1988. (Campbell also was an innovator in politics. After serving terms in the Colorado state legislature and the House of Representatives, he was elected to the U.S. Senate in 1992, the first Native American to serve in that chamber in sixty years.)

Following the classification scheme of art historians Wade and Strickland, the individualists among contemporary Native American artists were the most innovative of all. Because their works were so thoroughly integrated into the mainstream of twentieth-century art, some critics complained that the individualists had abandoned altogether their "Indian roots" in favor of absolute artistic freedom. Yet even here there are suggestions of traditional sources and values. James Havard (Choctaw/Chippewa) earned an international reputation in a style known as abstract illusionism, seemingly distant from the world of traditional Indian art. His canvases rendered abstract designs as three-dimensional realities, bits of acrylic scribblings appearing suspended above the plane of the canvas. But close observers of his work also detected "directional arrows and graffiti-style scrawls . . . reminiscent of New Mexico sandpaintings" and "zig-zag patterned bars curved to resemble 'medicine sticks.'" The works of individualist Jaune Quick-to-See Smith (Cree/Shoshone) are equally as abstract and offer more substantial hints of the artist's Indian identity. Influenced by such modernists as Miro and Klee, she also acknowledged "a commitment to address her heritage as a Native American" and adamantly defended herself against critics who said her works were "not Indian enough." Smith described herself as a "bridge builder" between two worlds.

The quintessential Native American individualist was George Morrison (Chippewa), an abstract expressionist whose paintings appeared to be totally unconnected to his Indian heritage. The sweeping, rhythmic pattern of lines in works like *New York* (1961) closely resemble the "drippings" of Jackson Pollock, while *The White Painting* (1971) employs the technique of pointillism to create the illusion of an all-white surface. Morrison was praised by one critic for having achieved "the most outstanding record of any Indian painter in the fine arts field." In recognition of his achievement, he was the first Native artist to be appointed to the faculty of a major art school, the Rhode Island School of Design. Echoing the sentiments of Fritz Scholder and R. C. Gorman, Morrison thought of himself as an "artist who is an Indian" rather than an "Indian artist." Yet, when asked to describe the Indianness in his art, Morrison was quick to respond:

> Certain Indian values are inherent—an inner connection with the people and all living things, a sense of being in tune with natural phenomena, a consciousness of sea and sky, space and light, the enigmas of the horizon, the color of the wind. I've never tried to prove my Indianness through my art. And yet there remains deep within some remote suggestion of the earth and the rock from which I come.

One of the most promising of the new generation of Native American artists was T. C. Cannon (Caddo/Kiowa), born in 1946 in Lawton, Oklahoma. After studying with Fritz Scholder at the Institute of American Indian Arts, Cannon had numerous solo exhibitions around the country before his early tragic death in an automobile accident in 1978. His works demonstrate a keen consciousness of such major figures in twentieth-century American art as Jasper Johns, Andy Warhol, Wayne Thiebaud, and Richard Diebenkorn, yet they also draw heavily upon the artist's Indian heritage. One of his earliest works is a portrait done while a student at IAIA in the mid-1960s; like many other student works from the period, the facial features in the portrait are blurred and fragmentary.

Cannon's *Mama and Papa Have the Going Home to Shiprock Blues* (1966) portrays an elderly Navajo couple in traditional dress but also lacking facial features. The faceless heads and multiple images in the work suggest that the artist (or Mama and Papa, or Indians in general) may have difficulty focusing on a single identity. The couple are border-town residents, caught between two cultures. Commenting on this powerful work, Patricia Janis Broder observed:

> Cannon has utilized techniques of abstract expressionism and pop art in order to express on both emotional and intellectual levels the paradoxical lives of [a people] suspended between two worlds. For the Indian artist living in modern America, life has many of the characteristics of a border-town. The artist is constantly called on to justify his personal identity and his role as an artist in both the Indian and non-Indian world.

The best-known and most provocative of Cannon's paintings is *Osage with Van Gogh* (1975), in which an Indian in traditional cloth-

ing (bear-claw necklace, beadwork, moccasins) is seated in a fashiona-
ble wicker chair on a Navajo rug (see the cover of this book). The
Indian art collector stares with narrowed eyes at the viewer, while on
the wall in the background is a reproduction of Van Gogh's *Wheat-
field*. The painting works on several levels, combining a pop art sensi-
bility with the basic elements of traditional Indian arts and crafts. It
also juxtaposes the world of European fine art and portraiture with the
lost world of Plains cultures before the arrival of the Europeans. To
appreciate fully the parody that Cannon intends, the viewer must be
familiar with several art-historical allusions in the work as well as the
stock features of late-nineteenth-century photographs of Native Americans stiffly posed in front of Victorian backdrops.

T. C. Cannon was an artist of considerable vision and insight. Like
his mentor Fritz Scholder, Cannon believed that contemporary Native
Americans must confront and refute the stereotypes that have reduced
the Indian in American popular culture to the status of a well-worn
cliché. "The mass media have forced so many fantasies and fortunes
on us that our art must counteract—act—and superimpose this influence," wrote Cannon in an exhibition catalogue in 1971. Carrying on
the tradition that began (at least) with Joe Herrera and Oscar Howe,
Cannon was determined to broaden the range of acceptable Indian
art. "I dream of a great breadth of Indian art to develop that ranges
through the whole region of our past, present and future." This
generosity of spirit calls to mind the communal approach to artistic
creation that had characterized Native American art for countless
generations. "Art is big and there's room for everybody. I used to
argue the old argument about the traditional painters and the modern
painters. . . . I don't think that kind of debate makes any sense any-
more. There's room for every kind of painter."

SOURCES AND SUGGESTIONS FOR FURTHER READING

Much of the material on the revival of Native American cultures is
drawn from periodicals. In addition to those cited for the previous
chapter, important sources include articles in *The Oregonian, Spokesman Review, Christian Century, Science News, U.S. News and World
Report,* and *Life*.

Harvey Arden and Steve Wall, *Wisdomkeepers: Meetings with Native
American Spiritual Elders* (1991) and Steve Wall, *Wisdom's Daugh-
ters: Conversations with Women Elders of Native America* (1993) reveal
the extent of Native religious practices. See also Robert A. Brightman,

"Toward a History of Indian Religion: Religious Changes in Native Societies," in Colin G. Calloway, *New Directions in American Indian History* (1988). The early peyote controversy is described in L. G. Moses, *The Indian Man: A Biography of James Mooney* (1984).

On the revival of Native languages, see the relevant chapter in Arlene Hirschfelder and Martha Kreipe de Montaño, *The Native American Almanac: A Portrait of Native America Today* (1993), and the summary articles in the *Los Angeles Times* (July 12, 1993), *San Francisco Examiner* (April 3, 1994), *Contra Costa Times* (March 29, 1995), and *News from Native California*, Special Report #2 (1994). Especially useful is Leanne Hinton, *Flutes of Fire: Essays on the Languages of Native California* (1993). The pages of *Native Peoples Magazine* are filled with articles on the revival of various aspects of Indian material culture. On the importance of woodcarving, see Diane Hoyt-Goldsmith, *Totem Pole* (1990) and Vickie Jensen, *Where the People Gather: Carving a Totem Pole* (1992). See also Charlotte Heth, ed., *Native American Dance: Ceremonies and Social Tradition* (1992). The recent fluorescence of intertribal gatherings is described in Michael Parfit, "Powwow," *National Geographic* (June 1994); Robert Crum, "Powwow," *Motorland: Travel and News Magazine of the West* (May/June 1994); and David Whitehorse, *American Indian Pow Wow* (1990). Joan Weibel-Orlando, *Indian Country, L.A.: Maintaining Ethnic Community in Complex Society* (1991) offers a comprehensive look at the preservation of traditional culture in the nation's largest urban community. James O. Olson and Raymond Wilson, *Native Americans in the Twentieth Century* (1984) places the cultural revival in historical context.

The discussion of the Native American fine arts movement is based mainly on four comprehensive art histories: Margaret Archuletta and Rennard Strickland, *Shared Visions: Native American Painters and Sculptors in the Twentieth Century* (1991); Patricia Janis Broder, *American Indian Painting and Sculpture* (1981); Jerry Jacka and Lois Essary Jacka, *Beyond Tradition: Contemporary Indian Art and Its Evolution* (1988); and Edwin L. Wade and Rennard Strickland, *Magic Images: Contemporary Native American Art* (1981).[1] On the development of

---

[1]The quotations from artists Bob Haozous (page 188), Oscar Howe (page 189), Fritz Scholder (page 192), Allan Houser (page 192), Millard Dawa Lomakema (page 193), Frank LaPena (page 194), Harry Fonseca (page 194), James Havard (page 195), Jaune Quick-to-See Smith (page 195), George Morrison (page 196), and T. C. Cannon (page 197) are from *Magic Images: Contemporary Native American Art*, by Edwin L. Wade and Rennard Strickland. Copyright © 1981 by the University of Oklahoma Press and Philbrook Art Center.

Southwest ceramics, see *Seven Families in Pueblo Pottery* (1974) and Richard L. Spivey, *Maria* (1979). Frank LaPena, "Contemporary Northern California Native American Art," *California History* (Fall 1992) is especially helpful on the artists of the Golden State.

See also J. J. Brody, *Indian Painters and White Patrons* (1971); Ralph T. Coe, *Lost and Found Traditions: Native American Art, 1965–1985* (1986); David M. Fawcett and Lee A. Callander, *Native American Painting: Selections from the Museum of the American Indian* (1982); and Edwin L. Wade, ed., *The Arts of the North American Indian: Native Traditions in Evolution* (1986).

HARBRACE
BOOKS
ON AMERICA

SINCE 1945

8

NATIVE AMERICAN VOICES

→ → → → → → → →

 A SIGNAL EVENT IN the recent cultural history of Native Americans was the awarding of the 1969 Pulitzer Prize for fiction to Kiowa writer N. Scott Momaday for his novel *House Made of Dawn* (1968). The Pulitzer jury declared that in making the award it was recognizing "the arrival on the American literary scene of a matured, sophisticated literary artist from the original Americans." The importance of Momaday's award, in fact, was far greater than that. It marked the beginning of a renaissance of Native American literature that would continue to grow and flourish throughout the remainder of the twentieth century. A great Niagara of novels, short stories, and poems began to flow from the pens (and word processors) of Indian authors across the country. Their writings offered bitter commentaries on the enduring problems that confronted Native Americans poised between two worlds and, with great insight, they analyzed the cultural and psychological implications of centuries of Indian-white interaction. Gifted Indian writers transformed the contemporary experiences of Native people into a literature of tremendous power and grace.

A central theme in this literary renaissance, like that of the Native American fine arts movement, was the search for an authentic Native American identity. Most of the major writers were people of mixed ancestry who had experienced life in both Native American and European American cultures. Their mixed-blood status heightened the sense of alienation and marginality that was common among Native peoples regardless of their "degrees of blood." Images of dislocated characters wrestling with their Indian identity fill the pages of contemporary Native American prose and poetry, just as they do the canvases of contemporary Native artists. Some succeed in discovering a satisfying sense of place and community, but others fail and remain lost in an alien and hostile world. Although the search for identity was a major theme, the complexity and diversity of contemporary Indian writing remained mind-boggling. "If you have an idea in mind what 'Indian literature' is, I suggest that you reconsider," cautioned Native writer Wendy Rose (Hopi/Miwok):

> If your idea is based on the observation of certain themes or images, consider that there is no genre of "Indian literature" because we *are* all different. There is only literature that is written by people who are Indian and who, therefore, infuse their work with their own lives the same way that you do.

Kenneth Lincoln, author of *Native American Renaissance* (1983), stressed the continuities between the earlier oral traditions of Native people and the literary flowering of the late twentieth century. Contemporary Indian novelists drew upon tribal storytelling traditions, as well as upon the pictographs of tribal histories recorded on rock walls, buffalo skins, birch-bark scrolls, and shell-beaded wampum belts. Native poets found inspiration in the songs and ceremonies of traditional spiritual leaders and healers. The oratory of ancient chiefs and council members contributed to the style and substance of modern Indian essayists. Through it all was a living connection between Native American literature and the context of tribal life, past and present. "The values and perceptions in older oral literatures underlie contemporary Indian writing," Lincoln concluded. "Without question a renaissance or 'rebirth' springs from roots deep in the compost of cultural history, a recurrent past."

Joseph Bruhac (Abenaki) questioned the use of the word "renaissance" to describe the works of contemporary Native American writers, but agreed that an essential quality of Native literature was its connection with the past. "Although what has been happening in the last few decades in North American Native writing has been described as a 'renaissance,' that word may be both inadequate and inaccurate in describing what has been happening," wrote Bruhac in *Returning the Gift* (1994). "A renaissance is a sort of reawakening, but contemporary Native writing is both something old emerging in new forms and something which has never been asleep." Northwest poet Elizabeth Woody (Wasco/Navajo) was one of the many Native writers to acknowledge in her work a sense of connection with earlier, preliterate traditions. "The petroglyphs on rock in the Columbia River Gorge," she commented in 1994, "are part of my literary heritage."

NOVELS

Although the Native American traditions of storytelling and pictography were rich and full, the record of earlier published writings was scant. Prior to the appearance of Momaday's *House Made of Dawn* in 1968, only nine novels by Indian authors had been published. The earliest was *The Life and Adventures of Joaquin Murieta* (1854) by mixed-blood Cherokee author John Rollin Ridge, a seminal novel not only because it was the first ever written by an Indian author, but also because it set the tone for much that would come later. As Louis Owens (Choctaw/Cherokee/Irish), author of *Other Destinies: Understanding the American Indian Novel* (1992), observed, the fiction of John Rollin Ridge demonstrates "the tension arising from conflicting identities that would emerge as the central theme in virtually every novel by a Native American author to follow."

Eighty years after the appearance of *The Life and Adventures of Joaquin Murieta,* mixed-blood Osage writer John Joseph Mathews published his novel *Sundown* (1934). Mathews was a graduate of the University of Oklahoma and also received degrees from Oxford and the University of Geneva. He served as a member of the Osage tribal council from 1934 to 1942, critical years when traditional values and the land itself were under relentless assault. The main character of *Sundown,* Challenge Windzer, is a mixed-blood who attempts to navigate a course between the demands of "civilization" and the "something that was not understandable and was mysterious" that drew him to the world of his Indian ancestors. Unable to put the disparate pieces of his life together, Chal often is rendered inarticulate. Witnessing the disintegration and impoverishment of the Osage people, he swears to himself, "I wish I didn't have a drop of God damn' Indian blood in my veins." Then, near the end of the novel, Chal stumbles through a drunken dance and sings what he imagines is an authentic song of his people. "He was fascinated by his own voice, which seemed clear and sonorous on the still air. . . . He was an Indian now."

Also published in the 1930s was D'Arcy McNickle's *The Surrounded* (1936). Born on the Flathead reservation of northern Montana and adopted into the Flathead tribe, McNickle was a mixed-blood who worked for years as an administrator for the Bureau of Indian Affairs. He helped found the National Congress of American Indians in 1944 and also served as the first chair of the department of anthropology at the University of Saskatchewan. *The Surrounded* tells the story of an assimilated half-blood wanderer named Archilde Leon who returns to his home on the Flathead reservation and attempts to re-enter the traditional, tribal world there. Yet Leon and other characters appear shackled by some inexorable fate, trapped forever between worlds and identities. They are surrounded by dominant and hostile forces that are too strong to resist. The novel ends with Archilde Leon being arrested for complicity in two murders. A government agent underscores the futility and frustration of contemporary Indian life by observing, "It's too damn bad you people never learn that you can't run away. It's pathetic—."

Although sales of *The Surrounded* were disappointing (the author's first royalty check amounted to only $8.33), the publisher encouraged McNickle to begin work on a second novel. McNickle labored on the manuscript, off and on, during the next four decades, and not until a year after his death was the novel finally published. The main characters in *Wind from an Enemy Sky* (1978) are two ill-fated brothers in the fictional Little Elk tribe, a people deeply divided by their responses to the dominant culture. Bull is a tribal leader who tries to live a traditional life and keep apart from the whites, but his older brother Henry Jim chooses to live the white man's way. Neither response proves to be successful. When Bull attempts to resist the encroachment of white civilization on land sacred to the Little Elk people, he fails miserably. He fires his rifle at a hydroelectric dam being built in a Little Elk "power place," but the gesture only proves the futility of resistance. When he requests that a sacred medicine bundle be "repatriated" to the tribe from a local museum, he is told that mice destroyed the bundle in the museum's basement. "There is nothing left to restore." Meanwhile, Henry Jim becomes thoroughly disenchanted with the white world. He moves out of his government-built house and into a tipi where he dies, no longer able (or willing) to speak English. As in *Sundown* and *The Surrounded,* there are hints in *Wind from an Enemy Sky* of the possibility of reconciliation and cross-cultural survival, but the overwhelming message is one of despair.

A more hopeful perspective informs the work of the central figure in the Native American literary renaissance of the late twentieth century, N. Scott Momaday. Born in Oklahoma in 1934, Momaday is Kiowa on his father's side and European American (and Cherokee) on his mother's. He first began writing and publishing poetry as an undergraduate at the University of New Mexico in the 1950s; he received a Stanford doctorate in American literature in 1963. He taught English and comparative literature at the University of California and at Stanford before joining the Native American Studies faculty at the University of Arizona.

The quest for identity—that central theme in the earlier novels of John Joseph Mathews and D'Arcy McNickle—was also an abiding concern in the poetry and prose of N. Scott Momaday. His own identity as a Native American was achieved through the active appropriation of his father's Kiowa heritage. "I think of myself as an Indian because at one time in my life I suddenly realized that my father had grown up speaking a language that I didn't grow up speaking," he once explained. "And so I determined to find out something about these things and in the process I acquired an identity; it is an Indian identity, as far as I am concerned." For Momaday, and the characters in his novels, the key to resolving the dilemmas and confusions of living in the modern world was to connect with the stories and traditions of one's ancestors. By knowing and telling those stories, one achieved a sense of identity that was certain and secure. "I think the storyteller in Indian tradition understands that he is dealing in something that is timeless," Momaday observed. "[When] I am telling a story, I am doing something that my father's father's father's father's father's father's father did."

House Made of Dawn (1968), Momaday's Pulitzer Prize–winning novel, begins and ends with the traditional Pueblo words for starting (*Dypahlo*) and concluding (*Qtsedaba*) a story. The novel tells the tale of Abel, a young man returning home to the Jemez Pueblo from a series of dislocations—from World War II, prison, and an urban ghetto in Los Angeles. Having been removed for so long from his family and community, Abel appears alienated and disconnected. His grandfather, Francisco, is the repository of the traditions of his people, and to him Abel is drawn. At first Abel tries "to speak to his grandfather, but he could not say the things he wanted; he had tried to pray, to sing, to enter into the old rhythm of the tongue, but he was no longer attuned to it. And yet it was there still, like memory, in the reach of his hearing."

KIOWA AUTHOR N. SCOTT MOMADAY WON THE PULITZER PRIZE FOR FICTION
FOR HIS NOVEL *HOUSE MADE OF DAWN* (1968).

The key phrase is *"yet it was there still."* As the novel progresses, Abel
finds himself increasingly reintegrated into the world of his grandfather. He runs in the annual Jemez dawn race, dances to the traditional drumming at feasts, purifies himself with ashes and water, and
sings the "house made of dawn" prayer from the Night Chant, a
healing ceremony that promises restoration of wholeness and balance. Thus Abel obtains a sense of harmonious self-definition, something denied so many other characters in the earlier writings of
Native Americans.

A year after the appearance of *House Made of Dawn,* Momaday
published his highly imaginative *The Way to Rainy Mountain* (1969).
Part personal memoir and part tribal history, *The Way to Rainy Mountain* describes the author's pilgrimage to the grave of his grandmother,
Aho, buried near Rainy Mountain in the Kiowa country of southwestern Oklahoma. Along the way, Momaday retraces the route his Kiowa
ancestors took centuries earlier as they migrated from the mountains
of the Yellowstone to the barren plains of Oklahoma. *The Way to Rainy
Mountain* is "preeminently the history of an idea," Momaday explains
in the prologue. As the Kiowa made their epoch journey, they came of
age as a people and "conceived a good idea of themselves; they dared
to imagine and determine who they were." This act of imagination,

Momaday believes, is essential to self-definition. "We are what we imagine. Our very existence consists in our imagination of ourselves." By the imaginative act of recalling Kiowa tribal history, Momaday joins himself to that story in the living present. "The journey herein re-called," he concludes, "continues to be made anew each time the miracle comes to mind, for that is peculiarly the right and responsibil-ity of the imagination."

After two decades of pursuing his successful academic career, and writing poetry and nonfiction, Momaday published a second novel deal-ing with the quest for an Indian identity. *The Ancient Child* (1989) chronicles the life of an orphaned half-blood artist named Locke Set-man, or Set, who grows up in San Francisco, severed from his father's Kiowa culture and bereft of any coherent sense of who he is. His crisis of identity is intensified when he returns to his father's grave in Kiowa country and begins to feel "as if some ancestral intelligence had been awakened in him for the first time." Set's crisis moves toward resolu-tion as he enters more fully into the world of his Kiowa relatives, accepting a medicine bundle that once belonged to his grandmother and retracing the migration path of his ancestors. *The Ancient Child* ends with what Louis Owens calls "one of the only full recoveries" in Native American literature: "Like Abel, and like Momaday himself, Set is reintegrated into the mythic reality of his tribe; he has come home."

No doubt, one of the reasons N. Scott Momaday's writings have been so highly acclaimed is that they fit well within the modernist canon of the New Critical approach to literature. His protagonists—like those of other leading twentieth-century writers—suffer from al-ienation and deracination (the isolation of a person from a native or customary culture or environment). Cultural contexts are fragmented, and structures seem threatened by chaos. But what makes Momaday's fiction so remarkable is that he infuses his work with a Native American perspective, showing that in the midst of late twentieth-century angst and anomie, an Indian world remains where ancient traditions endure and identities may be affirmed.

A similar hopeful quality is evident in the first novel of James Welch (Blackfeet/Gros Ventre), a writer who succeeded N. Scott Momaday to become the most significant Native American novelist of the 1970s. Welch's *Winter in the Blood* (1974) describes the painful awakening of a sense of Indian identity in a nameless narrator who has lived for years within the confines of the dominant European American culture. The novel opens as the narrator visits an abandoned homestead on the Blackfeet reservation of Montana and confesses his own lost identity and alienation: "I was as distant from myself as a hawk from the moon." Only as the narrator moves into the world of his ancestors does he discover a coherent, centered sense of personal and cultural identity. A more pessimistic vision darkens Welch's second novel, *The Death of Jim Loney* (1979), a book reminiscent of the works of McNickle, Mathews, and other earlier Native writers. The protagonist, Jim Loney, is a half-blood whose isolation and despair move him slowly toward self-destruction. Loney tries in vain to appropriate the identity of his Indian ancestors, "to create a past, a background, an ancestry— something to tell him who he was," but he fails at every turn and is left feeling empty and confused.

In *Fools Crow* (1986), a historical novel set in the 1870s, Welch returns to the traditional world that was only glimpsed in *Winter in the Blood.* Here Welch convincingly reconstructs the traditional world of the Blackfeet, making it accessible to himself and his contemporaries. European Americans (*Napikwans*) are the ones who are "marginalized" in this account, a threatening presence just over the horizon. The novel ends with the reassuring (and metaphorical) springtime return of the buffalo herds to the northern plains: "The blackhorns had returned and, all around, it was as it should be." *The Indian Lawyer* (1990), Welch's fourth novel, is set in the contemporary world and tells the story of yet another deracinated protagonist who struggles to find his place between two worlds. Sylvester Yellow Calf is a successful lawyer who fails to achieve his goal of being elected to Congress and turns his back as well on a critical element of traditional Blackfeet culture. His grandmother offers him her grandfather's ancient medicine bundle but he refuses to take it. Yellow Calf looks in the mirror and tries to imagine himself as his warrior ancestors once were, but all he sees is "a man whose only war, skirmish, actually, was with himself." A war of a different sort is the subject of Welch's first book of nonfiction, *Killing Custer: The Battle of the Little Bighorn and the Fate of the Plains Indians* (1994), a retelling of a familiar tale that gives full credence to Indian oral accounts and challenges the reliability of white sources.

The contemporary Native American novelist most closely akin to N. Scott Momaday is Leslie Marmon Silko (Laguna Pueblo). She, too, is a mixed-blood writer whose central concern is the establishment of an authentic identity. "I suppose at the core of my writing is the attempt to identify what it is to be a half-breed or mixed blooded person," she once observed, "what it is to grow up neither white nor fully traditional Indian." Her novel *Ceremony* (1977) parallels in many ways Momaday's masterpiece, *House Made of Dawn*. Both novels describe the homecoming of a mixed-blood World War II veteran, a protagonist seeking to reestablish his Indian identity. Like Momaday's Abel, Silko's Tayo returns home in a state of confusion and fragmentation. His mind is a jumble of conflicting voices and memories, "tangled up like colored threads from old Grandma's wicker sewing basket." What he needs is a healing ceremony, a rediscovery of the stories and a reemersion in the traditions of his people. "You don't have anything," Silko writes, "if you don't have the stories." Aided by a mixed-blood medicine man, his grandmother, and other sympathetic helpers, Tayo spends seven years (as did Abel) reestablishing his identity and place in the Pueblo world. By the novel's end, Tayo has achieved wholeness and health, realizing that "nothing was lost; all was retained between the sky and the earth and within himself." At last he is invited by the elders to enter the kiva, the spiritual center of Pueblo life.

Leslie Marmon Silko's celebration of the role of the mixed-blood is echoed in the works of the nation's most prolific Native American writer, Gerald Vizenor (Chippewa). Born in Minneapolis of mixed-blood parents in 1934, Vizenor has published more than twenty-five books as well as dozens of essays, poems, and stories. After graduating from the University of Minnesota, he taught and studied at various colleges before becoming a professor of Native American literature at the University of California, Berkeley. Like Silko, Vizenor is fascinated with defining a twentieth-century role for people of mixed Indian and white heritage. He identifies the mixed-blood with the trickster of Indian oral tradition, that "shape shifter" who appears in countless forms in the stories of various tribes. Trickster may be human or take on the guise of Coyote, Hare, or Raven. He is at once footloose and irresponsible, lustful and callous, yet also sympathetic and even lovable. In Vizenor's writings, the mixed-blood/trickster figure is the one who mediates between worlds, challenging static definitions of culture and reminding everyone that change and adaptation are essential qualities for personal or communal identity. Echoing the sentiments of Native artists Fritz Scholder and T. C. Cannon, Vizenor rejects the "terminal creeds" of a fixed identity that leave Indians "stuck in coins and words like artifacts." His mixed-blood/trickster figures demand a constant "reinvention" of what it means to be an Indian.

Vizenor's *Darkness in Saint Louis Bearheart* (1978) is a novel-within-a-novel, a surrealistic tale in which two of the main characters are identifiable tricksters. Proude Cedarfair is an irreverent mixed-blood shaman, whereas Benito Saint Plumero (also known as Big Foot) is a joker and a menace. The novel begins during the American Indian Movement's occupation and ransacking of the Bureau of Indian Affairs headquarters in Washington, D.C. A minor bureaucrat named Saint Louis Bearheart passes on to a young activist a manuscript of his novel, *Cedarfair Circus: Grave Reports from the Cultural Word Wars*. Bearheart's novel tells of the pilgrimage of Proude Cedarfair and other refugees from the fictional Cedar Circus reservation. They are fleeing the plundering of their reservation by unscrupulous tribal officials ("bigbellies") and avaricious corporations bent on exploiting the Circus cedar. The pilgrims travel westward through the wasteland that America has become, heading for the vision window in New Mexico's Chaco Canyon where they can glide into the "fourth world" as bears at the winter solstice. Along the way they are confronted with the essential question, "What does Indian mean?" And they receive the answer, "Indians are an invention." Vizenor's message is clear and unmistakable: Just as the survival of Indian cultures in the past depended upon their ability to adapt and change to new circumstances, the psychic survival of individuals today (mixed-bloods in particular) depends upon their willingness to engage in new acts of creative self-imagining.

Vizenor's subsequent works—especially *Griever: An American Monkey King in China* (1987), *The Trickster of Liberty* (1988), and *Manifest Manners: Postindian Warriors of Survivance* (1994)—continue to insist upon the necessity of invention and imagination as the true path to liberation. *Griever* chronicles the experiences of a mixed-blood Native American teacher in China, where the spirit of the Indian trickster is merged with that of Monkey, the immortal trickster of Chinese mythology. Neither white nor Indian (or is he both?), the composite mixed-blood trickster in the guise of Griever de Hocus challenges fixed cultural identities and opens wide the possibilities of new creations. In *The Trickster of Liberty*, Vizenor carries his campaign against "terminal creeds" even further. Here he takes on white scholars and other "friends of the Indian" who would relegate Native Americans to the world of collectible artifacts and colorful ancient times. He also spurns contemporary Indian activists who attempt to fulfill white fantasies of resurrected mythic warriors. Vizenor's hilarious but devastating portrait of Coke de Fountain, an "urban pantribal radical," is a thinly veiled parody of the American Indian Movement's Dennis Banks. De Fountain is a paroled felon whose "tribal career unfolded in prison, where he studied tribal philosophies and blossomed when he was paroled in braids and a bone choker." Vizenor continues the attack in *Manifest Manners*, charging that the media lionize radical Indian activists while ignoring the ongoing struggle of tribal leaders. He offers the term "postindian" as an antidote to the stereotypes and misconceptions spawned by half a millennium of Indian-white contact. In *Manifest Manners*, as in all his writings, Vizenor fights "those values he despises, but he fights them obliquely and with wit rather than directly with confrontation." As Alan Velie, author of *Four American Indian Literary Masters* (1982), observed, "Vizenor's weapon is satire and humor; he plays the clown while launching his attacks."

The greatest commercial success in the 1980s and 1990s was enjoyed by the Native American novelist Louise Erdrich (Chippewa). Born in Minnesota of mixed-blood parents, Erdrich published a quartet of highly acclaimed novels exploring the marginal zone of American society where (in the words of Louis Owens) "fullbloods, mixedbloods, and non-Indians meet and merge." Erdrich's first installment, *Love Medicine* (1984), outsold any previous novel by a Native American author and received a host of critical awards, including the *Los Angeles Times* award for best novel of the year. It tells the complex story of three generations of Chippewa families in which some members gain a coherent sense of self, while others remain displaced and deracinated. In the tradition of McNickle, Momaday, Welch, and Silko, Erdrich begins the story with a homecoming. June Kashpaw, a middle-aged Chippewa woman, is heading home from an oil boomtown to her reservation but is caught in a blizzard and freezes to death. Later, as if in an artful mirror, Nector, the patriarch of the Kashpaw family, spoofs the Indian identity he was assigned as an extra in a Hollywood movie: " 'Clutch your chest. Fall off that horse,' they directed. That was it. Death was the extent of Indian acting in the movie theater." Far more satisfying was the authentic identity of Albertine, taught by her mother the stories and ways of her ancestors. "I raised her an Indian," says Albertine's mother, "and that's what she is."

The Beet Queen (1986), Erdrich's second novel, is peopled with lost souls adrift in a small town near the Minnesota–North Dakota border during the years 1932 to 1972. Identities are confused among the leading characters, Indian and white, and a sense of community seems to have vanished. Gradually, a renewed feeling of collective identity coalesces around the mixed-blood character Dot, fated to be crowned someday the Beet Queen. Erdrich's third novel, *Tracks* (1988), is set in the early twentieth century and describes the beginnings of the disintegration that will plague the characters of *Love Medicine* and *The Beet Queen*. Yet even here the people are connected in a fragile web of relationships that gives them a sense of identity. The stories told by the elders confirm a pattern that is not evident in the rush of daily events. "There is a story to it the way there is a story to all, never visible while it is happening. Only after, when an old man sits dreaming and talking in his chair, the design springs clear." *The Bingo Palace* (1994), Erdrich's final novel of the quartet, begins once again with the familiar scene of a homecoming. Lipsha Morrissey returns from the city in search of an authentic life, is smitten by a beautiful dancer at a pow-wow, and becomes entangled in his uncle's scheme to build a gambling palace on the shore of a sacred lake. After a series of mystical encounters, Lipsha learns the "bingo life" is an attraction that "has no staying power, no weight, no heart."

The central theme in the works of Louise Erdrich, as in those of her many colleagues in the Native American literary renaissance, is the anguished and heroic attempt by individuals and whole communities to hold on to what is left of their fragmented identities. "There's a quest for one's own background in a lot of this work," Erdrich once commented. "You look back and say, 'Who am I from?' You must question. . . . All of our searches involve trying to discover where we are from."

SHORT STORIES

Native American writers in the late twentieth century were as prolific in their production of short stories as they were of novels. Less well known to the general reading public than the major novels, Indian short stories were equally as rich and expressive of the themes found in the longer works. As Craig Lesley, editor of *Talking Leaves: Contemporary Native American Short Stories* (1991), observed, the enduring values in Indian short fiction include "respect for the land and tribal elders, a sense of history and tradition, awareness of the powers inherent in storytelling, and a closeness to the spiritual world." Native writer Clifford E. Trafzer (Wyandot), editor of *Earth Song, Sky Spirit: Short Stories of the Contemporary Native American Experience* (1992), concurred. Twentieth-century Indian writers, he explained, "understand clearly that they are part of today's world but that their tribal traditions, languages, ceremonies, and stories create a relationship to this land that is unmatched by others." The search for an authentic Indian identity took many forms in the short stories—traditional myths are reworked in contemporary settings, spiritual powers are invoked in moments of crisis, contemporary problems are confronted and overcome, old ways are preserved in the midst of conflicting pressures, and the mythical image of the Indian is dismissed with good humor and disdain.

The reworking of traditional myths was central to the work of Paula Gunn Allen (Laguna Pueblo/Lakota), a writer and scholar whose anthology of short stories, *Spider Woman's Granddaughters* (1989), was awarded the American Book Award. Her story "Deer Woman" is about two young men, Ray and his pal Jackie, who get more than they bargain for when they pick up a couple of strikingly beautiful young women at a "stomp dance" on a sultry summer's day in Oklahoma. The two women turn out to be incarnations of Deer Woman, a spirit who leads the bewildered men to the mountain home of Thunder. The experience makes sense only when Ray remembers the stories that his great-uncle used to tell: "He said that Deer Woman would come to dances sometimes, and if you weren't careful she'd put her spell on you and take you inside the mountain to meet her uncle. He said her uncle was really Thunder, one of the old gods or supernaturals, whatever the traditionals call them." In "Spirit Woman," from *The Woman Who Owned the Shadows* (1983), Allen narrates a mystical encounter between a contemporary Indian woman named Ephanie and the spirit of Old Woman. The spirit tells Ephanie of the creation of the universe and charges her with keeping the story alive: "Pass it on, little one. Pass it on."

A similar intersection of ancient myth and contemporary reality forms the basis of Gloria Bird's "Turtle Lake." Bird, a widely published Spokane poet, was a founding member of the Northwest Native

American Writers Association. In "Turtle Lake" she tells the story of two ice fishermen, Sklemucks and Tapete, who reflect mournfully on the devastation by the *suyapi* (whites) of the timber reserves on their reservation. As they fish on a frozen lake their conversation turns to the old stories of "Stick Indians" that they had heard as children. "Do you think the old folks made up those stories just to scare us kids with?" asks Sklemucks. Suddenly, the ice begins to crack and the two fishermen race for the shore, making it to safety just in time. What had happened? "Asshole here started talking about Stick Indians so loud," explains Tapete, "that he woke them up!"

Traditional myth is also at the center of "Diamond Island: Alcatraz," a short story by Darryl Babe Wilson (A-Juma-We/Atsuge-We). The narrator of the story visits his centenarian grandfather and learns from him the legend of the Mouse Brothers who traveled long ago from the Pit River country of northeastern California to Alcatraz Island (*Allisti Ti-tanin-miji*) where they discovered a healing treasure for all people. The brothers returned with the treasure, but now it is lost. Grandfather's story is mixed with recollections of his own confinement on Alcatraz in the days when it was a military prison for California Indians. He remembers his escape from Alcatraz, riding on his mother's back through the treacherous waters that swirled around the island. The narrator is confounded by what his grandfather tells him, not knowing what to believe. Years later, long after his grandfather's death, he realizes that such stories are an important part of his heritage and identity. "Perhaps a generation approaching will be more aware, more excited with tradition and custom and less satisfied to being off balance somewhere between the world of the 'white man' and the world of the 'Indian,' and will seek this knowledge." In anticipation of that day, Wilson collected several hundred traditional stories of California Indians. Typical was "Akun, Jiki Walu: Grandfather Magician," a story of "long ago when magic was a large part of the everyday life of the native people of 'California.'"

The central importance of spiritual knowledge and power is the message of dozens of Native American short stories. Anita Endrezze (Yaqui) combines traditional myth with her story of Rosa, a half-blood woman seeking a cure for her blind eye and a reaffirmation of her faith. In "The Humming of Stars and Bees and Waves," Endrezze, a professional storyteller and teacher, describes the spiritual challenges that face the modern half-blood. "You have to believe that trees and rocks and birds talk," she explains, "and you have to have faith in glass-walled elevators and voices that are transmitted from space." Seeking to regain her sight, Rosa accepts the call of Spider Woman to come to a sacred cave with offerings of cedar, tobacco, and corn. ("No walkie-talkie. No flashlight.") Once in the cave, she regains her sight, both physical and spiritual. "Her eye is clear. There is no division between the worlds of seeing and believing." In "Marlene's Adventure," Endrezze tells of a comparable crisis that comes when the head of an Indian family collapses and is rushed to the hospital for emergency surgery. Unlike Rosa, Marlene has no healing encounter with Spider Woman. Her life, instead, "hung on a series of meaningless ifs" and "was falling apart."

In a similar vein, Anna Lee Walters (Pawnee/Otoe-Missouria) opens her story "Bicenti" with an all-encompassing statement of spiritual disjunction, "*THINGS WEREN'T RIGHT.*" The setting is a suburban neighborhood near Santa Fe where two Indian women, Maya and Wilma, encounter a series of mysterious phenomena. "What's happening?" Maya asks in disbelief. A man appears at her front door, eerily gyrating in ways that were not humanly possible. "He bobbed up and down, as if there were springs in his legs and feet. He waved his arms imitating a grounded bird, and he contorted his face into grotesque masks that changed and flitted away as quickly as they settled over his features." This encounter with a shape-shifting trickster convinces Maya that she must seek the help of Bicenti, a tribal medicine man whom she convinces to come to her suburban home. Once there, she was sure, he "would bind the tiniest fracture in infinite space and time. Then, he would go silently away, until the next time."

The message of Anita Endrezze and Anna Lee Walters is that spiritual powers are still present and effective for those who believe. The works of Diane Glancy (Cherokee), a professor of creative writing and Native American literature at Macalester College, hold out the same hope. In "Aunt Parnetta's Electric Blisters," Glancy uses a broken refrigerator as a metaphor for spiritual frigidity and for the frustrations of contemporary Indian life. When the refrigerator stops working, Uncle Filo loads his rifle like an old-time warrior and sends a bullet through it. "Had to stand against civilization," he says. Aunt Parnetta sees the failure of the refrigerator as part of a larger pattern: "Everythin' against uz." Hemmed in on all sides, Parnetta seeks the Great Spirit in a dream, hoping for a healing not only of her broken refrigerator but also of the coldness and alienation in her own heart. She confesses that she is a stranger in this world, "An Indian in a white man's land."

The short stories of Native American writers also confront directly the contemporary social and economic problems of Indian people, demonstrating the reserves of strength that are available to individuals as they struggle to survive and prevail. Duane Niatum (Klallam), in his evocative story "Crow's Sun," describes the prejudice and verbal abuse that a young Indian sailor faces as he enters a Marine Corps brig. The white sergeant pummels the sailor and tells him, "Down home where I come from, we fry niggers like ya' in chicken fat and feed the remains to the hogs." The sailor stays calm, reaching deep within himself for the strength given him by his father and grandfather. "When the world's too broken for the heart, live in the cave inside your skull: follow hummingbird's flight through the yellow light to the center of our birth." Life behind bars is also the subject of "Going Home," a short story by Abenaki writer and publisher Joseph Bruhac. Harold Buffalo, a medicine man, insists that he be allowed to build a sweat lodge for his fellow Indian inmates at the Fort Grant "rehabilitation center." When the warden denies his request, Buffalo escapes to a nearby mountaintop to build a fire and pray. After being recaptured, Buffalo again confronts the warden with his request and this time he prevails. "When something like that is going to happen," says the medicine man, "you can't stop it."

Ed Edmo (Shoshone-Bannock) is a traditional storyteller and writer who also addresses the personal indignities that Native Americans often must endure. In "After Celilo," Edmo describes the dispersal of Indians displaced by the building of a freeway and dam at Celilo Falls on the Columbia River. After being relocated to an all-white community, the narrator recalls being humiliated by a little girl who spat on him and told him to go back to where he had come from. "I couldn't go back because there was a freeway where my house used to stand," he remembers thinking. "I couldn't understand why she said that." Later, when he hitchhikes his way to Portland, a friendly driver drops him off at a bridge where the transients and homeless stay. The driver, with unconscious irony, instructs him, "Walk across the bridge, kid, an' you'll find your people."

Although the ravages of poverty are presented with unflinching honesty, the short stories by Native writers often portray Indian people surviving with their dignity intact. Nooksack writer Mickey Roberts' story "The Indian Basket" describes three generations of Native women going door-to-door bartering baskets for bits of cast-off white clothing. She emphasizes that although these women were losing a valuable part of their material heritage not all was lost. "As we peddled our treasures in those early years, we probably appeared to be a pitiful people. We were, however, living in as dignified a manner as possible while selling a part of our culture."

The debilitating problems of alcohol and drug abuse also appear in Native American short stories, but often are accompanied by a hope of healing and recovery. In "Northern Lights" by Joy Harjo (Creek), a Vietnam veteran is wounded while "flying on heroin." After the war, he pawns his service medals for a quart of alcohol and becomes "an acrobat of pain in the Indian bars of Kansas." Years later he dances once again in "the circle of hope" and speaks proudly of his daughter, "sober after drinking away adolescence," who shares with him the "intimate knowledge of survival from the abyss." Likewise, Beth Brant (Bay of Quinte Mohawk) describes the successful struggle of a mixed-blood alcoholic woman to remain sober. In "Swimming Upstream," she portrays Anna May as the grieving daughter of an alcoholic father who has just lost her own son in a drowning accident. Anna May stops by a deserted river bank where she is tempted to get drunk, but is distracted by the struggle of a salmon spawning upstream against the powerful current. "Make it, damn it, make it!" she cries as the battered fish leaps over the final obstacle. From this transformative experience— this reemergence in the natural world—Anna May finds the strength to resist the lure of the bottle.

As in the novels by Native Americans, the most common path to the discovery of an authentic Indian identity leads the protagonists of the short stories to some encounter with traditional culture. Elders and ancestors are the revered source of knowledge necessary for individuals to survive in a rapidly changing world. Elizabeth Woody (Wasco/Navajo) recalls with deep appreciation the stories and songs of her grandmother in the short story "HomeCooking." Woody confesses that she did not know any songs "or even know Indian," but from her grandmother she learns much. Granma tells her of the old days when "our people knew how to do everything for themselves. Not like nowadays, where we have to hire big shots to come in and boss us around." The stories and songs Woody learns from her grandmother are magical and filled with power; they give her a feeling of connection with the magic that is "this soft rumble of blood-life, laughter, our great heart under the land." The power is still there for those who have eyes to see. "I see segments of this power," Woody writes, "hanging from the hands of old ladies as they dance at gatherings."

Similar acts of recovery and affirmation are described in Vickie Sears's "Dancer" and Roger Jack's "The Pebble People." Sears, a Cherokee writer and therapist, tells the story of a displaced five-year-old foster child named Clarissa who is "full up with anger and scaredness." When her new foster parents take Clarissa to a powwow, she is fascinated by the dancing of an old woman in her seventies. As Clarissa learns the traditional dances and songs, the "angry part of her slowed down." She proudly announces one night at supper, "I'm an Assiniboin." Roger Jack (Colville), a graduate of the Institute of American Indian Arts in Santa Fe, portrays eight-year-old Ben Adams as a youngster intent on repeating with exactitude what he had learned from his uncle about the proper discipline necessary for performing the dances of his people. Like Clarissa, Ben finds traditional culture to be a deeply satisfying part of his young life.

The narrator of "Aunt Moon's Young Man" by Linda Hogan (Chickasaw) is likewise drawn to the wisdom and knowledge of a tribal elder. Aunt Moon lives alone, wears her long hair braided "in the manner of the older Chickasaw women," prepares medicine herbs, and knows well the ancient stories of her people. She passes her knowledge on to the young narrator, teaching her creation stories and explaining that the soul is a small woman who lives inside the eye. She gives her a bag of herbs and an old eagle feather "that had been doctored by her father back when people used to pray instead of going to church." The story ends with the narrator leaving home, strengthened by all that she has received and ready to meet the larger world. "I had Aunt Moon's herbs in my bag, and the eagle feather wrapped safe in a scarf. And I had a small, beautiful woman in my eye."

Although many of the short stories of Native Americans are filled with characters establishing their own authentic identities, others tell of Native people who confront and refute the stereotypical images of Indians that litter the dominant culture. Thomas King's "A Seat in the Garden" is an uproarious romp through the minefields of cross-cultural misperception. King, a Cherokee professor of American studies at the University of Minnesota, describes the vision of two white men who think they see the spirit of a "big Indian" in their garden. Joe Hovaugh and Red Mathews are puzzled by this apparition that some-

how reminds them of Ed Ames, Sal Mineo, Victor Mature, and An-
thony Quinn—white actors who often portrayed Indians in Hollywood
films. When Red suggests they seek the help of some local Indians, Joe
replies, "There aren't any Indians around here." Red points out three
vagabond Indian men who collect cans for recycling, but Joe does not
consider these flesh-and-blood people to be real Indians: "They don't
count." In desperation, Joe and Red ask the men for help, but the
Indians claim they cannot see any spirit in the garden. King's humor
cuts both ways. The white men, whose vision is distorted by seeing too
many Hollywood Indians, have difficulty seeing the real Indians before
them. The Indians, whose vision is clear enough, cannot see the image
conjured up by the white men's imagination.

Images and stereotypes are also at the heart of "It's All in How You
Say It" by Mickey Roberts, a story that begins with the author's child-
hood encounter with an inaccuracy in a school textbook. The textbook
stated that dried fish, a delicacy of many Native people, tasted "like an
old shoe, or was like chewing on dried leather." Roberts, who knew
otherwise, objected. She showed the textbook to her father who "told
me in his wise and humble manner that the outside world did not
always understand Indian people, and that I should not let it hinder
me from learning the good parts of education." Years later, the author
remembers her father's wise counsel when she is told by a tactless and
unthinking white man that a group of "professional Indians" will be
brought in to perform at the county fair. The words hurt deeply, for
Roberts knew the "professional Indians" were not Indians at all. She
comforts herself with the words of her father—words that may also
serve as a challenge to all who have not yet heard the eloquent voices
in Native American literature—"They just don't understand Indian
people."

POETRY

One of the most remarkable features of the Native American literary
renaissance was its profusion of poetry as well as prose. Leading Indian
novelists and short story writers proved themselves to be accomplished
poets also, writing in multiple genres with equal skill. Their themes
remained consistent, raising questions of identity and commenting on
the problems of contemporary Indian life. Yet the poetry of Native
Americans was largely ignored by the general public and by the arbiters
of American literary taste. As Alan R. Velie has pointed out, several

major anthologies of American verse—including *The Harvard Book of Contemporary American Poetry* and *The Norton Anthology of American Literature*—contained no Indian poetry. Perhaps part of the explanation was the relatively recent appearance of Indian poetry. Writing in 1983, Kenneth Lincoln conceded that "less than twenty years ago, there simply were no acknowledged, much less published, Native American 'poets' in America."

Prior to the literary renaissance of recent decades, the poetry of Native Americans was known only to a few. George Copway's *The Ojibway Conquest* (1850), the first volume of Indian poems published in the United States, appeared in the same decade as the first Indian novel. Its circulation was limited, as were the published poems of Alexander Posey (Creek) and E. Pauline Johnson (Mohawk) during the early years of the twentieth century. Indian origin myths, songs, and stories were translated and presented in verse form in various anthologies, such as George Croynyn's *The Path on the Rainbow* (1918) and Margot Astrov's *The Winged Serpent* (1946), but these volumes did little to acknowledge the work of contemporary Indian poets. Many of the archaic "poems" in such collections were later rediscovered and reprinted in anthologies of Native American literature during the heyday of the literary renaissance.

The first showing of contemporary Indian poetry was in a variety of small journals published in the late 1960s and early 1970s. Special issues of the *South Dakota Review* contained some of the earliest works, as did the limited-edition publications of the Blue Cloud Abbey, a Benedictine monastery in Marvin, South Dakota. Other important venues included the poetry pages of *Akwesasne Notes*, the newspaper published by the Mohawks of upstate New York, and *Sun Tracks*, a literary magazine founded in 1971 by the American Indian Student Club and the department of English at the University of Arizona in Tucson.

Anthologies of Native American poetry soon began to appear, bringing to a wider audience the work of contemporary Indian poets. Nineteen seventy-four was a particularly important year because three major collections of Indian poetry were published. *American Indian Prose and Poetry: We Wait in the Darkness*, edited by Gloria Levitas, Frank Vivelo, and Jacqueline Vivelo, was hailed by Kenneth Lincoln as "the first significant cross-section of Native American poets now writing." *Come to Power: Eleven Contemporary American Indian Poets*, edited by Dick Lourie, included the writings of familiar figures such as Leslie Marmon Silko, Joseph Bruhac, and Duane Niatum.

Writing in the introduction, Bruhac cautioned that *Come to Power* was a mere sampling of what was being produced. "For me, at least, a good anthology is always a reminder of how much more there is in store, like picking one berry at the edge of the woods and knowing from its taste that a whole summer of berries is ahead." As if to prove Bruhac's point, there soon appeared *Voices from Wah'Kon-Tah: Contemporary Poetry of Native Americans,* a treasury of verse gathered from the pages of small journals and magazines published across the country. The foreword by Vine Deloria, Jr., observed that contemporary Indian poets now were bridging "the gap between Chief Joseph and Russell Means," portraying artfully the dissolution of a "glorious past" into a "desperate present."

The most widely anthologized Native American poet was N. Scott Momaday, whose verse has been brought together in *The Gourd Dancer* (1976). After publishing his first poems as an undergraduate at the University of New Mexico, Momaday was strongly influenced by poet Yvor Winters at Stanford. Just as the paintings of Native artists Joe Herrera and Oscar Howe illustrate the "cross-fertilization" of primitivism and modernism in twentieth-century art, the poetry of Winters and Momaday reveal a similar interplay in literature. Winters was one of several modern poets inspired by Indian poetry, especially by a collection of poems adapted from translated Chippewa songs. Momaday, in turn, acknowledged Winters as a prime source of his poetic technique.

Momaday's poems point repeatedly to the unique experiences of his Kiowa ancestors, remembering times past and facing the changed world of the present. In "The Fear of Bo-talee" he recalls the mounted warrior who rode easily among his enemies, seemingly fearless. Yet when the battle was over, he could say "Certainly I was afraid. I was / afraid of the fear in the eyes of my enemies."[1] A sense of foreboding permeates "The Burning," in which the coming of a fire across the prairie is an omen of other tragic invasions to come. "Shapes in the shadows" were approaching, "Always, and always alien and alike."

> *In the numb, numberless days*
> *There were disasters in the distance,*
> *Strange upheavals. No one understood them.*[2]

---

[1]From *In the Presence of the Sun: Stories and Poems, 1961–1991,* N. Scott Momaday; Copyright © 1992 by N. Scott Momaday, St. Martin's Press, Inc., New York, NY.

[2]From *In the Presence of the Sun: Stories and Poems, 1961–1991,* N. Scott Momaday; Copyright © 1992 by N. Scott Momaday, St. Martin's Press, Inc., New York, NY.

The juxtaposition of what Deloria called the "glorious past" and the "desperate present" is most evident in Momaday's "The Great Fillmore Street Buffalo Drive." Images of those vanished herds of "great, humpbacked animals" and their "wild grace" are superimposed on the grim realities of the streets of San Francisco.[3]

The poetry of James Welch, the Blackfeet/Gros Ventre novelist, is also heavily laden with symbolism and surrealistic juxtapositions. Surrealism corresponds well to Welch's interest in dreams and visions as a basis of spiritual life. His "Magic Fox" is a surrealistic poem in which the trickster changes dreams into nightmares and transposes the reality of horses, fish, and stars. Likewise, in "Getting Things Straight," Welch describes in naturalistic detail the "rising, circling" hunting practices of a hawk and the vision quest of an Indian giant who "had his vision / came back to town and drank himself / sick." But the real and the unreal are confusing, uncertain. "What does it mean?" asks the poet; and as for that hawk, "Is he my vision?"[4] The fallen giant of "Getting Things Straight" is just one of the many broken souls who appear in Welch's poetry. In "The Man from Washington," a tour de force of compressed history, Welch offers a devastating synopsis of the ill effects of federal treaty making and dispossession. Packed away "in some far corner of a flat world," the Indians receive a visit from a "slouching dwarf with rainwater eyes" who promises them

> *that treaties would be signed, and everyone—*
> *man, woman and child—would be inoculated*
> *against a world in which we had no part,*
> *a world of money, promise and disease.*[5]

Anger is often not far below the surface of Native American poetry, but harsh realities are also treated with irony and humor. Maurice Kenny (Mohawk) was one of the most successful Indian poets of the 1980s, a decade in which five volumes of his verse were published. For *The Mama Poems*, he received the American Book Award in 1984. He directed his razor-sharp wit at the inequities and injustices around

---

[3]From *In the Presence of the Sun: Stories and Poems, 1961–1991*, N. Scott Momaday; Copyright © 1992 by N. Scott Momaday, St. Martin's Press, Inc., New York, NY.

[4]James Welch. From *Riding the Earthboy 40* by James Welch. Harper & Row; Copyright © 1974 by James Welch. All rights reserved.

[5]James Welch. From *Riding the Earthboy 40* by James Welch. Harper & Row; Copyright © 1974 by James Welch. All rights reserved.

him, with results that were both insightful and hilarious. In "Corn Planter," he describes seven years of fruitless planting when ravens and heat, locusts and moles, devour his seeds. In the eighth year, the corn planter succeeds in getting a crop, but when he takes it to market he finds that "The people of my village are too poor to buy it." Abandon ing the natural life, he succumbs to the false images of the dominant culture and succeeds well enough to fail.

> *The ninth spring I make chicken feather headdresses,*
> *plastic tom-toms and beaded belts.*
> *I grow rich,*
> *buy an old Ford,*
> *drive to Chicago,*
> *and get drunk*
> *on welfare checks.*[6]

Perhaps the most important contemporary Native American poet was Simon J. Ortiz (Acoma Pueblo), a writer whose works are winsome and casual, yet filled with a powerful, biting wit. His search for identity and meaning took him on a cross-country odyssey in the mid-1970s, a trip reminiscent of the one N. Scott Momaday described in *The Way to Rainy Mountain*. Ortiz's *Going for the Rain* (1976) is a collection of short poems about the spiritual dimensions of his quest. The traveler-as-seeker, Ortiz writes in the preface, sometimes finds meaning and sometimes does not. "But he continues; he must. His travelling is a prayer as well, and he must keep on." In "Washyuma Motor Hotel" he imagines ancient spirits conspiring to cause the concrete foundations of a motel to crumble. The American tourists brush their teeth and fall into a dreamless sleep in their motel rooms, unaware that in the earth beneath them "ancient spirits tell stories / and jokes and laugh and laugh."[7] "The Significance of a Veteran's Day" describes the poet "waking up on concrete" one cold morning and "calling for significance / and no one answered." He finds the strength "to survive insignificance" by recalling (and believing) what his grandfather had taught him. He places himself within an ancient continuum:

[6]From Maurice Kenny, *Between Two Rivers: Selected Poems, 1956–1984*. Reprinted with permission from White Pine Press, Fredonia, NY 14063.
[7]Selected and excerpted lines are from poems in *Going for the Rain*, © 1976. Permission is granted by the author, Simon J. Ortiz.

. . . I am a veteran of at least 30,000 years
when I travelled with the monumental yearning
of glaciers, relieving myself by them,
growing, my children seeking shelter
by the roots of pines and mountains.[8]

Like Momaday, Ortiz believed in the central importance of stories as a source of individual and corporate identity. In the preface to *A Good Journey* (1977), an anonymous voice asks the poet, "Why do you write?" The answer comes quickly: "The only way to continue is to tell a story . . . your children will not survive unless you tell something about them." Ortiz wrote poems to teach his children, Raho Nez and Rainy Dawn, about the values of their Pueblo ancestors. "Be patient, child, be kind and not bitter." Ortiz's own father had taught him the patience and attentiveness necessary for the building of stone walls and the carving of wood, virtues that still have the power to bind a people together.

All these, working in the mind,
the vision of weaving things
inwardly and outwardly
to fit together, weaving stone
together, my father tells me
how walls are built.

Raho Nez, he writes, will be "tasting forever" the ancient dust of the stones at Canyon de Chelly, where Native people have lived continuously for thousands of years. To his daughter Rainy Dawn he writes,

relish
the good wheat bread your mother makes,
taking care that you should think
how her hands move, kneading the dough,
shaping it with her concern,
and how you were formed and grew in her.[9]

Ortiz's *After and Before the Lightning* (1994) is a collection of verse written during a winter spent teaching at Sinte Gleska College on the

---

[8]Selected and excerpted lines are from poems in *Going for the Rain,* © 1976. Permission is granted by the author, Simon J. Ortiz.

[9]Selected and excerpted lines are from poems in *A Good Journey,* © 1977. Permission is granted by the author, Simon J. Ortiz.

Rosebud Sioux reservation in South Dakota. Ortiz experienced anew the sense of being adrift in a vast landscape (geographic and human), where meaning was elusive yet attainable. Caught in the bitter cold and driving snow of a prairie wind "feels like being somewhere between South Dakota and 'there,' perhaps at the farthest reaches of the galaxy." Through the act of writing, Ortiz was able to center himself and get his bearings. "I needed a map of where I was and what I was doing in the cosmos," he explained. "Writing this poetry reconnected me to the wonder and awe of life." Likewise for the reader, Ortiz's poems are a beacon of hope and a challenge for the future. *After and Before the Lightning,* in the judgment of Leslie Marmon Silko, is "a symphony of poems of celebration and prayers for survival in America's prairie winter of the soul."

Evidence that the teachings of poets like Simon J. Ortiz were hitting home was found in the writings of the latest generation of young Native American poets. Their search for an authentic identity led them also to rediscover the strengths of family and tradition. In 1986 a fifth-grade Crow student from Montana wrote a poem called "As I Dance" in which she describes her joy in wearing the traditional Crow regalia of feathers and elk teeth and dancing as her grandmother watches. Three years later a Navajo eighth-grader wrote about his renewed faith in the Great Spirit and his sense of fulfillment singing the traditional songs of his people. His poem "Going Up the Mountain" first appeared in the *Wingate Elementary School Poetry Calendar* (1989), part of a federally-sponsored writing project at his school in New Mexico. A San Carlos / Taos Pueblo eighth grader wrote a similar poem in 1990 paying tribute to the "Apache People and Their Heritage." Her poem, first published in an anthology of student verse, describes in lively detail the sights and sounds of a proud people trying to keep alive the ways of their ancestors. Likewise, a Native American tenth-grader wrote movingly about his rediscovery of the traditional culture of his people on the plains of southern Montana. In "Under One Sun," published in *A Tree Full of Leaves Which Are Stars* (1990), this young poet awakens to a new understanding of the meaning of the drums he has heard beating at a powwow.

So it was that the literary renaissance that began with the awarding of the Pulitzer Prize to N. Scott Momaday in 1969 showed no sign of diminishing. The eternal search for identity, the unceasing reflection and questioning, continued among a new generation of young poets. Their writings, filled with vivid images of their heritage, bear eloquent witness to the importance of their quest. In their poetry we hear what Carla Willetto, a Navajo student at the Rough Rock School in Arizona, has called "Rising Voices":

> *Rising from the monolithic monuments,*
> *purple mountains and rolling grasslands,*
> *The moaning winds carry a soft*
> *but steadily rising voice . . .*
> > *A voice made of many voices*
> > *of proud men and women*
> > *with a hope and a question. . . .*
> > *Will we make it? . . . Listen!*
> > > *The Voice—our Voice—is getting stronger*
> > > *Rising to the turquoise sky—*
> > > *Listen! You will hear it soon . . .*
> > > *very soon. . . .*[10]

SOURCES AND SUGGESTIONS FOR FURTHER READING

The Native American literary renaissance has been chronicled and analyzed by several scholars, and it is upon their work that this chapter is based. The single most important source for the first section of the chapter is Louis Owens's brilliant analysis, *Other Destinies: Understanding the American Indian Novel* (1992). Of nearly equal importance are Charles R. Larson, *American Indian Fiction* (1978); Kenneth Lincoln, *Native American Renaissance* (1983); Gerald Vizenor, ed., *Narrative Chance: Postmodern Discourse on Native American Indian Literature* (1989); Alan R. Velie, *Four American Indian Literary Masters: N. Scott Momaday, James Welch, Leslie Marmon Silko, and Gerald Vizenor* (1982); and Alan R. Velie, ed., *American Indian Literature: An Anthology* (1991).

Leslie A. Fiedler, "The Indian in Literature in English," in Wilcomb E. Washburn, ed., *History of Indian-White Relations,* vol. 8, *Handbook of North American Indians* (1988), provides a brief overview. See also Brian Swann and Arnold Krupat, eds., *Recovering the Word: Essays on Native American Literature* (1987); Kenneth Lincoln, *Ind'n Humor* (1993); A. LaVonne Brown Ruoff, *Literatures of the American Indian* (1991); Anna Lee Stenstand, *Literature by and*

---

[10]Reprinted with permission from Carla Willetto, "Rising Voices," in *Rough Stones Are Precious Too,* vol. 2 (Chinle: Navajo Curriculum Center, 1982).

about the American Indian (1979); and Gerald Vizenor, ed., *Native American Literature: An Anthology* (1995).

The discussion of Native American short fiction is based on the introduction and selections in Craig Lesley, ed., *Talking Leaves: Contemporary Native American Short Stories* (1991), and Clifford E. Trafzer, ed., *Earth Song, Sky Spirit: Short Stories of the Contemporary Native American Experience* (1992). See also Greg Sarris, ed., *The Sound of Rattles and Clappers: A Collection of New California Indian Writing* (1994); Joseph Bruhac, ed., *Returning the Gift: Poetry and Prose from the First North American Native Writers Festival* (1994); and Elizabeth Woody, *Luminaries of the Humble* (1994).

The two main sources for the consideration of Indian poetry are Kenneth Lincoln's *Native American Renaissance* and Alan R. Velie's *American Indian Literature*. See also Joseph Bruhac, *Survival This Way: Interviews with American Indian Poets* (1987). The selections from the next generation of Indian poets are taken from Arlene B. Hirschfelder and Beverly R. Singer, eds., *Rising Voices: Writings of Young Native Americans* (1992).

9

THE CHANGING IMAGE

→ → → → → → →

 DURING THE YEARS after World War II, the image of the Indian in American popular culture continued to bear the burden of centuries of European American mythmaking and misconception. Yet the image was hardly static. Old stereotypes were challenged by reports of Native Americans serving with valor in the nation's armed forces, organizing and petitioning their government for a redress of assorted grievances, and demanding to be heard in a series of spectacular and dramatic demonstrations. For a time in the 1960s and early 1970s, stories about Indians were routinely on the front pages of the nation's newspapers and featured at the top of the hour on the six o'clock news. Then, as the strident rhetoric and militant actions of the Red Power movement began to fade, new voices were heard from the Native American fine arts movement and literary renaissance. Old prejudices continued their grip on the popular imagination, but the non-Indian image of the Indian slowly became more positive and more sophisticated.

As the twentieth century neared its close, Native Americans seized the initiative in shaping their own image. Activists and artists, traditionalists and tribal leaders, all shared an unwillingness to allow others to fashion the image by which they were known. They realized the stakes were too high for that; they knew that from perception (or misperception) flowed the actions of individuals as well as the policies of governments. "Just about everybody would agree that the *image* of a culture is as important, especially in this high-tech world of global telecommunications, . . . as whatever lies in the *actual* truth of that culture," wrote Native author and film critic David Seals in 1991.

Indians have often been victims of stereotyping—Custerism, I call it—
and this reduction of the image of people kills as surely as any real-life,
Wounded Knee–type massacre. What is this Custerism? The celluloid
residuals of Manifest Destiny, played out as emotional climax.

THE INDIAN IN POPULAR CULTURE

The first signs of an increased European American interest in Native
Americans came at the end of World War II with the flourishing of what
came to be called the Indian hobbyist movement. Hobbyists were non-
Indians who were fascinated with "Indian lore," especially with Indian
arts and crafts, dancing, and singing. The roots of the movement lay in
several youth organizations formed in the early 1900s, most notably the
Boy Scouts of America. Boys who joined the ranks of Scouting were
encouraged to learn Indian costume making, sign language, and a variety of putative Indian customs. The Indian Lore Merit Badge gave
formal recognition for achievement in using "Indian methods in so far
as possible" to fashion drums ("tom-toms"), bow and arrows, and war
clubs. The national Scout fraternity, the Order of the Arrow, used ceremonies based on Indian themes to initiate its members, and provided
local chapters with Indian names. The official Scout manual, *Handbook
for Boys* (1948), was adorned on its cover with the image of a mystical
blue Indian materializing from the smoke of a campfire, while inside it
advised Scouts to follow Indian custom in building such a fire: "White
man make-um big fire—no get-um close . . . ugh! Indian make-um
small fire, get-um close, heap plenty warm . . . how!"

As William K. Powers, author of *Here Is Your Hobby: Indian Dancing and Costumes* (1966), observed, some Boy Scout troops devoted
so much attention to their Indian lore programs that the national
Scout office directed them to broaden their approach or to leave
Scouting. Those who left the Scouts formed the core of other hobbyist
groups. In 1954 one former Scout began publishing *The American
Indian Hobbyist*, a monthly magazine that continued for nearly a decade to promote the activities of hobbyists. Throughout the 1950s
hobbyists became increasingly sophisticated in their mastery of such
recondite skills as the making of yarn leg wraps, blanket capotes, and
split-horn bonnets. They also attempted to reach out to Indian communities and to involve Native Americans in their programs. The very
term *hobbyist* was rejected by some as being derogatory or patronizing
to the people whose cultures they admired.

Indian hobbyists in the 1960s and 1970s came under increasing criticism from Native Americans who objected to being "relegated to a kind of human stamp-collecting." Indians protested especially the continued and indiscreet use of sacred dances and ceremonies by non-Indian hobbyists. "Every dance or ceremony the indigenous people of this country partake in has a special meaning to them," explained California Native John Walker.

> The honor of wearing a headdress is not meant for non-Indians since they cannot completely understand the full meaning that it bestows, which comes from the heart, not a book that is read. . . . Being a Native American is not a game; it is a way of life, it is our culture.

Mohawk artist Richard Glazer Danay, expressed the discomfort of many Native people with his oil painting of an actual letter by a third-grader: "My favorite hobby is Indians. I like to read about them very much. I collect books about them and also plastic ones that I play with. . . . Indians are a fun hobby."

The years after World War II also were a time of increased scholarly interest in Native Americans. The GI Bill encouraged thousands of veterans to enroll in the nation's colleges and universities, and many were attracted to courses that offered to satisfy their newly awakened curiosity about the diverse peoples of the world. Departments of anthropology, in particular, experienced a postwar boom. New undergraduate courses were added to the curriculum, new faculty were hired, and new graduate-level field schools were developed. Before the war the majority of American anthropologists and archaeologists had concentrated their studies on Indian cultures; so it was only natural that after the war they directed their new students to Indian communities as appropriate places to hone their research skills. Tribes in the Plains and the Southwest soon were swamped by professors of anthropology and their students. One joke making the rounds in the early 1950s was that "the average Navajo family consisted of a father, mother, three children, and an anthropologist."

The inundation of the reservations led to a breakdown of relations between anthropologists and Native Americans. In the early 1960s, Native people began to complain that not only were their communities being saturated with scholars, but also that the scholars' research was not especially useful or beneficial. Indians disdained anthropologists who seemed more interested in studying the distant past than in helping them solve the serious social, economic, and political problems they faced in the present. Indian activists disrupted archaeological digs, denounced archaeologists as "grave robbers," and condemned linguists for "stealing our languages too." The word *anthro* became a term of opprobrium among youthful members of such organizations as the National Indian Youth Council and the American Indian Movement. As anthropologist Nancy Oestreich Lurie acknowledged, "Indian hostility toward anthropology became a generalized, ideological rallying point in the cause of Indian unity."

Individual anthropologists and the discipline as a whole responded to their Native American critics in the late 1960s and 1970s by seeking new ways to improve relations. Cooperative ventures were formed with tribal governments and researchers established partnerships with Native scholars. Anthropologists paid closer attention to Indian sensibilities in their publications and monitored more carefully their field studies to avoid needless duplication. Curators of anthropological museums showed a greater willingness to cooperate with the requests of tribes for the repatriation of items in their collections and to assist tribes in the development of their own museums. The American Anthropological Association allied itself with Native groups in opposing policies that threatened the vital interests of the Indian people.

Native Americans also held a special fascination for adherents of the counterculture that flourished in the 1960s. Calling themselves "hippies" and "freaks," members of the counterculture demonstrated their sense of alienation by wearing colorful or outlandish clothing, experimenting with a variety of psychedelic drugs, and engaging in highly visible protests against racial discrimination and the war in Southeast Asia. As Stewart Brand, publisher of the *Whole Earth Review,* remarked, hippies viewed the Indians as a people who were "ecologically aware, spiritual, tribal, anarchistic, drug-using, exotic, native and wronged, the lone genuine holdouts against American conformity and success." Canvas tipis materialized at countercultural gatherings in city parks and at hippie communes deep in the hinterland. Young men wore their hair long ("Indian style"), and a headband and beads were part of the preferred attire for hip men and women of all ages. Some hippies christened themselves with new names, often with romantic or imagined Indian allusions such as "Morningstar" or "Sundove." San Francisco was the great mecca of the counterculture, and it was there in 1967 that a "Human Be-In" was held, billed as "A Gathering of the Tribes."

While the hippies and the hobbyists shared an enthusiasm for all things Indian, members of the counterculture embraced parts of the Native American world that were beyond the ken of most Boy Scouts. In the summer of 1962, hippies from San Francisco traveled to the foothills of the Sierra Nevada to meet with California Natives who guided them in the use of peyote. Others gathered in Santa Fe, where in 1968 they joined Indians from throughout the Southwest to form the American Church of God. The white members mastered more than forty peyote songs and learned peyote rituals from their Indian coreligionists. Activist Leonard Crow Dog (Sioux) oversaw a mixed congregation in Rosebud, South Dakota, and welcomed the participation of non-Indian peyotists: "If they can take it, they can take it." Members of the counterculture also participated in the political protests of young Indian activists. Hippies and campus radicals in the San Francisco Bay Area supplied food to the activists who occupied Alcatraz Island, and rock bands such as the Grateful Dead and Big Brother and the Holding Company held benefit concerts. Stewart Brand aptly characterized the relationship between the hippies and the Indian activists as one of "mutual reinforcement." Members of the counterculture supported the activists in their political struggle, while the Indians "provided the counterculture with a living identity base."

Relations were not so symbiotic on the reservations where hippies were as unwelcome as "anthros" and other uninvited interlopers. Lured by romantic images of Native American life in the underground press of San Francisco, Los Angeles, and New York, members of the counterculture flocked to the reservations where they imagined they would be welcomed into a permissive society. Conditions on the Hopi reservation in Arizona were typical. There the "hippie invasion" of the late 1960s provoked a strong reaction from local residents who objected to the newcomers' exhibitionism, personal hygiene, and boisterous and meddlesome ways. "Those hippies offended our way of life," recalled Peter Nuvamsa, Sr. (Hopi).

> They hugged each other and kissed in public as if they didn't have anything else to do and nowhere else to go. I went out there and spoke to some of them. I said, "Why are you here? Why do you behave like this, doing anything that comes into your head? We do not like the way you are behaving. It's not our way. It's improper."

THE RETURN OF
THE VANISHING AMERICAN

The 1960s were also a decade when the image of the Indian returned to the center of attention in American literature. In the words of literary critic Leslie Fiedler, it was a time when "the vanishing American unexpectedly re-appeared." During the earlier decades of the twentieth century, the Indian as a subject for fiction had been left primarily to regional writers and to popular authors without literary pretensions. Pulp Westerns of the 1950s—not far removed from the dime novels of the previous century—were filled with images of bloodthirsty savages attacking settlers' cabins and wagon trains crossing the plains.

The best-selling Western writer of all time, Louis L'Amour, published dozens of novels in the conventional mode in which agents of white civilization advance bravely into the wilderness. Hostile Indians are just one of the many obstacles to be overcome by L'Amour's protagonists, but his works also deviated significantly from the stereotypical treatment of the Indian-as-savage. L'Amour consistently upheld the values of family and reverence for the land, two values that he credits the Indians with sharing. Indian warriors often are portrayed as family men, returning to their lodges and their families after a battle. In one of L'Amour's earliest and best-known works, *Hondo* (1953), hostile Apaches are an ever-present danger yet also are an admirable people because of their great knowledge of the land and their ability to live thoughtfully in it. Hondo, the central character, is able to bridge the world of Indians and whites because he has lived for years among the Apaches. Filled with ethnographic and historical details on various western tribes, the novels of Louis L'Amour present a balanced view of Native Americans unusual among the more sensational (and subliterary) works of Western fiction.

The return of the Native American to the center of American literature in the 1960s was part of the era's questioning of fundamental assumptions about the nation's direction and history. Feelings of discontent grew in the face of an accumulation of disquieting realizations—the prospect of nuclear annihilation, the persistence of racial and economic inequalities, and the pervasive sense of anonymity and alienation in a mass society. From this discontent grew questions about historical progress, the moral superiority of "white civilization," and the validity of rational or scientific analysis. As in the seventeenth century, when the image of the so-called noble savage first appeared, American writers in the 1960s employed the image of the Indian primarily as a vehicle for social criticism. The details of Native American culture were neglected as the Indian became a symbolic or representative figure of an alternative reality. As historian Robert F. Berkhofer, Jr., author of *The White Man's Indian* (1978), observed:

> The latest . . . use of the Indian reflects some Whites' disquietude with their own society and indicates that even today's sympathetic artists chiefly understand Native Americans according to their own artistic needs and moral values rather than in terms of the outlook and desires of the people they profess to know and depict.

Among the major American writers to use Native American images in the 1960s were John Barth, Ken Kesey, Thomas Berger, and Arthur Kopit. Barth's novel *The Sot-Weed Factor* (1960) was one of the first to place the encounter between whites and Indians at the narrative center. Set in the early colonial period, the novel systematically debunks the notion of progress in American history. The civilization that Europe transplants abroad is shown to be filled with shameless debauchery, chicanery, and betrayal. The assumed moral superiority of the white colonizers is discredited through the scandalous revelations of a spurious "secret diary" of Captain John Smith. The compass with which Smith impresses Powhatan, leader of an Algonquian confederacy, contains pornographic pictures, and among Smith's gifts to the Indian people is the practice of sodomy. Thus the corruption of the continent begins as the original Americans fall victim to a conquering society of moral degenerates bent on destruction and exploitation. The future of the republic is darkly foreshadowed with portents of escalating catastrophes and atrocities.

A more personal, but equally dark vision informs Ken Kesey's anti-establishment novel, *One Flew Over the Cuckoo's Nest* (1962). The setting is a mental ward where the central character, a trickster named McMurphy, wages a futile battle against the debilitating forces of conformity in modern society. Nurse Ratchett is the unwitting emblem of all that has gone wrong in the world of rationality and control, while the stoic Indian, Chief Bromden, stands as the natural man who has the strength to resist the straitjackets and therapies of the dominant culture. In the moral universe of Ken Kesey, the opposing forces are clear-cut. The mechanized, systematized, bureaucratized modern world is crushing the human spirit that once was nurtured in an earlier, simpler, more natural mode of existence. Thus the novel's hydroelectric dam is life destroying whereas its Indian fishing village is life affirming. The narrator sounds a note that echoes not only the reality of the mental ward, but also the despoiling of a continent and the demise of its Native people: "You think this is too horrible to have really happened, this is too awful to be the truth!"

Thomas Berger's *Little Big Man* (1964) uses the device of a 121-year-old narrator to offer a comic yet macabre view of Indian-white relations in the old West. Jack Crabb reminisces about his life as a young white pioneer, adopted by the Indians, who witnessed the Battle of the Little Big Horn. Crabb's reminiscences are noteworthy for their tone of moral ambiguity and uncertain identity, elements that are conspicuously absent in the traditional Western. Crabb moves back and forth so often between the white and Indian worlds—never seeming to understand either fully—that he is left puzzled about whether he is "really" a white man or an Indian. The shifting points of view allow the reader to see the struggle for the continent from both Indian and white perspectives, with a clear preference for the former. Berger presents Native American culture with sympathy and understanding; his Indian characters, portrayed with a touch of nostalgia and sentiment, emerge as fully rounded "Human Beings" (as Jack Crabb's Cheyenne relations call themselves).

One of the most powerful indictments of Indian-white relations in American literature is Arthur Kopit's play *Indians,* first performed in 1968. Like Barth's *The Sot-Weed Factor, Indians* is a self-conscious attack on the accepted legends and myths of American history. Written at the height of the war in Southeast Asia, Kopit once remarked that his inspiration for the play came while listening to General William Westmoreland's comments on the "accidental tragedies" of American military action. As Kopit later recalled:

> I knew almost instantly that I would write a play that would explore what happens when a social and political power imposes itself on a lesser power and creates a mythology to justify it, as we did with the Indians, as we have tried to do in Vietnam.

Indians presents a montage of historical scenes from the 1870s and 1880s, portraying sympathetically the Indians' loss of land and their difficulties defending themselves against the vagaries of federal Indian policy. The impresario Buffalo Bill Cody appears on stage as a man of compassion for the Indians, yet whose Wild West show is presented as the prototype of a long series of attempts to package American history in a way that justifies the Indians' demise. Like the characters in Cherokee author Thomas King's short story "A Seat in the Garden," Kopit's Bill Cody is a man haunted by images of Indians appearing and reappearing in the grass, rocks, and trees. The Indians of *Indians* are like that, ghosts from a time past that continue to haunt the European American conscience.

Several works of nonfiction about Native Americans also gained widespread popularity in the late 1960s and early 1970s. Especially popular among members of the counterculture were a series of books by anthropologist Carlos Castaneda describing his encounter and apprenticeship with Don Juan, a Yaqui shaman from Sonora, Mexico. *The Teachings of Don Juan: A Yaqui Way of Knowledge* (1968), *A Separate Reality: Further Conversations with Don Juan* (1971), and *Journey to Ixtlan: The Lessons of Don Juan* (1972) present Castaneda's exploration of the mystical, spiritual world opened to him by Don Juan and his ingestion of peyote and other hallucinogens. Don Juan leads Castaneda to question the adequacy of scientific rationalism as a worldview and attempts to restore the irrational as the true "path of knowledge."

The Teachings of Don Juan became an immediate underground best-seller at colleges and high schools, where disaffected young people were eager for confirmation of their own rejection of the values and lifestyle of the dominant culture. Yet the Don Juan of the first (and most popular) volume of Castaneda's trilogy is a curiously disembodied Indian, a man whose teachings seem to exist in a cultural vacuum. The reader is given very little specific information about the Yaqui way of life. The subsequent volumes place Don Juan in broader cultural context, leading Paul Riesman to conclude that Castaneda's works are "among the best that the science of anthropology has produced." Other critics were not so certain. Novelist Joyce Carol Oates raised the possibility that Don Juan's "teachings" were fiction, and *New York Times* critic Weston LaBarre dismissed Castaneda's writings as "pseudo-profound, sophomoric, and deeply vulgar . . . frustratingly and tiresomely dull, posturing pseudoethnography and, intellectually, kitsch."

Meanwhile two other works of nonfiction were published during the heyday of Castaneda's popularity that offered a hard look at the real world of Native Americans, past and present. Stan Steiner's *The New Indians* (1968) was the first book to tell the story of the Red

Power movement, defined on the dust jacket as "a revolt against the white man's culture and its debasement of the tribal way." Steiner traveled through the American heartland on a 20,000-mile trek over a twenty-year period, and observed firsthand the stirrings of discontent among young university-educated Indian activists as well as among tribal elders and traditionalists. Three years after *The New Indians* appeared, historian Dee Brown provided "deep background" for Steiner's portrait of contemporary Indian America. *Bury My Heart at Wounded Knee: An Indian History of the American West* (1971) became a number-one best-seller and brought to a large audience the story of broken treaties, massacres, and heroic acts of defiant resistance that marked Indian-white relations in the late nineteenth century. Brown's intent was to offer an Indian perspective that would challenge the popular image of "Indians stereotyped in the American myth as ruthless savages." What Arthur Kopit and John Barth attempted in fiction, Dee Brown accomplished in this tour de force of unrelenting historical narrative. *Newsweek* critic Geoffrey Wolff said that reading *Bury My Heart at Wounded Knee* "made me realize for once and all that we really don't know who we are, or where we came from, or what we have done, or why."

Following the awarding of the Pulitzer Prize for fiction to Kiowa author N. Scott Momaday in 1969, the momentum in writing about Indian affairs shifted from European Americans to Native Americans. Indian scholars in a variety of disciplines produced pioneering studies of Native cultures, tribal histories, and surveys of Indian-white relations. (Indeed, this book is based in part on the works of such diverse Native writers as Lawrence Baca, Raymond Butler, Robert Burnette, Edward D. Castillo, Duane Champagne, Ward Churchill, Donald L. Fixico, Rayna Green, Charlotte Heth, Louis Owens, and Russell Thornton.) Indian writers joined forces to encourage one another in the Wordcraft Circle of Native Writers and Storytellers in Washington, D.C., and the American Indian Historians Association formed in Spokane, Washington, in 1978. The proliferation of Native American studies programs at colleges and universities offered expanded opportunities for Indian scholars, as did the creation of courses in Native American history and literature. In 1987 Jeannette Henry and Rupert Costo (Cahuilla) established at the University of California, Riverside, the nation's first endowed chair in American Indian history.

Teaching at the Riverside campus in the 1990s was one of the most prolific and insightful of Native American scholars, Clifford E. Trafzer

(Wyandot). Author or editor of more than twenty books on the history of Native peoples, including the award-winning *Renegade Tribe: The Palouse Indians and the Invasion of the Inland Pacific Northwest* (1986) and *The Kit Carson Campaign: The Last Great Navajo War* (1982), Trafzer also served as chair of the university's ethnic studies department and secretary of the California Native American Heritage Commission. In his published works and professional activities, Trafzer encouraged his fellow historians to consider the importance of consulting the widest possible range of Native sources. "American Indian history must be approached through Indian sources as well as white sources," Trafzer explained, "and with an understanding of the oral tradition, religious beliefs, language, and other aspects of the specific Indian group one studies."

Also teaching at the multicampus University of California were several other distinguished Native scholars, including Terry P. Wilson (Potawatomi) at Berkeley and Jack D. Forbes (Powhatan/Lenape) at Davis. Wilson's published works included *The Underground Reservation: Osage Oil* (1985), *Teaching American Indian History* (1993), and several tribal histories for children. He also served as editor of *The American Indian Quarterly*, an interdisciplinary journal of history, literature, folklore, anthropology, and the arts. Among his proudest achievements was the creation of a new course at Berkeley, "People of Mixed Race Descent," an exploration of many of the same issues found in the fiction of contemporary mixed-blood writers. In words reminiscent of novelist and Berkeley colleague Gerald Vizenor, Wilson regarded people of mixed ancestry as important "cultural brokers" of human identity. "They weren't caught between two cultures," Wilson explained in 1994. "They were *in* both cultures." Likewise, Jack D. Forbes explored the multicultural and multiracial dimensions of American history in such works as *Apache, Navajo, and Spaniard* (1960) and *Tribes and Masses: Explorations in Red, White, and Black* (1978). Forbes served as a member of the board of trustees of nearby D-Q University and contributed to the international reputation of the Native American studies program at Davis. In 1993 the University of California accorded the program full departmental status, the first Native American studies department in the state and one of only a few such departments in the nation.

Michael Dorris (Modoc) played a similar role at Dartmouth College in New Hampshire where he founded and chaired the Native American studies program. Author of several works of critically acclaimed fiction and nonfiction, including *A Guide to Research on North American Indians* (1983), Dorris was best known for his prize-winning study of fetal alcohol syndrome, *The Broken Cord* (1989). Based on his own experiences with an adopted son, the book describes in wrenching detail the physical and behavioral impairments caused by FAS. Dorris also achieved considerable success as a novelist, chronicling the story of a child of mixed African American and Native American ancestry in *A Yellow Raft on Blue Water* (1989) and collaborating with his wife Louise Erdrich (Chippewa) on his second novel *The Crown of Columbus* (1991).

Foremost among the ranks of Indian nonfiction writers in the late twentieth century was Vine Deloria, Jr. (Standing Rock Sioux), author of several widely read commentaries on contemporary Native American issues. Deloria became the primary spokesman for the advocates of Indian cultural nationalism and political sovereignty. His first and most popular book, *Custer Died for Your Sins: An Indian Manifesto* (1969), offers a devastating critique of federal Indian policy and a thoughtful treatise on Native American political ideology. Professing to be nauseated by the traditional image of the Indian in popular culture, Deloria attacks forthrightly the "wigwam stereotyping" of Native people. Anthropologist Nancy Oestreich Lurie commented that the book should "shake a patronizing public" into realizing that "the day is past when we can talk or write as if Indians were either illiterate or extinct, no matter how benevolent or objective our intentions."

Deloria's second book, *We Talk, You Listen: New Tribes, New Turf* (1970), presents the argument for a "retribalization" of Native Americans. Buttressed by extensive legal analysis, Deloria attempts to explain the nature of Indian sovereignty as he envisions it. He also issues a sweeping pronouncement on what non-Indians must do to survive: "The only answer will be to adopt Indian ways. . . . For the white man even to exist, he must adopt a total Indian way of life." N. Scott Momaday was among those who remained uncertain of Deloria's vision and was disappointed that he failed to evoke "that spirit and mentality which distinguishes the Indian as a man and as a race." As if in response to Momaday's complaint, Deloria went to the heart of the "Indian spirit" in *God Is Red* (1973), his unmerciful attack on the Judeo-Christian tradition and a soul-searching explication of Native American spirituality. Deloria returns to political analysis in *Behind the*

Trail of Broken Treaties: An Indian Declaration of Independence (1974), his behind-the-scenes account of the occupation of the headquarters of the Bureau of Indian Affairs in 1972 and the shoot-out at Wounded Knee the following year.

Non-Indians who continued to write about Indian affairs were warned by Native Americans like Vine Deloria, Jr., that it was no longer possible to carry on with business as usual. Distorted images, negative stereotypes, and romantic idealizations all were to be avoided in favor of clear-sighted portraits of real Indian people, presented accurately and with their humanity intact. European American author Ruth Beebe Hill learned to her dismay how serious this new mandate could be. Her novel *Hanta Yo* (1979) was based ostensibly on years of research and purported to be the story of a Lakota band in the early nineteenth century. Praised by white critics for its engrossing narrative style and vivid language, the novel soon became a best-seller. Reaction among the Sioux, however, was negative. The faculty senate of the tribally controlled community college at Sinte Gleska, South Dakota, denounced Hill for falsifying Lakota religion and sexuality and for creating "new and defamatory stereotypes . . . of American Indians." Anthropologists also condemned the book for its depiction of the culture of the fictional Mahto band of Sioux. Native American critic David Seals reported that the publication of *Hanta Yo* had caused "some Skins to swear they'd kill author Ruth Beebe Hill if she ever showed her face in Sioux Country."

Far more successful in satisfying Native American and European American critics was novelist Tony Hillerman. Beginning with *The Blessing Way* (1970), Hillerman produced more than a dozen detective novels in which he deftly describes the Navajo worldview and introduces his readers to Navajo folkways, ceremonies, and family relationships. He portrays honestly the ongoing tragedies of poverty and discrimination, but lifts up the Navajo concept of *Hózhó,* "a sort of blend of being in harmony with one's environment, at peace with one's circumstances, content with the day, devoid of anger, and free from anxieties." Hillerman's two main characters, Navajo police officers Joe Leaphorn and Jim Chee, are intent on restoring the harmony and peace disturbed by various nefarious criminal acts. Jim Chee, speaking in *The Ghostway* (1985), summarizes the spiritual balance needed by all people: "All is part of totality, and in this totality man finds his *hozro,* his way of walking in harmony, with beauty all around him." Hillerman neither idealizes nor patronizes his Native American subjects, and for this achievement the Navajos honored him with the title "Special Friend to the Dineh," the Navajo people.

NATIVE CHALLENGES

Throughout the last third of the twentieth century, Native Americans directed their campaign against Indian stereotypes at an ever-widening range of targets in American popular culture. Native critics were especially vigilant in challenging demeaning stereotypes and inaccurate images of Indians in school textbooks. As Nooksack writer Mickey Roberts suggested in her short story "It's All in How You Say It," the textbook images showed clearly that "the outside world did not always understand Indian people." In 1964 Jeannette Henry (Eastern Cherokee) and Rupert Costo (Cahuilla) founded the American Indian Historical Society in San Francisco and began lobbying for the publication and adoption of textbooks that contained more accurate information about Native Americans. Critiques of existing textbooks filled the pages of *The Indian Historian,* published by the society from 1964 to 1980, and were expanded in a special report prepared by Henry and Costo, *Textbooks and the American Indian* (1970). Major publishers, including McGraw-Hill Book Company, issued guidelines to its textbook authors to banish offensive words like "squaw" and to avoid the pitfalls of ethnocentrism.

Some of the most glaring stereotypes, as noted by folklorist Rayna Green (Cherokee), were those associated with Indians used as mascots for schools and athletic teams. Often chosen because of their identification with aggressive behavior, proud bearing, and (ironically) an ability to win, Indian mascots included comic caricatures, costumed dancers, and "Indian war chants" as team cheers. Beginning in the late 1960s, Native Americans called for the modification or elimination of all such usages. Dartmouth College dropped its Indian mascot shortly after its bicentennial in 1969, and the following year Stanford University banned a comic Indian caricature that Native American students regarded as "a gross misconception of the Indian." Undergraduate Native American Lorenzo Stars called upon Stanford officials to recognize that "the mascot is a group of people and not an animal." The university dropped its Indian mascot altogether in 1972, and plans were made to change the names of its alumni contributor categories in the Stanford Buck Club (Brave, Buck, Big Buck, Chief, Big

"THE STANFORD INDIANS," COMIC CARICATURES THAT GRACED SWEATSHIRTS, WINDOW DECALS, AND OTHER SOUVENIR PRODUCTS AT CALIFORNIA'S STANFORD UNIVERSITY UNTIL THEIR BANISHMENT IN 1970. NATIVE AMERICAN STUDENTS OBJECTED TO THE USE OF SUCH INDIAN IMAGES AS SCHOOL MASCOTS.

Chief, Super Chief). Syracuse University likewise dropped its "Saltine Warrior" mascot after vigorous protests from Native American students and alumni. "Army had a mule for a mascot, Navy had a goat, Georgia had a bulldog and Syracuse had an Indian," recalled Syracuse alumnus Oren Lyons (Iroquois). "It was as if we were less than human." Members of the National Indian Youth Council (NIYC) also scored a victory at the University of Oklahoma when the administration agreed to halt the use of the name "Little Red" for the school's mascot.

Among those who resisted the efforts of Native Americans to eliminate Indian mascots was the University of Illinois, where for sixty years "Chief Illiniwek" entertained football crowds at Memorial Stadium in Champaign. The chief, almost always a European American dressed in a feathered headdress, stamped his way through allegedly authentic Indian dances during half-time. James Yellowbank (Winnebago), member of a Native American advocacy group in Chicago, was among those who took offense. "It's a racist, degrading figure that demeans our heritage," he said.

No one would tolerate a phony priest performing a mockery of Communion in the San Diego Padres dugout. Yet the university encourages a phony Indian to prance around with the band in a burlesque of our sacred ceremonial dances. My Indian friends all call him Little Red Sambo.

When Indian and non-Indian students, faculty, and administrators demanded that Chief Illiniwek be banished in 1989, the university chancellor refused, saying that the chief was "a dignified, respected, even revered symbol." The state legislature passed a resolution commending the university for "its commitment to preserve the esteem of Chief Illiniwek." Indian students were left disheartened and confused. "These people keep telling us how much they love Indians," said one Native American fine arts student. "Yet when we criticize the mascot, we're hushed like small children or harassed by the community."

The battle over mascots was also waged in communities across America where countless elementary and secondary schools had teams named "Chiefs," "Warriors," "Indians," and "Braves." Boards of education and school officials generally acceded to the requests of Native Americans that such appellations be changed. In Sonoma, California, the principal of Altimira Middle School changed the school mascot in 1993 from "Apaches" to "Wolves" after Native people complained. "We're not going to please everyone, but we can't ignore the request of the American Indians and all those who are offended," said the principal. "It's not respectful." Also in 1993 the Washington State Board of Education ordered the state's schools to review their mascots and logos to make sure they were free of bias against any group. Issaquah High School was among those that began seeking an alternative for its Indian mascot. Andy de los Angeles, chairman of the local Snoqualmie tribal council, offered to help. "Our tribe can help you pick out a name, pick out a mascot," he said. "But the name 'Indian' is not appropriate."

Native Americans were far less successful in winning the cooperation of professional sports franchises in changing their names. Russell Means and other members of the American Indian Movement filed an unsuccessful $9 million lawsuit against the Cleveland Indians in the early 1970s, alleging that the baseball team's name and comic mascot ("Chief Wahoo") defamed American Indians. Twenty years later, Indians were rebuffed in their attempt to have media mogul Ted Turner's Atlanta Braves change its name, retire its dancing mascot ("Chief Noc-a-Homa"), and banish forever its notorious "tomahawk chop."

Likewise, the Washington Redskins football team retained its much maligned name, but did agree to eliminate a reference to scalping from a cheer that Native Americans found offensive: "Hail to the Redskins / Hail Victory / Braves on the Warpath / Fight for old D.C. / Scalp 'em, Swamp 'em, We will take 'em big score / Read 'em, Weep 'em, Touchdown we want heap more." Calling for greater sensitivity in professional sports, an editorial in *Sports Illustrated* in 1990 suggested that it was time to listen more carefully to what Native Americans were saying. "The Indian has nothing to do with football," wrote Franz Lidz, "and everything to do with what's sacred to the Native American heritage."

The battle over images and names also was joined in the interpretation of historic sites, from Plymouth Rock to the California missions. One of the most protracted controversies centered on the site of the defeat of Colonel George Custer and his Seventh Cavalry by Sioux forces led by Sitting Bull and Crazy Horse at the Little Bighorn River, Montana, in 1876. Ever since the 1920s, Native Americans had attempted to have a monument erected at the site that would provide an Indian perspective on the battle. The issue simmered for the next half century, reaching a boiling point when Russell Means attempted unsuccessfully to install a plaque at the battlefield in 1972, 1976, and 1982. Means and other members of the American Indian Movement finally succeeded in 1988 in placing a small steel plate at the site, honoring the "Indian patriots" who had fought there "in order to save our women and children from mass murder."

Three years later, in 1991, Congressman Ben Nighthorse Campbell (Northern Cheyenne) won passage of legislation authorizing a more permanent Indian monument at the site and changing its name from the Custer National Battlefield Monument to the Little Big Horn National Battlefield Monument. Conservatives denounced the proposed monument as a "sacrilege," and right-wing radio commentator Rush Limbaugh likened it to putting up a memorial to the Japanese pilots who died at Pearl Harbor. But Campbell and his supporters were jubilant. "Some people tell me that the monument and the name change are not important because they're only symbolic. . . . The fact is," declared Campbell, "symbolism is important."

Undeterred by those who criticized their efforts as nothing more than an exercise in multicultural "political correctness," Native Americans in the 1990s persisted in attacking stereotypes whenever they encountered them. Members of the Shinnecock tribe on Long Island,

New York, objected in 1994 to a local school's production of the play *Peter Pan* because it contained offensive Indian caricatures. Particularly upsetting was the song "Ug-a-Wug," in which children portraying Indians sang of "the brave noble redskin" and uttered nonsense doggerel such as "Bibbity, Bibbity, Sab!" When the school canceled the production, the *New York Times* ran a story with the lead "Multiculturalism has grounded Peter Pan."

Meanwhile, Native Americans also took exception to a seminar on Indian spirituality being offered by a European American calling himself "Blue Snake" on American Online, one of the country's largest on-line computer services. Telecommunications engineer J. Lightfoot Fry (Mohawk) began monitoring the seminar and found that Blue Snake was "mixing in rituals borrowed from various tribes, New Age hocus-pocus and his own philosophy. It had nothing to do with true Native American culture—in fact, it was cultural theft of the worst kind." To combat such misappropriation, Fry and other Indians formed the Native American Communications Council in 1994, a comprehensive computer network by, for, and of Indians. Rick Phillips (Eastern Cherokee) described the network as "what the information superhighway should be all about." He envisioned it as the most effective means yet of dispelling stereotypes and misinformation about Native people:

> We'd provide real information in real time on a grass-roots level. . . . I see a time when a black kid in New Jersey who really wants to know about Native American culture can link up with a 12-year-old Oglala Sioux on the Pine Ridge reservation in South Dakota.

The observance of the quincentennial of Christopher Columbus's epoch-making voyage of 1492 sparked a national debate about colonialism in the Western Hemisphere and, more specifically, about the nature of Indian-white relations in the United States. As the quincentennial approached, Native Americans became increasingly outspoken in their opposition to a traditional celebration feting the glories of "the Admiral of the Ocean Seas." In a 1991 *Newsweek* article entitled, "I Won't Be Celebrating Columbus Day," Suzan Shown Harjo (Cheyenne/Arapaho) expressed the hope that the anniversary would be a time when 500 years of suffering by Native people would at last come to an end. Similar sentiments were expressed by Indian writers in articles published in periodicals as diverse as *USA Today* ("We Can No Longer in Good Faith Celebrate Columbus") and the *Utne Reader*

("Columbus Quincentennial Is Nothing to Celebrate"). "When we see people honoring Christopher Columbus, it's the same as what Jewish people see when they see people honoring Adolf Hitler," remarked Native American activist Bobby Castillo in 1992. And Russell Means went even further: "Columbus makes Hitler look like a juvenile delinquent."

Several nationally prominent Native Americans urged Indian people to use the quincentennial as a means of dispelling stereotypes and educating the general public about contemporary Native concerns. Kiowa writer N. Scott Momaday viewed the anniversary as a "wonderfully important time to reflect upon the meaning of Columbus's voyages to America." He hoped that its observance in 1992 "would produce greater awareness of Native cultures, the importance of those cultures, and indeed the indispensable importance of them in the light of the twenty-first century." Journalist Tim Giago (Oglala Lakota), editor of *Indian Country Today* in Rapid City, South Dakota, agreed. It was his hope that 1992 would be the year when "white America can make an effort to see this nation through the eyes of the Indian people." Likewise, Rayna Green, director of the American Indian Program at the Smithsonian's National Museum of American History, regarded the quincentennial as an "extraordinary opportunity" for Indians to redefine the event for their own purposes.

The controversy surrounding Columbus led to the cancellation or scaling back of many commemorative activities planned for the quincentennial. The U.S. pavilion at Seville's "Expo '92," the largest international Columbian celebration, was drastically cut back after fund-raising faltered. Plans for a major celebration in San Francisco—including a visit by replicas of Columbus's three ships—were scrapped amidst criticism from local Native American leaders. San Franciscan Lee Sprague (Huron Potawatomi) said, "We want the general community to acknowledge what happened. . . . The genocide instituted by Christopher Columbus continues today." Across the bay in Berkeley, Columbus Day was officially renamed Indigenous Peoples Day, prompting ridicule from CNN as "the most outrageous story of the week" and winning praise from activist Dennis Banks (Chippewa): "It's nice to get just one day out of 500 years of days." Meanwhile, Banks' colleague in the American Indian Movement, Russell Means, was in Denver leading a successful campaign to have the city's 1992 Columbus Day parade canceled. (Means had been arrested the previous year for pouring a red liquid on a statue of Columbus in downtown Denver.)

The attention of many Native Americans was focused on the first day of the quincentennial year when the annual Tournament of Roses parade in Pasadena, California, was to be led by Grand Marshal Cristóbal Colón, a Spanish duke and direct descendant of Christopher Columbus. The response by Native people to the selection of Colón was immediate and overwhelmingly negative. "This man has no part in this land, much less the parade," declared Vera Rocha (Gabrielino). "Columbus didn't discover America. We were already here, but wherever he set foot, his men spoiled the land and disgraced our people." Helen Anderson, chair of the California Alliance of Native Americans, agreed: "We don't like to come down on somebody's parade, but the fact of the matter is that a lot of our people are dead based on the era that man brought [to America]."

The potentially explosive issue was defused when the directors of the Tournament of Roses issued an invitation to Native American Congressman Ben Nighthorse Campbell to share the honors with Colón as the parade's "co-Grand Marshal." Campbell accepted the invitation only on the condition that he be allowed to ride ahead of Colón. "We were here first," Campbell reminded the tournament directors. He also insisted on being able to hold in-depth interviews with the media to discuss contemporary Native American issues. Campbell was among those who believed that the quincentennial was an excellent opportunity for Native people to attract attention to their concerns. "We need to participate and be able to tell our story; that simply can't be done if we drop out of the system." And Campbell certainly succeeded in attracting attention when he led the tournament parade on January 1, 1992. Wearing his eagle feather headdress with double trailer, beaded buckskins, and riding astride a spirited pony, Campbell was an impressive reminder to the estimated 450 million viewers in more than ninety countries that the Indian people, indeed, "were here first." As the *Los Angeles Times* observed, "The symbols are important—the issue serious."

Ben Nighthorse Campbell also played an important role in the establishment of the Smithsonian's National Museum of the American Indian (NMAI), "the first national museum dedicated to changing forever the way people view Native peoples of this hemisphere and to demonstrating how Indian culture has enriched the world." Campbell sponsored legislation in 1989 authorizing the NMAI, which was to include a major new museum in Washington, D.C., a cultural resources complex in Maryland, and an exhibition center in New York City. W. Richard West, Jr., (Cheyenne/Arapaho), son of the Native

UNITED STATES SENATOR BEN NIGHTHORSE CAMPBELL (CHEYENNE)
RIDING IN THE INAUGURAL PARADE OF DEMOCRATIC PRESIDENT
BILL CLINTON ON JANUARY 20, 1993. CAMPBELL WAS THE FIRST
NATIVE AMERICAN TO SERVE IN THE SENATE IN SIXTY YEARS.

artist who had directed the art program at Bacone College, was chosen
director of the NMAI.

The importance of changing the image of the Indian was upper-most in the minds of those who were charged with the responsibility of fulfilling the museum's mandate to become the nation's leading public interpreter of Native cultures. The Smithsonian's secretary, Robert McC. Adams, looked to the NMAI "to alter beyond all expectation public understanding of American Indian people," and the chair of the museum's fund-raising campaign, Gene A. Keluche (Wintu), believed that it "can do more to promote understanding and reconciliation between Native American and non-Indian worlds than any other enterprise I know."

The core of the collection of the National Museum of the American Indian was to be the more than one million objects assembled by New York banker George Gustav Heye between 1903 and 1954. Heye's appetite for Indian artifacts was so voracious that he collected items representing virtually every aspect of Native American material cultures. As writer Joseph Bruhac (Abenaki) recalled, Native people once said that after Heye visited an Indian community, "If he left us with our underclothes we were lucky!" An important part of the mission of the NMAI, therefore, was to cooperate fully with tribal leaders who sought to have items in the collection repatriated. Clara Sue Kidwell (Choctaw/Chippewa), an assistant director of the museum, was committed to returning:

> Sacred and ceremonial objects necessary to the practices or revitalization of Native religions, communally owned property which could not have been legally disposed of by any individual member of a tribe, and abundant objects of which the museum has multiple examples.

The first evidence of the museum's innovative approach to altering the public perception of Native Americans was a "preview" exhibition in 1992 at the museum's center in New York. Called "Pathways to Tradition," the exhibition was planned, organized, and curated by Native Americans. Native American "selectors"—tribal elders, artists, performers, educators, and religious leaders—spent a week going through the vast collection of the museum, selecting items for the exhibition. "We deliberately set out to break a lot of rules which normally apply to exhibition development," explained NMAI director W. Richard West, Jr. "However, it is this museum's role to insure that the interpretation of objects and culture stems directly from the peoples who make up that culture." The museum's innovative approach was taken not only to honor Indians but also to allow non-Indians to see the exhibition from a Native perspective. As director West explained, "One of the missing perspectives for many, many years—almost from the beginning of museums—has been the voice of Native peoples themselves."

The centerpiece of the NMAI was a major museum in Washington D.C., to be built on the last available spot on the Mall, near the National Air and Space Museum. Congress agreed to provide two-thirds of the estimated $110 million in construction costs, but only if the NMAI first raised the initial one-third. In 1994 the museum received a big boost from the Mashantucket Pequots of Connecticut, who donated $10 million from the profits of their huge Foxwoods Casino. Once the fund-raising campaign was completed, the museum was scheduled to open its doors by the year 2001. The essence and the hope of this twenty-first century institution was best expressed by its director:

> It is, in the end, a national institution of living culture. It is about a group of peoples and cultures that continue to exist right now and draw upon a lengthy and deep cultural past to maintain a present and to build a cultural future.

THE MOVIES, AGAIN

In spite of the best efforts of Ben Nighthorse Campbell, W. Richard West, Jr., and scores of other Native Americans dedicated to challenging popular stereotypes, distorted images of Indians continued to appear in the one source most relied on for information about Native people, the movies. As film historians Michael T. Marsden and Jack Nachbar pointed out, the tradition of portraying the Indian either as a fearsome bloodthirsty savage or a romantic noble savage continued unbroken from the earliest days of filmmaking through the late twentieth century. Film images of the Indians also remained locked in the past; only a few hinted that Native people might still be living or have stories today worth telling on the silver screen.

Gradually the most racist of images, such as those found in the early Westerns of John Ford or King Vidor's *Northwest Passage* (1940), were replaced by images more sympathetic. Portrayals of hostile Indians were tempered with an acknowledgment that European Americans may have been the true cause of Indian-white conflict. *Duel in the Sun* (1946), starring Jennifer Jones as the mixed-blood Pearl Chavez, details the psychological damage caused by racial prejudice. And two John Ford films of the late 1940s demonstrated a more mature understanding of the sources of Indian hostility than was evident in his earlier efforts. "Your word to a breechclothed, savage, illiterate, uncivilized murderer and treaty breaker?" smirked the imperious commander, portrayed by Henry Fonda, of *Fort Apache* (1948). "There is no question of honor between an American officer and Cochise." Such unbridled contempt led the commander into a battle with Cochise and his Apache warriors in which the commander's troops are slaughtered. Likewise, a remarkable even-handedness is evident in the portrayal by John Wayne of a seasoned cavalry officer and by John Big Tree (Seneca) of an aging chief in *She Wore a Yellow Ribbon* (1949). Both men are unable to contain their younger, more willful followers, and they find a common ground of mutual respect in their longing for peace and retirement.

The romantic image of the noble savage (what Marsden and Nachbar have called the "Noble Anachronism") was relegated in the films of the late 1940s largely to the role of loyal helpmate, as in Tonto the "faithful Indian companion" of the Lone Ranger. The adventures of the Masked Rider of the Plains and his Potawatomi squire appeared in numerous films in the late 1940s and in a popular television series, running from 1949 to 1965. The character Little Beaver projected a similar image of a loyal, if exasperating, helpmate in the nearly thirty Red Ryder films made between 1940 and 1949. Both Tonto and Little Beaver were decidedly secondary roles, and it was the antics of the latter that made him the more apt figure to bear the name of the former, meaning "fool" or "numbskull" in Spanish.

The watershed movie of the postwar period was Delmer Daves's *Broken Arrow* (1950), a critically acclaimed film that set a new standard for the sympathetic portrayal of Native Americans while also perpetuating some of the old clichés. The bloodthirsty savage is present in the guise of Geronimo (Jay Silverheels); Cochise (Jeff Chandler) takes on the mantle of the noble savage. The leading character, played by James Stewart, attempts some meaningful cross-cultural communication to bring an end to Indian-white hostilities. Cochise is presented as a decent and fair-minded man, passionately devoted to peace. By the film's end, it is evident that he is the true tragic hero of the story.

Broken Arrow promoted the noble savage—an altogether admirable figure doomed to extinction by the advance of white civilization—to first rank in future American feature films, and it was that image that steadily rose to dominance by the 1960s. In *The Devil's Doorway* (1950), for instance, an eastern Shoshone dies fighting for his land, and in *Hiawatha* (1952) the title character of Longfellow's epic poem is shown in the role of peacemaker. *Crazy Horse* (1952), *Sitting Bull* (1954), and *Geronimo* (1962) all portray the leaders of Indian resistance with far greater sympathy than they had been accorded in earlier film treatments. Even twentieth-century Native Americans find their stories presented with understanding and empathy, although typecast as tragic victims of the dominant culture. *Jim Thorpe, All American* (1951) tells the story of an Indian athlete, portrayed by Burt Lancaster, who is stripped of his two Olympic gold medals; *The Outsider* (1961) features Tony Curtis as Ira Hayes (Pima), the hero of Iwo Jima who dies alone and desperate; and *Tell Them Willie Boy Is Here* (1969) recounts the story of an outlaw Paiute-Chemehuevi who is pursued into the desert and killed.

The sympathetic portrayal of Native Americans reached something of a climax in 1970 with the release of four major films with Indian subjects. Ralph Nelson's *Soldier Blue*, like Arthur Kopit's play *Indians*, was inspired by the war in Southeast Asia. The excruciating savagery of racism in the film, loosely based on the Sand Creek Massacre of 1864, was clearly intended as an indictment of more recent American military action as well. Likewise, the comedy *Flap* was not just a sympathetic portrait of Indian resistance, it was also a parable of American protest demonstrations of the 1960s. The biggest box-office success of 1970 was Arthur Penn's *Little Big Man*, based on Thomas Berger's novel, starring Dustin Hoffman in the role of Jack Crabb. Film critic Stanley Kauffmann praised *Little Big Man* as a "unique film with American verve, about some of the things American verve has done," and Native actor Chief Dan George (Squamish) was honored with an Academy Award nomination for best supporting actor. The most controversial film of the year proved to be *A Man Called Horse*, a movie purporting to show the tribal life and customs of the Sioux as encountered by an Englishman taken captive in the 1820s. Native American critics objected, however, to numerous inaccuracies in the film. The pivotal scene, showing the Sun Dance ceremony (recreated by the filmmakers from the practices of the Mandan, arch rivals of the Sioux), is erroneously presented as a test of courage rather than a sacred ritual.

NATIVE AMERICAN ACTOR IRON EYES CODY (CHEROKEE) SHEDS A TEAR FOR THE ENVIRONMENT IN THIS ANTIPOLLUTION POSTER FROM 1972. CODY ALSO APPEARED IN A SERIES OF TELEVISION COMMERCIALS THAT INVOKED THE IMAGE OF THE NOBLE SAVAGE IN HIS FAMILIAR ROLE AS A VEHICLE FOR SOCIAL CRITICISM.

One exasperated Native critic suggested the film might have been more aptly titled *A Man Called Horse Shit*.

The most common image of the Indian in the films of the 1970s continued to be a variant of the noble savage. Motivated by the same discontent that had informed the image of the Indian in American literature, filmmakers often employed the noble savage as a vehicle for social criticism. Native people were presented as admirable, if doomed, characters whose natural virtues contrasted sharply with the rapacious and destructive propensities of European Americans. This image was repeated endlessly in a series of television commercials, featuring actor Iron Eyes Cody (Cherokee), in which the Indian is the natural man whose ecological sensibilities are offended by the pollution created by the thoughtless modern (white) man. Ken Kesey's novel *One Flew Over the Cuckoo's Nest* was brought to the screen in 1975, with Native actor Will Sampson in the role of Chief Bromden, the stoic Indian whose very presence makes the white man's world seem all the more insane. Likewise, Robert Altman's *Buffalo Bill and the Indians, or Sitting Bull's History Lesson* (1976), a film loosely based on Arthur Kopit's play *Indians,* portrays Native Americans as spiritually and morally superior to the incompetent and arrogant Bill Cody. So too in *Eagle's Wing* (1979), a Comanche chief (Sam Waterson) becomes a symbol of natural harmony and freedom, qualities that elude a city-bred trapper (Martin Sheen) who competes with the chief for a magnificent white stallion.

Related perhaps to the popularity of Carlos Castaneda's *Don Juan* series, several films of the 1970s and 1980s featured Indians as possessors of special spiritual powers. A Sioux medicine man in *The Manitou* (1978) performs a successful exorcism; vampire bats are liberated through tribal sorcery in *Nightwing* (1979); the title character of *Windwalker* (1980) returns from the dead; and a young Sioux becomes his tribe's savior in *Mystic Warrior* (1984), a made-for-television film based on Ruth Beebe Hill's ill-fated novel *Hanta Yo.* As film historians Marsden and Nachbar pointed out in 1987, this emphasis on the "spiritual exoticism" of Native Americans brought the movie image of the Indian full circle. Just as the earliest films of the late nineteenth century "were sold to audiences eager to view the strange otherness of Native peoples, so too do audiences in the 1980s go to the movies for the pleasure of seeing Indians whose mystical lore makes them fascinatingly different."

The most successful Indian movie of all time was released in 1990 and led to a revival of interest in Native American subjects in the last decade of the twentieth century. Nominated for twelve academy awards and winning seven, Kevin Costner's *Dances with Wolves* ranks with *Broken Arrow* and *Little Big Man* as a milestone in the history of images of Indians in the movies. The film tells the story of a disenchanted cavalry lieutenant who comes west to escape the horrors of the Civil War and ends up identifying completely with his Lakota neighbors at a lonely frontier outpost on the northern plains. In the face of the bloody cruelty and wanton destructiveness of his fellow European Americans, the young lieutenant finds the burden of his own whiteness unbearable. His transformation to an Indian identity is complete as he utters the words of his rebirth, "I am Dances with Wolves!"

In spite of its gaggle of academy awards and booming box-office success, *Dances with Wolves* was sharply criticized from a variety of perspectives. Philip French in *The Observer* put it down as "long, simplistic, and lacking in irony," while Aims McGuinness in *The New Republic* condemned director Kevin Costner for merely turning on its head "the old red-and-white" dualism of evil and good. "This time around, the Indians are the cowboys and the cowboys are the Indians."

Dances with Wolves received mixed reviews from Native Americans who were expert now at spotting stereotypes and unwilling to allow them to go unchallenged, no matter how "sympathetic" they might appear. Historian Edward D. Castillo (Cahuilla/Luiseño), in a generally favorable review published in the prestigious *Film Quarterly*, praised the film for its "sensitive exploration of a native culture" but also noted that it contained a number of historical inaccuracies. Michael Dorris said that he wished the film's screenwriter "had resisted the temptation to plug every positive stereotype about Native Americans. The characters, alternately stoic, are ecologically aware and brave. Even Hollywood Indians don't have to be like this." Among the Sioux of South Dakota, where the film was shot and set, concern was expressed that the filmmakers had ignored the historical realities of post–Civil War Indian life in favor of "some very poetic and nature-loving Indians." Especially disturbing was the lack of any reference to the critical Fort Laramie Treaty of 1868, the basis for activists' demands a century later for a reassertion of tribal sovereignty. Full-blood elders Dave Bald Eagle and Dave Yakima Chief, both of whom appeared in the film, complained that the screenplay's Lakota dialogue had the male characters generally speaking the feminine form of the language. Lakota spiritual leader Arvol Looking Horse and the ruling elders' council objected unsuccessfully to the representation in the film of a ceremonial pipe, the "sacred Canupa of White Buffalo Calf Maiden."

Native Americans also found it disappointing that once again a film portrayed Indians as part of some heroic past, diverting attention from the harsh realities of the present. As Native writer David Seals, author of *The Powwow Highway* (1990), pointed out, the film's perfect village of tipis was located along the Belle Fourche River, a river whose water was currently undrinkable and polluted from nearby mine tailings. Seals, who coined the term *Custerism* for the practice of Indian stereotyping, charged that *Dances with Wolves* spawned more of the same old clichés: "Where the Old Custerists didn't mind blatantly stereotyping Indians as savages, for New Custerists the sentimentality and romance must not be sullied."

Two years later, in 1992, James Fenimore Cooper's classic novel *The Last of the Mohicans* was brought to the screen for the third or fourth time. What made this latest version remarkable was that filmmaker Michael Mann cast American Indian Movement leader Russell Means in the title role of Chingachgook. Means, long a critic of the distorted images of Indians in American popular culture, accepted the role only after being assured that he would not be asked to portray his character in any "stereotypical" way. True to form, Means led a walkout of 150 Indian actors to protest discriminatory treatment on the set by the film's production staff. He reproved non-Indian staffers for calling Native cast members derogatory names such as "Chief" and "Redskin" and for referring to an Indian choker as a "dog collar." Yet for all that, Means found the experience to be a positive one. He came to see the potential of film—with proper involvement by Native Americans—as a powerful means for correcting past images. "It's a tremendous voice, a tremendous tool."

Also appearing in *The Last of the Mohicans,* as the ever-threatening Magua, was another talented up-and-coming Native American actor, Wes Studi (Cherokee). A horse trainer by profession, Studi starred the following year in Walter Hill's film biography of *Geronimo: An American Legend* (1993). Preparing for the part, Studi immersed himself in his character, determined to present as accurately as possible the elusive Chiricahua Apache during the years he was pursued and finally captured by federal troops. "As an Indian myself, I felt an obligation to give him dignity," said Studi, "because he did have dignity, even when he was being hunted." The film was criticized by some viewers for sanitizing Geronimo, making few references to the hostility he stirred among his fellow Apaches and leaving out altogether his infamous drunken binges. Film critic Richard Schickel placed *Geronimo* squarely in the noble savage tradition, with stock figures recognizable (at least) from the days of *Broken Arrow.* Included were a callow young army officer who respects his enemy, a greenhorn who wants to learn more about the Apaches, and the Indian-as-tragic-hero, "noble, misused and off the reservation because promises have been broken."

Another retelling of the story of Geronimo was part of entertainment tycoon Ted Turner's "Indian initiative" in the early 1990s, the most ambitious effort ever made to combat stereotypes in the media. "The Native Americans: Behind the Legends, Beyond the Myths" was a $40-million multimedia venture, the first time that all of the various components of Turner's entertainment empire were dedicated to a single subject. "Most of the contact that non-Indian America has had with Indians is through movies," Turner explained, "many of which promote the stereotype of Native Americans as savages." His intent was to provide alternative images consistent with the highest degree of cultural authenticity and presented from a consistently Indian point of view. Turner and his wife Jane Fonda were members of the International Founders Council of the National Museum of the American Indian (NMAI), and "The Native Americans" was also intended to help create the visibility and support necessary to complete the museum's fund-raising campaign.

The project was launched in the fall of 1993 with two feature films broadcast on Turner Network Television (TNT). The first was *Geronimo,* starring Native actor Joseph Runningfox as the young Apache leader, followed by *The Broken Chain,* the story of the eighteenth-century Iroquois Confederacy, featuring Buffy Sainte-Marie (Cree), Graham Greene (Oneida), Floyd Westerman (Sioux), and Wes Studi. *Lakota Woman,* produced by Jane Fonda, was broadcast on TNT the next year and told the real-life story of Mary Crow Dog, a contemporary woman caught up in the Indian activism of the late 1960s and early 1970s. Meanwhile, Turner's Cable News Network (CNN) began broadcasting a series of in-depth news reports, "The Invisible People," on current Native issues. In 1994 Turner Publishing released *The Native Americans,* a lavishly illustrated volume of Indian history, coinciding with the broadcast on Turner Broadcasting System (TBS) of a six-hour documentary series of the same name. (Turner's initiative was followed in 1995 by two decidedly pro-Indian documentaries, Ric Burns's *The Way West* on PBS and Kevin Costner's *500 Nations* on CBS.)

Critical reaction to all this was predictable. Some European Americans lauded Turner for providing a much-needed corrective to conventional stereotypes, while others accused him of overkill. *San Francisco Chronicle* television critic John Carman described the opening segment of the TBS documentary as "a visual dud combined with a verbal scold. The message is that if you are not an American Indian, you are unworthy and must be hectored." Native Americans, willing to overlook Turner's Atlanta Braves and their tomahawk-chopping fans, were more generous in their response. Hanay Geiogamah (Kiowa/ Delaware), a producer of the TNT movies, praised Turner for allowing Native people to tell their own stories. "This is something we always dreamed about. The man is doing what he said he's going to do." By insisting on an Indian perspective in his prime-time dramatic features, documentaries, and news reports, Turner was offering to "deliver us from the delusion of stereotypes and bigotry." Such a deliverance was just what Native Americans—and European Americans—desperately needed. "Now we can give an even better image of us to non-Indians," said Geiogamah, "a clearer image of who we were and how strong we were, how strong we had to be to survive."

Native American participation in Ted Turner's "Indian initiative" was clear evidence of the increased involvement by Native people in virtually every aspect of the film industry. Indeed, the growing level of Native activity in the industry contributed to Turner's decision to launch his initiative in the first place. "A big part of the reason this is happening is that Indians have been pushing for it for years, and getting professionally prepared to participate in it," explained Hanay Geiogamah. "Now we're seeing the first really tangible fruits of our efforts." Since at least the late 1960s, Native actors had been active participants in shaping their roles on the screen. Jay Silverheels (Mohawk), famous for his portrayal of Tonto on the Lone Ranger television series, formed two groups in Los Angeles in 1966 to encourage Native actors. The Indian Actors Workshop offered Native performers the chance to improve their skills, and the Indian Actors Guild promoted the use of Native people in Indian roles. Native American performing artists also started their own drama and dance companies, such as the Red Earth Theatre in Seattle and the Native American Theatre Ensemble in New York. In 1975 the American Indian Film Festival was founded in Seattle and later moved to San Francisco, to showcase new works by and about Native people. Typical of the works was *Dance Me Outside* (1995), a poignant film that features an all-Indian cast and gives an inside look at contemporary Native American life from an Indian point of view. By the mid-1990s, an estimated 300 veteran Indian actors were regularly employed in theater, film, and television. Especially encouraging was the casting of Native actors in prime-time television series, such as D. Martin Pera (Apache) on *Northern Exposure* and Rodney A. Grant (Omaha) on *Hawkeye*.

Tribes also became more aggressive in the marketing of their reservations as locations for films. The Navajo Nation Film Office was created in 1994 to take advantage of such scenic resources as Monument Valley, beloved by generations of cinematographers. The proceeds from tribal location fees were used to encourage Navajos interested in the film industry. "We have a lot of young people on our reservation who are interested in filmmaking," explained Mary Whitehair, administrator of the film office. "So we try to help them when it's possible."

Native Americans also raised their voices as forceful critics of the continuing presence of Indian stereotypes in the media. They applauded the decline of the image of the bloodthirsty savage but were chagrined to find it so often replaced by an equally unreal version of the noble savage. Even the sentimental image of the Indian maiden continued to pull on the heartstrings of America, as witnessed by the box-office success of Walt Disney Studio's 1995 animated feature film *Pocahontas*. (Activist-turned-actor Russell Means is the voice of "Chief Powhatan.") Native critics longed for the day when Indian people would be presented on the screen routinely as real people, complete with all the virtues and vices common to humanity. "There's been such abominable ignorance about us," commented Native American professor Vi Hilbert of the University of Washington. "What I'd like to see is both sides of native culture shown, good and bad. You don't have to dwell on the bad things or make the good saccharine sweet. You can be honest, but that hasn't happened very often." Actor D. Martin Pera, of *Northern Exposure*, concurred that while media images of Indians were steadily maturing, they still tended to fall into two categories: "It's either a warrior going 'Grrrrrrr . . .' or a shaman saying, 'If you listen to the sun you'll hear the animals.' There's no medium."

Kiowa/Delaware producer Hanay Geiogamah suggested that such stereotypes were perpetuated because, until recently, so few Indian people were involved in the film industry:

> We Indians really have had no part in creating any of these clichés. We're just human beings like everyone else. Yes, we want to use our Native American traditions and ways. But ours has always been a more simple approach to life than these romantic images make it out.

Geiogamah was especially contemptuous of his fellow filmmakers' insistence on making Indians into spiritual exotics: "When you hear the tinkling reverb music on the movie soundtrack, you know some Indian's going to have a vision. We don't live like that, and we never did."

Michael Dorris agreed that movie images of Indians were more like a mirror reflecting the needs and concerns of the dominant culture, rather than a lens through which moviegoers could gain a realistic view of Native Americans. Thus it was that Indians were presented in films "not as they were but as they 'had' to be—from a European point of view. They were whisked out of the realm of the real and into the land of the make-believe. Indians became invariably super- or subhuman, never ordinary." *Seattle Times* theater critic Misha Berson summed up the equally distasteful alternatives: "The subhuman were bloodthirsty scalpers, treacherous scouts, inscrutable squaws. The superhuman: noble primitives, beatified victims, New Age-y healers—seen through a mist of white guilt and awe."

Native critics also expressed the hope that filmmakers would focus more attention on the stories of contemporary Native Americans, rather than dwelling on those of the distant past. Echoing sentiments once expressed by his outspoken father, historian Phil Deloria (Standing Rock Sioux) regarded the public preference for the "long-ago Indian" as a cop-out. Deloria explained:

> We can all feel good about the nineteenth century now, because it's our shared history. But what about the present? All the Indian writers I know are much more interested in focusing on today than on yesterday. And I worry that when you lose that nineteenth-century context, Indians lose their glamour and are seen as yet another lower-class American people. And Hollywood could care less about that.

Yet surely the history of Native Americans in recent times could provide the material for countless dramatic presentations that would stir the imagination (and the soul) of a wide audience. The story of the Navajo code talkers in World War II, the struggle for self-determination, the emergence of Indian activism, and the cultural renaissance among Native Americans all are stories of tremendous power and drama. Surely the works of a dozen or more contemporary Native authors could be transformed into screenplays with enormous potential as blockbuster films. Hanay Geiogamah was optimistic that such stories someday would be brought to the screen.

I think there are human interest stories among our people that will be universally attractive to people everywhere. There's this legacy, this heritage we have that no one has really shown yet and it's just waiting for us. It's like having a billion dollars in the bank. . . . We'll never run out of material.

The richness of that bank account should be sufficient for the image makers of the twenty-first century to put aside stereotypes and present the story of real people living in the here and now. As the old century drew to a close, there were encouraging signs that the well-worn clichés about Native Americans were buckling under the weight of new truths. "I think some myths have been put away," said Cherokee actor Wes Studi, "and replaced by facts that are just as entertaining as the myths."

SOURCES AND SUGGESTIONS FOR FURTHER READING

Much of this chapter is based on articles in various periodicals, most of which have been cited for chapters 6 and 7. Additional material comes from articles in the *Albuquerque Journal, Christian Science Monitor, Oakland Tribune, USA Today, New York Review of Books, New York Times Magazine, New York Times Book Review, New Yorker, Utne Reader, The Nation, The New Republic, Film Quarterly, Saturday Review, Smithsonian, The Christian Century, Commonweal,* and *The New Statesman.*

Three articles in Wilcomb E. Washburn, ed., *History of Indian-White Relations,* vol. 8, *Handbook of North American Indians* (1988) are the main source for the first part of this chapter: William K. Powers, "The Indian Hobbyist Movement in North America"; Nancy Oestreich Lurie, "Relations between Indians and Anthropologists"; and Stewart Brand, "Indians and the Counterculture, 1960s–1970s." On the "hippie invasion," see also Harry C. James, *Pages from Hopi History* (1974) and Peter Nabokov, ed., *Native American Testimony: A Chronicle of Indian-White Relations from Prophecy to the Present, 1492–1992* (1991).

The most important sources for the discussion of the image of the Indian in American literature are Leslie Fiedler, *The Return of the Vanishing American* (1969); Robert F. Berkhofer, Jr., *The White Man's Indian: Images of the American Indian from Columbus to the Present* (1978); Brian W. Dippie, *The Vanishing American: White Attitudes and United States Indian Policy* (1982); and Robert F. Berkhofer, Jr., "White Conceptions of Indians"; and Leslie A. Fiedler, "The

Indian in Literature in English," in Wilcomb E. Washburn, ed., *History of Indian-White Relations*. The discussion of specific authors is based on their works and on reviews quoted in *Contemporary Literary Criticism* and *Contemporary Authors*. See especially G. Clarke Chapman, "Crime and Blessing in Tony Hillerman's Fiction," *The Christian Century*, November 13, 1991.

The account of Indian stereotypes in popular culture comes largely from periodical literature and Rayna Green, "The Indian in Popular American Culture," in Wilcomb E. Washburn, ed., *History of Indian-White Relations*. Of particular importance is Franz Lidz, "Not a Very Sporting Symbol," *Sports Illustrated* (September 17, 1990) and "Degrading Native American Sports Mascots," in Arlene Hirschfelder and Martha Kreipe de Montaño, *The Native American Almanac: A Portrait of Native America Today* (1993). On the controversy over the Columbian quincentennial, see Kirkpatrick Sale, *The Conquest of Paradise: Christopher Columbus and the Columbian Legacy* (1990); Martin Espada, "Putting Columbus in His Place," *Christian Science Monitor* (March 11, 1992); Tim Giago, "Our Past Is a Part of Our Tomorrow," *Christian Science Monitor* (March 27, 1992); Simon Schama, "They All Laughed at Christopher Columbus," *The New Republic* (January 6, 1992); and Darryl Babe Wilson, ed., *Dear Christopher: Letters of Contemporary Native Americans to Christopher Columbus* (1992). The story of the conflict over the Little Big Horn National Battlefield Monument and the Tournament of Roses is based on Herman J. Viola, *Ben Nighthorse Campbell: An American Warrior* (1993). A brief introduction to the National Museum of the American Indian is provided in Joseph Bruhac, "The Heye Center Opens in Manhattan with Three Exhibitions of Native Arts," *Smithsonian* (October 1994) and in a series of special reports in *Native Peoples Magazine* (1992–1994).

The premier source for the discussion of the Hollywood image of Indians is Michael T. Marsden and Jack G. Nachbar, "The Indian in the Movies," in Wilcomb E. Washburn, ed., *History of Indian-White Relations*. Also important are Robert F. Berkhofer, Jr., *The White Man's Indian;* Gretchen Bataille and Charles L. P. Silet, eds., *The Pretend Indians: Images of Native Americans in the Movies* (1980); Raymond W. Stedman, *Shadows of the Indian: Stereotypes in American Culture* (1982); and James A. Sandos and Larry E. Burgess, *The Hunt for Willie Boy: Indian Hating and Popular Culture* (1994). Among the many articles and reviews commenting on the topic, see especially David

Seals, "The New Custerism," *The Nation* (May 13, 1991) and Edward D. Castillo, review of *Dances with Wolves, Film Quarterly* (Summer 1991). Most of the quotations near the end of this chapter are drawn from Misha Berson's perceptive analysis, "Native American Images," in *The Seattle Times* (April 10, 1994), © The Seattle Times Co.

PICTURE CREDITS

➤ ➤ ➤ ➤ ➤ ➤ ➤ ➤

Page 7 From the collections of The National Archives: U.S. Marine
Corps #69889-A

Page 31 AP/Wide World Photos

Page 44 From the collections of The National Archives: RG75N-Reloc-G

Page 48 AP/Wide World Photos

Page 66 UPI/Bettmann Newsphotos

Page 79 AP/Wide World Photos

Page 96 Photo by Ed McCombs©

Page 111 Courtesy of the National Indian Youth Council, Inc.

Page 115 © The News Tribune, Tacoma, WA/1964

Page 128 UPI/Bettmann

Page 132 AP/Wide World Photos

Page 144 AP/Wide World Photos

Page 148 Photo by Ed McCombs©

Page 186 Photo by Tyler Dingee

Page 191 "Indian, 1976", Fritz Scholder, Mission, Print, Photographed
by Larry Phillips, Courtesy of the Institute of American Indian
Arts Museum, MS-40.

Page 206 AP/Wide World Photos

Page 243 Stanford Daily, Stanford University

Page 249 Glenn Asakawa/Rocky Mountain News

Page 254 Keep America Beautiful, Inc.

INDEX

→→→→→→→→→

A-Juma-We, 214
Abenaki, 202, 216, 250
Abrahamson, Rose Ann (Shoshone-
    Bannock), 183
Acculturation, 90–91, 93–94, 126
    decline of Native languages,
    175–176
    tribal governments, 106–107
    during World War II, 10–11. *See
    also* related topics
Acknowledgment of tribal status,
    158–159
Acoma Pueblo, 223–225
Acquired immunodeficiency
    syndrome (AIDS), 87
Actors, 256, 257–260, 262
Adams, Robert McC., 250
Advocates for Indigenous California
    Language Survival (AICLS), 178
African Americans, 6, 39, 97, 101,
    117–119, 127, 239
After and Before the Lightning
    (1994), 225
Agriculture, 150–151
AIDS. *See* Acquired
    immunodeficiency syndrome
    (AIDS)
AIM. *See* American Indian
    Movement (AIM)
Air pollution, 142–143
Ak-Chin Community, Arizona,
    150–151
Akwesasne Notes, 125, 154, 220
Akwesasne Mohawk, 110–111, 113
Alabama, 118
Alaska, 66–67, 176
Alaska Federation of Natives (AFN),
    66
Alaska Native Claims Settlement Act
    (1971), 66–67
Alaska Native Tourism Council, 151
Alaska Natives, 55, 66–67, 90, 151,
    179, 180
Albuquerque, New Mexico, 14, 47,
    75, 87, 100

Alcatraz Island, occupation of
    (1969), 69, 105, 121–123, 124,
    135, 214, 233
Alcohol
    abuse of, 85–87, 217
    alcoholism, 81, 87, 150
    fetal alcohol syndrome (FAS), 86,
    240
    forbidden in Native American
    Church, 174
    public intoxication, 15
    right to purchase, 19
Aleut, 66, 151, 179
Algonquian, 235
Allegheny River, 108
Allen, Elsie (Pomo), 176
Allen, Paula Gunn (Laguna Pueblo /
    Lakota), 213
Allisti Ti-tanin-miji (Alcatraz
    Island, California), 214
Allotment policy, 27–30
All–Pueblo Council, 15, 29
Altman, Robert, 255
Ambler, Marjane, 149
America Online, 246
American Anthropological
    Association, 232
American Church of God, 233
American Committee for the
    Preservation of Archaeological
    Collections (ACPAC), 166–167
American Indian Capitol
    Conference on Poverty (1964),
    57
American Indian Defense
    Association (AIDA), 30
American Indian Federation, 34,
    106
American Indian Film Festival, 259
American Indian Historians
    Association, 238
American Indian Historical Society,
    125, 242
*American Indian Holocaust and
    Survival* (1987), 89

American Indian Movement (AIM), 69, 153, 171, 211, 232, 257
  advent of, 120–121
  interpretation of historic sites, 245
  mascot issue, 244
  Trail of Broken Treaties, 126–129, 210
  Wounded Knee occupation, 129–136
  repatriation issue, 165–166
American Indian Music and Cultural Festival, 159
American Indian Painting and Sculpture (1981), 185
American Indian Policy Review Commission, 69
American Indian Press Service, 125
American Indian Prose and Poetry (1974), 220
American Indian Quarterly, 239
American Indian Religious Freedom Act (1978), 163–164, 172, 175
American Indian Theatre Ensemble, 259
American Indians and World War II (1991), 10
American Indians United, 120, 122
American Jewish Committee, 175
The American West Transformed (1985), 11
American Women's Voluntary Service, 6
Anasazi, 184–188
The Ancient Child (1989), 207
Anderson, Helen, 248
Anderson, Wallace "Mad Bear" (Tuscarora), 108–109, 117, 127, 147, 172
Anthropology, 17, 29, 37, 55, 78, 80, 109, 110, 204, 237, 239, 240, 241
  and improved relations with Native Americans, 231–232
  postwar boom, 231–232
  and reparation issue, 165–169
Anti-Indian backlash, 159–162
Anti-sovereignty movement, 159–162

Apache, 1, 25, 58, 225, 234, 252, 258
  actors, 260
  artists, 188, 190, 192
  economic development, 141–142, 146, 151, 155
  suicide among, 90
  termination policy, 42
  traditional culture, 173–174, 182
  unemployment, 80
  during World War II, 14, 15. *See also* names of individuals
Apache, Navajo, and Spaniard (1960), 239
Arapaho, 14, 26, 73, 145, 165, 172, 246, 250–251
Archaeology, 167, 231–232
Archambault, JoAllyn (Standing Rock Sioux), 184
Archuleta, Margaret, 188
Area Redevelopment Act (1961), 55, 57
Arizona, 1, 13, 16, 17, 19, 46, 47, 57, 58, 66, 67, 72, 80, 84, 89–90, 94, 95, 97, 140–141, 142–143, 150–151, 153, 155, 164, 173, 180, 181, 220
Arizona State University, 57, 181
Arizona v. California (1983), 72
Armed forces, 4–13, 17–20
Artists, 184–197
Artists Hopid, 192–193
Assimilation, 10–11, 15–16, 70–71, 73, 75, 90–91, 92–93, 106, 153, 181
  as goal of early American Indian policy, 24–29
  during Collier era, 30–35
  religion, 173–174
  relocation policy and, 46–50
  termination era, 35–46. *See also* related topics
Assiniboine, 5
Astrov, Margot, 220
Athapaskan, 67
Atlanta Braves (baseball team), 244, 259
Atlanta, Georgia, 118, 244, 259

Atsuge-We, 214

Babbitt, Bruce, 75
Baca, Lawrence (Pawnee), 71, 238
Bacone Junior College, Oklahoma,
   186, 250
Bad Heart Bull, Wesley (Sioux),
   129–130
Baghdad, Iraq, 158
Bald Eagle, Dave (Sioux), 256
Banks, Dennis (Chippewa), 120,
   127, 130–131, 211, 247
Barth, John, 235, 236, 238
Battle of the Little Big Horn
   (1876), 3, 5, 114, 208, 236, 245
Bay of Quinte Mohawk, 217
Bear Butte, South Dakota,
   164–165
Bear, Little Light (Creek), 47–49
Beatty, Willard, 91, 92
The Beet Queen (1986), 212
Begay, Harrison (Navajo), 187
Behind the Trail of Broken Treaties
   (1974), 240–241
Bell, Terrel, 100
Bellecourt, Clyde (Chippewa), 121,
   127
Bellecourt, Vernon (Chippewa),
   121, 126, 127
Belle Fourche River, South Dakota,
   257
Bennett, Robert (Oneida), 59–60
Berger, Thomas, 235, 236, 253
Berkeley, California, 183, 247. *See
   also* University of California,
   Berkeley
Berkhofer, Robert F., Jr., 4, 235
Bernal, Paul (Taos Pueblo), 38
Bernstein, Alison R., 10, 13, 47
Berson, Misha, 261
Bibby, Brian, 170
Big Brother and the Holding
   Company, 233
Big Horn Mountains, Wyoming,
   172
Bighorn River, Montana, 160
Bigman, Art (Crow), 172
Big Mountain, 147

Big Tree, John (Seneca), 252
Bingo. *See* Indian gaming
The Bingo Palace (1994), 212
Bird, Gloria (Spokane), 213–214
Bison, 180
Black Hills Alliance (BHA), 146
Black Hills National Monument,
   South Dakota, 124
Black Hills, South Dakota, 124,
   145–146
Black Legs Society (*Tokonga*), 18
Black Mesa, Arizona, 140–141,
   142–143, 147
Black Panther Party, 120
Black Power, 118, 119
Blackfeet, 14, 53, 58, 72, 83, 94,
   122, 176, 207–208, 222
Blatchford, Herbert (Navajo), 109,
   110–112, 114
The Blessing Way (1970), 241
Bloodthirsty savage, image of, 2–3,
   234, 251, 252, 260–261
Blue Dog, Kurt (Sioux), 158–159
Blue Eagle, Acee (Creek/Pawnee),
   186
Blue Lake, New Mexico, 38, 65, 66,
   69, 123
Boarding schools, 27, 29, 30, 40,
   91, 99, 176
Boat-building, traditional,
   178–179
Boldt, George H., 115–116, 160
Bommelyn, Loren (Tolowa), 178
Borrego Pass, New Mexico, 95
Bowen, J.R. (Yurok), 183
Bowman, Ellison (Navajo), 10
Boy Scouts of America, 230, 233
Brand, Stewart, 232, 233
Brando, Marlon, 114
Brant, Beth (Bay of Quinte
   Mohawk), 217
Breaking the Iron Bonds (1990),
   149
Brennan, William J., 163
Bridge of Respect Law (1989),
   166–167
Broder, Patricia Janis, 185,
   192–193, 196

Broken Arrow (1950), 252–253, 255, 257
The Broken Chain (1993), 258
The Broken Cord (1989), 86, 240
Brophy, William, 35
Brown, Cosey (Navajo), 5–6
Brown, Dee, 130, 238
Brown, Raymond (Navajo), 96
Bruce, Louis R. (Mohawk / Sioux), 64, 127–129
Bruhac, Joseph (Abenaki), 202–203, 220–221, 250
Brule, 125
Bruner, Joseph (Creek), 34, 106
Buffalo, 180
Buffalo Bill and the Indians (1976), 255
Buffalo Gap, South Dakota, 129–130
Bureau of Indian Affairs, 14–15, 16, 23, 26, 27, 82, 83, 92–93, 99–100, 106, 111, 116, 124, 133, 141, 162, 174, 176, 190
  acknowledgment process, 159
  Clinton administration, 74–75
  Collier era, 29–35
  Indian gaming, 154
  Kennedy administration, 54–56
  Nixon administration, 64–70
  occupation of headquarters by activists, 105, 126–129, 210, 241
  termination policy, 35–46
  relocation policy, 46–50
Burke Act (1906), 28
Burnette, Robert (Sioux), 107, 116, 126, 127, 238
Burns, Ric, 258
Bury My Heart at Wounded Knee (1971), 130, 238
Bush, George, 74
Butler, Raymond (Blackfeet), 53, 83, 238

Cabazon Band of Mission Indians, 153–154
Cable News Network (CNN), 247, 258

Caddo, 196–197
Cahuilla, 94, 107, 125, 181, 238, 242
California, 8, 10, 14, 25, 37, 40, 46, 47–49, 54, 72, 78–80, 87, 93–94, 97, 120, 121–123, 125, 126, 140, 142, 153–154, 156, 159, 174, 214, 248
California Indian Education Association, 94
California Indians, 37, 38, 59, 94, 107, 125, 181, 231, 233
  acknowledgment process, 151
  artists, 194
  economic development by, 153
  gaming, 153–154, 156
  G-O Road controversy, 162–163
  language revival, 176, 177–178
  Point Conception controversy, 163–164
  poverty of, 78–80
  reparation issue, 166–168
  traditional culture preservation, 181, 183
  writers, 214. *See also* names of individuals and individual tribes
California Mission Indian Federation, 107
California-Nevada Indian Gambling Association, 156
California State Advisory Commission on Indian Affairs, 78
California Wilderness Act (1980), 162
Cambra, Rosemary (Ohlone), 167
Campbell, Ben Nighthorse (Northern Cheyenne), 194–195, 245, 248–249, 251
Camp Pendleton, California, 8
Canada, 26
Cannon, T. C. (Caddo / Kiowa), 196–197, 209
Canyon de Chelly, Arizona, 152
Captivity narratives, 3
Carlisle Indian Industrial School, Pennsylvania, 90
Carman, John, 258–259

Carmichael, Stokley, 127
Carter, Jimmy, 72–73, 163
Casinos, 153–157, 162, 212, 251
Castaneda, Carlos, 237, 255
Castillo, Adam (Cahuilla), 107
Castillo, Bobby, 247
Castillo, Edward D. (Cahuilla /
   Luiseño), 238, 256
Central Arizona Project, 150
Central Washington State
   University, 94
Ceramics, 185, 194
Ceremony (1977), 209
Chaco Canyon, New Mexico, 210
Chahta Enterprises, Mississippi,
   150
Champagne, Duane, 238
Chandler, Jeff, 252
Chemehuevi, 162, 178, 253
Cherokee, 54, 89, 90, 159, 176,
   205, 238
   actors, 255, 257, 262
   allotment policy, 28
   economic development by, 151,
      157
   relocation policy, 49
   removal policy, 24–25
   writers, 203, 215–216, 218–219,
      242. See also names of
      individuals
Cheyenne, 14, 73, 125, 155, 172,
   176, 186, 236, 245, 246, 250,
   artists, 180, 250
   economic development by, 140,
      141, 143, 145
   education, 102
   repatriation issue, 168–169
   termination policy, 53, 56
   traditional culture, 180. See also
      names of individuals
Cheyenne River Sioux, 16, 165,
   172–173
Chicago, Illinois, 34, 47, 50, 55,
   85, 86–87, 109–110, 120, 150,
   175, 243
Chickasaw, 90, 218
"Chief" (form of address), 10, 12,
   244, 257

Children, 72–73, 90–102, 161,
   176, 179, 181–184. See also
   Education, Infant mortality
Chinle, Arizona, 94–95, 152
Chino, Wendell (Apache), 62
Chippewa, 75, 250
   activists, 120–121, 122, 124, 221,
      247
   artists, 195–196
   education, 95, 97
   gaming, 154
   termination policy, 42
   during World War II, 10, 14
   writers, 209–212. See also names
      of individuals
Chiricahua Apache, 188, 190, 192
Choctaw, 80, 90, 150, 195
Christianity, 11, 24, 27, 30,
   173–174, 240
Chumash, 163–164, 177
Church of Jesus Christ of Latter-
   Day Saints (Mormons), 173
Churchill, Ward (Creek / Cherokee
   Métis), 238
Cisneros, Henry, 75
Citizens Equal Rights Alliance
   (CERA), 160
Citizenship, 5, 19, 27
Civil rights, 19–20, 30
Civil Rights Act (1968), 62
Clarke, Blake, 37
Clearfield, Utah, 13
Cleveland Indians (baseball team),
   244
Cleveland, Ohio, 47, 244
Clinton, Bill, 74–75, 157
Coal resources, 139–143
Coalition of Indian Controlled
   School Boards, 95
Cochise (Apache), 252
Coconino National Forest, Arizona,
   164
Code talkers, 7–9, 18, 140, 193,
   261
Cody, Iron Eyes (Cherokee), 255
Cody, William F. "Buffalo Bill,"
   236–237, 255
Coeur d'Alene, 43, 118, 161

Collier, John, 6, 16, 23, 55, 91, 107, 176, 186
  background, 29–30
  resignation, 34–35
  tenure as Indian Affairs Commissioner, 29–35
Collins, Anita Whitefeather (Walker River Paiute), 181
Colón, Cristóbal, 248
Colorado, 14, 107, 124, 126, 142, 195, 247
Columbia River, 114, 203, 216
Columbus quincentennial (1992), 246–248
Colville Confederated Tribes, 155
Colville reservation, Washington, 49, 59
Comanche, 49, 140, 183, 255
Come to Power (1974), 220
Community Action Projects, 57, 65
Community Health Representatives (CHRs), 84–85, 88
Concerned Community Indian Movement, Los Angeles, 182
Confederated Tribes of the Siletz and Grand Ronde, 277
Confederated Tribes of the Warm Springs, 151–152, 177
Congress of Industrial Organizations (CIO), 14
Connecticut, 154, 251
Cooper, James Fenimore, 257
Copway, George, 220
Cornell University, 84
Cornplanter (Seneca), 108
Costner, Kevin, 255–257, 258
Costo, Rupert (Cahuilla), 94, 107, 125, 238, 242
Council of Energy Resource Tribes (CERT), 140–142, 146, 147–148
Counterculture, 232–233, 237
County of Oneida v. Oneida Indian Nation (1985), 72
The Covered Wagon (1923), 3
Covington, Lucy (Nez Perce), 59
Cow Creek Band of Umpquas, 159
Coyote, 87, 194, 209–210

Coyote in the Mission (1989), 194
Coyote's Penis (1990), 87
Crawford, James, 176
Crazy Horse (Sioux), 245
Crazy Horse (1952), 253
Cree, 95, 115, 195
Creek, 34, 38, 186
  allotment policy, 28
  gaming, 154–155
  relocation policy, 47–49
  writers, 217, 220. *See also* names of individuals
Crescent City, California, 178
Crow, 54, 145, 160, 172, 182
  economic development by, 125, 140–141
  rejection of Indian Reorganization Act, 32
  termination policy, 56
  during World War II, 16, 18. *See also* names of individuals
Crow Dog, Leonard (Sioux), 233
Crow Dog, Mary (Sioux), 258
The Crown of Columbus (1991), 240
Croynyn, George, 220
Crumbo, Woodrow Wilson (Creek/Potawatomi), 186
Cummins, John (Crow), 54
Curtis, Tony, 253
Custer Died for Your Sins (1969), 240
Custer, George Armstrong, 5, 114, 208, 230, 257
Custer National Battlefield Monument, Montana, 245
Custer, South Dakota, 130, 131

D-Q University, California, 97, 239
Da, Tony (Pueblo), 194
Dallas, Texas, 47
Danay, Richard Glazer (Mohawk), 231
Dance, 11–12, 15, 18, 26, 181, 182, 203, 225, 230–231, 259
Dance Me Outside (1995), 259
Dances with Wolves (1990), 255–257

Dark Night of the Lakota, 172
Darkness in Saint Louis Bearheart
(1978), 210
Dartmouth College, New
Hampshire, 239, 242
Daves, Delmer, 252
David, Neil (Hopi), 193
Davis, California, 97. *See also*
University of California, Davis
Dawes Act (1887), 27, 106
Dawes, Henry L., 27
The Death of Jim Loney (1979), 208
Declaration of Indian Purpose
(1954), 108
Declaration of Indian Purpose
(1961), 110
Deer, Ada (Menominee), 67, 74
Deer Rattle-Deer Dancer (1981),
194
Defense industry employment,
13–17
Delaware, 176, 259, 260
Deloria, Phil (Standing Rock
Sioux), 261
Deloria, Vine, Jr. (Standing Rock
Sioux), 35, 59, 60, 69, 116, 117,
125, 171, 221, 222, 240, 261
De los Angeles, Andy (Snoqualmie),
244
Demmert, William G., Jr. (Tlingit /
Sioux), 100
Denver, Colorado, 14, 46, 107,
126, 247
Deschinny, Daniel (Navajo), 168
Desert Willow, Arizona, 84
The Devil's Doorway (1950), 253
Diabetes, 89, 180
Dick, John (Navajo) 95
Diet, 179–180
Dime novels, 3
Discrimination
in the armed forces, 9–10
during wartime employment, 14,
39
Disease, 28–29, 78, 81–82, 83, 88,
89, 180
Division of Economic
Development, 56

Dorris, Michael (Modoc), 86,
239–240, 256, 261
Driving Hawk, Ed, 59
Ducheneaux, Lester (Lakota), 180
Duel in the Sun (1946), 252
Dunn, Dorothy, 187, 188

Eagle Dancer (1981), 192
Eagle feathers, 74, 168, 218, 248
Eagle's Wing (1979), 255
Earth Mother (1990), 194
Earth Song, Sky Spirit (1992), 213
Eastern Cherokee, 125, 151, 238,
242
Echo-Hawk, Walter (Pawnee), 165
Economic development, 56, 68
agriculture, 51
energy resources, 139–150
gaming, 153–157, 162
manufacturing, 149–151
tourism, 151–153
Economic Development
Administration, 57
Economic Opportunity Act (1964),
56–57
Education, 40, 73, 75, 77, 78–81,
90–102, 105
assimilation, 27, 28, 90, 92
cultural pluralism, 30
expansion in Collier era, 31–33
Native American initiatives,
93–96
preservation of traditional culture,
183–184
postwar opportunities, 18–19. *See
also* Boarding Schools,
Children, GI Bill, Indian Self-
Determination and Education
Assistance Act, Native
American Studies, Textbooks,
Tribally controlled Indian
colleges
Education and the American Indian
(1974), 91
Edmo, Ed (Shoshone-Bannock),
216
Eisenhower, Dwight, 40, 41, 43,
44, 55

Elementary and Secondary
    Education Act (1965), 93
Ellis Island, New York, 124
Emergency Conservation Works, 32
Emmons, Glenn, 40–41, 47
Employment, 31, 46, 49, 58,
    77–81
  during World War II, 13–18
  postwar problems, 17–18
*Employment Division of Oregon v.
    Smith* (1990), 175
Endrezze, Anita (Yaqui), 214–215
Energy resources, 139–149
Environmental protection, 142,
    145, 161
Erdrich, Louise (Chippewa),
    211–212, 240
Ervin, Sam, 62
Eskimo, 66–67, 151
Esselen, 177

FAS. *See* Fetal alcohol syndrome
    (FAS)
Federal Bureau of Investigation
    (FBI), 135
Ferron, Roberta (Rosebud Sioux),
    86
Fetal alcohol syndrome (FAS), 86,
    240
Field Museum, Chicago, 166
Film images, 1–4, 12, 211–212,
    251–262
Film Quarterly, 256
Fine arts movement, Native
    American, 171, 184–197, 229
Firearms, right to purchase, 19
Fisher, Llevando (Northern
    Cheyenne), 169
Fishing rights, 44–45, 72,
    112–116, 159, 160–161
Fish-ins, 114–116, 117, 119, 127
Five Civilized Tribes, 68
Fixico, Donald L. (Creek / Seminole /
    Shawnee / Sac and Fox), 38, 50,
    238
Flagstaff, Arizona, 46, 143
The Flaming Frontier (1926), 3
Flap (1970), 253

Flathead, 40, 173, 204–205
Flathead reservation, Montana, 160
Florida, 40, 153
Fonda, Jane, 115, 258
Fonda, Henry, 252
Fools Crow (1986), 208
Fools Crow, Frank (Oglala Sioux),
    134
Forbes, Jack (Powhatan / Lenape),
    69, 239
Ford, Gerald, 70
Ford, John, 2, 4, 251–252
Fort Apache (1948), 252
Fort Berthold Mandan, 80, 141
Fort Bliss, Texas, 10
Fort Laramie Treaty (1868), 122,
    133, 256
Fort Lawton, Washington, 124
Fort Peck reservation, Montana, 5
Fort Sill, Oklahoma, 7
Fort Wingate, Arizona, 13, 14
*Four American Indian Literary
    Masters* (1982), 211
Four Corners, 142–143
Foxwoods Casino, Connecticut,
    154
Francis, David (Passamaquoddy),
    177
Freeland, Daniel (Navajo), 87
French, Philip, 256
Fry, J. Lightfoot (Mohawk), 246
Fund for the Republic, 78

Gabrielino, 248
Gaiashkibos (Lake Superior
    Chippewa), 75
Gallup, New Mexico, 6, 17, 110
Gambling. *See* Gaming
Gaming, 153–157, 212, 251
Garment, Leonard, 134
Garrison, Minnesota, 154
Garry, Joseph (Coeur d'Alene), 43,
    46, 118
Gasquet-Orleans Road controversy.
    See G-O Road controversy
Geiogamah, Hanay (Kiowa /
    Delaware), 259, 260–262
General Allotment Act (1887), 27

George, Chief Dan (Squamish), 253
Georgia, 25, 29, 118
Gerard, Forrest J. (Blackfeet), 72
Geronimo (Apache), 25, 252, 257
Geronimo (1962), 252
Geronimo (1993), 257–258
The Ghostway (1985), 241
Giago, Tim (Oglala Lakota), 247
GI Bill of Rights (1944), 18, 92,
    106, 231
Gila River, Arizona, 151
Gila River reservation, Arizona, 16
Gilbert, Madonna (Sioux), 146
Gilstrap, L. L., 12
Glancy, Diane (Cherokee), 215
God Is Red (1973), 240
Going for the Rain (1976),
    223–224
The Good Journey (1977), 224
Gorman, R. C. (Navajo), 193, 196
G-O Road controversy, 162
Goseyun, Carla (White Mountain
    Apache), 173
The Gourd Dancer (1976), 221
Grand Canyon, Arizona, 66, 152
Grant, Rodney A. (Omaha), 260
Grant, Ulysses S., 26, 29
Graves, Theodore D., 86
The Grateful Dead, 233
Great Smoky Mountain National
    Park, North Carolina, 151
Green, Rayna (Cherokee), 238,
    242, 247
Green River, Washington, 114
Greene, Graham (Oneida), 258
Gregory, Dick, 114
Griever (1987), 210
Gros Ventre, 207–208, 222
*Guide to Research on North
    American Indians* (1983), 240
Gulf Oil Company, 141

Häagen-Dazs ice cream, 150
Hagan, William T., 28
Hale, Albert (Navajo), 156
Hamline University, Minnesota,
    168
Handbook for Boys (1948), 230

Hanta Yo (1979), 241, 255
Harjo, Joy (Creek), 217
Harjo, Suzan Shown (Cheyenne /
    Arapaho), 73, 246
Harris, LaDonna (Comanche), 140
Harvard University, Massachusetts,
    167
Haskell Indian Nations University,
    Kansas, 100
Hastings, Dennis (Omaha), 122
Havard, James (Choctaw /
    Chippewa), 195
Havasupai, 66
Hawkeye, 260
Hayes, Ira (Pima), 17, 253
Health, 28–29, 33, 45, 58, 73, 75,
    77–81, 81–90, 91, 105, 150,
    154
Heard Museum, Arizona, 181
Henry, Jeannette (Eastern
    Cherokee), 94, 125, 238, 242
Here Is Your Hobby (1966), 230
Herrera, Joe (Cochiti Pueblo),
    188–189, 197, 221
Heth, Charlotte (Cherokee), 238
Heye, George Gustav, 250
Heye Center, 250–251
Hiawatha (1952), 253
Hickel, Walter J., 65
Hilbert, Vi, 260
Hill, John (Crow), 172
Hill, Ruth Beebe, 241, 255
Hill, Walter, 257
Hillerman, Tony, 241–242
Hinckley, Minnesota, 154
Hinton, Leanne, 177
Hippies, 232–233
Historic sites, interpretation of, 245
Hitler, Adolph, 4, 5
HIV. *See* Human immunodeficiency
    virus (HIV)
Hobbyist movement, 230–231
Hoffman, Dustin, 253
Hogan, Linda (Chickasaw), 218
Hohokam, 184
Honanie, Delbridge (Hopi), 193
Hondo (1953), 234
Hoover, Herbert, 29

Hopi, 152, 164, 233
  artists, 185, 187, 190–191,
    192–193
  Cultural Preservation Office, 181
  economic development by, 125
  environmental protection, 142,
    143
  gaming decision, 156–157
  land dispute with Navajo,
    146–147
  writers, 202. *See also* names of
    individuals
House Concurrent Resolution 108
  (1953), 40–46, 59–60, 107,
  repudiation of, 61, 64–65
House Made of Dawn (1968),
  201–203, 205–206, 209
Houser, Allan (Chiricahua Apache),
  190, 192
Housing, 15, 58, 77–81, 83–84,
  105, 120, 150
Howard, Edgar, 30
Howe, Oscar (Yanktonai Sioux),
  188, 189, 194, 197, 221
Hózhó, 241
Hualapai, 152
Human immunodeficiency virus
  (HIV), 87
Humphrey, Hubert, 61
Humqaq (Point Conception,
  California), 163–164
Hupa, 94, 153, 162, 166, 178, 183
Huron Potawatomi, 247

Ickes, Harold, 12, 15–16, 30
Idaho, 43, 58, 94, 146, 181
Illinois, 34, 47, 50, 55, 85, 86–87,
  109–110, 120, 124, 150, 175,
  243–244
Images of Native Americans
  American literature, 234–238
  films, 1–4, 211, 251–262
  popular culture, 230–233
  shaped by Native Americans,
    238–242
  during World War II, 12–13
Income, 14, 77–81, 150
Indian (1976), 191–192

Indian Actors Workshop, 259
Indian Alcohol and Substance
  Abuse Prevention and Treatment
  Act (1968), 87
Indian Arts and Crafts Board,
  31–32, 40, 186
Indian Business Development
  Program, 68
Indian Centers, 119, 120, 121, 122,
  183
Indian Child Welfare Act (1978),
  72–73
Indian Civil Rights Act (1968),
  62–63, 71
Indian Claims Commission (ICC),
  35–38, 65, 77, 124
Indian Country (1984), 162
Indian Country Today, 247
Indian Education (1969), 98
Indian Education Act (1972),
  98–99
Indian Financing Act (1974),
  68
Indian Gaming Regulatory Act
  (1988), 154, 155
Indian Health Care Improvement
  Act (1976), 88
Indian Health Service (IHS),
  82–90
The Indian Historian, 242
Indian Lawyer (1990), 208
Indian Nations at Risk (1991),
  100–101
Indian Reorganization Act (1934),
  30–33, 68, 70, 106, 107, 133,
  134
Indian Revolving Loan Fund, 68
Indian Rights Association, 33
Indian Self-Determination and
  Education Assistance Act
  (1975), 70–71, 74, 88, 99, 159,
  183
The Indian Wars (1913), 3
Indian with a Beer Can (1969),
  191–192
Indians (1968), 235, 236–237,
  238, 253, 255
Indians of All Tribes, 122–123

Infant mortality, among Native
Americans, 45, 78, 88, 161
Inn of the Mountain Gods, New
Mexico, 151
Institute of American Indian Arts
(IAIA), 100, 190–192, 196, 218
International Indian Treaty
Council, 158
Inter Tribal Bison Cooperative
(ITBC), 180
Inupiat, 180
Iroquois, 152–153, 182–183, 258
Iroquois Social Dance Group,
182–183
Iwo Jima, Battle of (1945), 6, 8–9, 17

Jack, Roger (Colville), 218
Jackson, Andrew, 24–25
Jackson, Henry, 59
Jackson, James (Quinault), 63
Japanese, 4, 8–10, 245
Japanese Americans, 6, 16, 39, 47
Jefferson, Thomas, 24
Jemez Pueblo, 205
Jemison, Alice Lee (Seneca), 34
Jenkins, Leigh, 181
Jewelry, 190, 194–195
Jicarilla Apache, 141–142
Jim, Russell (Yakama), 146
Jim Thorpe, All American (1951),
253
Job Corps Conservation Centers,
58
Johnson, E. Pauline (Mohawk), 220
Johnson, Lyndon B., 56–63, 64,
65, 121
Johnson-O'Malley Act (1934), 91,
93, 99
Johnston, Philip, 8
Jones, Jennifer, 252
Jones, JoAnn (Winnebago), 75
Jones, Mary (Konkow), 178
Jones, Myron (Tuscarora), 94
Jonson, Raymond, 188
Jorgensen, Joseph G., 80
Josephy, Alvin M., Jr., 72, 112
Journey to Ixtlan (1972), 237
Juaneño, 166

Kabotie, Fred (Hopi), 187
Kabotie, Mike (Hopi), 193
Kachinas, 143, 164, 185
Kah-Nee-Ta Lodge, Oregon,
151–152
Kansas, 40, 100
Karuk, 162, 178, 183
Kauffmann, Stanley, 253
Keeler, W. W. (Cherokee), 54
Keluche, Gene A. (Wintu), 250
Kennedy, Edward, 98
Kennedy, John F., 54–56,
70–71, 110
Kennedy Report (1969), 97–98
Kennedy, Robert, 97–98, 120
Kenny, Maurice (Mohawk),
222–223
Kesey, Ken, 235–236, 255
Khus, Pilulaw (Chumash), 164
Kickapoo, 159, 176, 181
Kidwell, Clara Sue (Choctaw/
Chippewa), 250
Kieffer, John (Spokane), 156
Kieyoomie, Joe Lee (Navajo), 8
Killing Custer (1994), 208
King, Martin Luther, Jr., 117–118,
120
King, Thomas (Cherokee),
218–219, 237
Kinzua Dam controversy, 108
Kiowa, 99, 183, 259, 260–261
artists, 196–197
relocation policy, 49
writers, 205–207, 221–222, 238
during World War II, 18. See also
names of individuals
Kisto, Tara (Pima), 181–182
Kit Carson (1903), 2
The Kit Carson Campaign (1982),
239
Klallam, 216
Klamath, 16, 31, 40, 45
Knox, Margaret L., 160
Kolina, Emms (Montana
Chippewa), 42
Kopit, Arthur, 235, 236, 238, 253,
255
Korean War, 109

Krauss, Michael, 176
Kuntsler, William, 131

LaBarre, Weston, 237
Laduke, Winona (Ojibwa), 146
La Farge, Oliver, 5
Laguna Pueblo, 208–209, 216
Lake Havasu, California, 162
Lake Superior Chippewa, 75,
  124
Lakota, 125, 164, 172, 173, 180,
  213, 241, 256
Lakota Woman (1993), 258
Lame Deer, Archie Fire (Lakota),
  164
L'Amour, Louis, 234
Lancaster, Burt, 253
Land controversies, 108–109, 124,
  203
  energy development, 145–147
  Bear Butte, 164–165
  G-O road, 162–163
  Penobscots and Passamaquoddies,
    150
  Point Conception, 163–164
Land transfers, 74
  during early years of American
    Indian policy, 24–28
  reversed in Collier Era, 30, 32–33
  under termination policy, 36–45
Languages, revival of traditional,
  175–178
LaPena, Frank (Wintu /
  Nomtipom), 194
Lassen National Park, California,
  124
The Last of the Mohicans (1992),
  257
Las Vegas, Nevada, 142
LaVelle, John (Santee Sioux), 165
Lawrence, Kansas, 100
Lawton, Oklahoma, 196
Leivas, Matthew (Chemehuevi),
  162
Lenape, 69–70, 239
Lesley, Craig, 213
Levitas, Gloria, 220
Lidz, Franz, 245

*The Life and Adventures of Joaquin
  Murieta* (1854), 203
Limbaugh, Rush, 245
Lincoln, Kenneth, 202, 220
Liquified natural gas (LNG),
  163–164
Literature, 201–202
  novels, 203–212
  short stories, 212–219
  poetry, 219–226. *See also* names of
    individual writers
Little Big Horn National Battlefield
  Monument, Montana, 245
Little Big Man (1964), 236, 253
Little Big Man (1970), 253, 255
Livermore, Earl (Blackfeet), 122
LNG. *See* Liquified natural gas
  (LNG)
Lohah, Charles (Osage), 140
Loloma, Charles (Hopi), 190–191
Lomakema, Millard Dawa (Hopi),
  193
Long Beach State University,
  California, 166
Longest Walk (1978), 147
Looking Horse, Arvol (Lakota),
  172–173, 256
Lookout, Fred (Osage), 42
Los Angeles, California, 14, 46,
  47–49, 50, 85, 121, 126, 142,
  173, 177, 182–183, 205, 233
Lotah, Kote (Chumash), 163
Lourie, Dick, 220
Love Medicine (1984), 211
Lower Brule reservation, South
  Dakota, 18
Luiseño, 190, 191–192
Lundgren, Dan, 156
Lurie, Nancy Oestreich, 37, 232,
  240
Lytle, Clifford, 35

Macalester College, Minnesota, 215
MacArthur, Douglas, 6
MacDonald, Peter (Navajo), 129,
  140–141, 147–149
Magic Images (1981), 193
Maidu, 194

Mail, Patricia, 88
Maine, 68, 150
Makah, 113
Mama and Papa Have the Going Home to Shiprock Blues (1966), 196
Mama Poems (1984), 222
A Man Called Horse (1970), 253–254
Mandan, 80, 253
Manifest Manners (1994), 210–211
The Manitou (1978), 255
Mankiller, Wilma (Cherokee), 75, 157
Mann, Michael, 257
Manpower Development and Training Act (1962), 55–56
Many Farms, Arizona, 95
Maricopa, 89
Marsden, Michael T., 3, 251, 252, 255
Marshall, Lyle (Hupa), 153
Martinez, Julian (Pueblo), 185
Martinez, Maria (Pueblo), 185, 194
Mascots, controversy over Indians as, 242–245
Mashantucket Pequot, 154, 251
Massachusetts, 27, 124, 125, 177
Massachusetts Institute of Technology (MIT), 177
Massayesva, Vernon (Hopi), 143
Material culture, revival of traditional, 178–180
Mathews, John Joseph (Osage), 203, 205, 208
Matthiessen, Peter, 162
Mayflower II, 124
McGovern, George, 61
McGuinness, Aims, 256
McKay, Marshall (Wintun), 156
McKinney, Roger (Kickapoo), 181
McNickle, D'Arcy (Flathead), 204, 208, 211
Means, Lanada (Oglala Sioux), 122
Means, Russell (Oglala Sioux), 121, 127, 130–135, 146, 147, 221, 244, 245, 247, 251, 260

Medicine Creek Treaty (1854), 112, 113
Medicine Crow, Joseph (Crow), 18
Medicine men, medicine women, 11, 125, 130, 134, 142, 147, 162, 163, 164, 168, 172–174, 175, 180, 202, 210, 255, 256,
Medicine Wheel, Wyoming, 172
Menominee, 40, 43–45, 67
Menominee Restoration Act (1973), 67–68, 158
Meriam Report (1928), 29, 35, 57, 78, 91, 98
Meriam, Lewis, 29, 78
Mescalero Apache, 15, 146, 151, 182
Mexico, 26, 174, 193
Miami, 37–38
Miles, Diane (Nez Perce / Paiute / Shoshone), 181
Mille Lac Chippewa, 154
Miller, Bill (Cheyenne River Sioux), 165
Mineral rights, 125
Mining, 125, 139–149
Minneapolis, Minnesota, 14, 85, 120, 121
Minnesota, 14, 41, 85, 97, 120–121, 122, 124, 154, 165–166, 168, 183, 212, 218
Mishongnovi, Arizona, 152
Mission Indians, 153–154
Missionaries, 24, 173
Mississippi, 24–25, 80, 118, 150
Missouri, 47
Mitchell, George (Chippewa), 120
Miwok, 202
Modoc, 68, 86, 158, 239–240
Mohave, 178
Mohawk, 13, 64, 153, 176, 246
  activists, 110–111, 113, 122
  actors, 259
  artists, 231
  economic development by, 153
  gaming, 155
  writers, 217, 220, 222, 223. *See also* names of individuals

Momaday, N. Scott (Kiowa), 201,
203, 205–207, 208, 209, 211,
221–222, 223, 225, 238, 240,
247
Montana, 5, 16, 30, 32, 40, 42, 45,
58, 94, 96, 97, 125, 141, 143,
145, 160, 172, 204, 208, 225,
245
Montana Chippewa, 42
Montgomery, Alabama, 117–118
Mormons. *See* Church of Jesus
Christ of Latter-Day Saints
Morongo reservation, California,
181
Morrison, George (Chippewa),
195–196
Morton v. Mancari (1974), 68–69
Morton, Rogers C. B., 68
Moses, Marya (Tulalip), 179
Motion pictures. *See* Film images
Mount Adams, Washington, 94
Mount Rushmore National
Memorial, South Dakota, 124,
125
Movement of Non-Aligned
Nations, 158
Movies. *See* Film images
Mundt, Karl, 34
Muskogee, Oklahoma, 186–187
Mussolini, Benito, 5
Myer, Dillon S., 39–40, 47, 92–93
Myers, Larry (Pomo), 166, 167
Mystic Warrior (1984), 255

Nabokov, Peter, 17
Nachbar, Jack, 3, 251, 252, 255
Nakai, Raymond (Navajo), 95, 140
Napikwans, 208
Narragansett, 159
Nash, Gerald D., 11, 107
Nash, Philleo, 55–56, 59
National Advisory Council on
Indian Education, 99
National Association of
Evangelicals, 175
National Congress of American
Indians (NCAI), 35–36, 46, 57,
59, 65, 75, 109–110, 116–117,
118, 126
advent of, 204
challenged by activists, 119–120
criticized Reagan policy, 73
fought termination policy, 43,
107–108
opposed Public Law 280, 62
opposed Wounded Knee
occupation, 131–133
supported self-determination
policy, 60, 61
tribal governments and,
107–108
National Council of Churches, 33,
175
National Council on Indian
Opportunity, 61, 65, 121
National Indian Education
Association (NIEA), 98
National Indian Youth Council
(NIYC), 118–119, 135, 232
advent of, 110–112
advocacy of fishing rights,
112–116
challenged by militants, 119
controversy over Indian mascots,
243
Trail of Broken Treaties, 126
National Museum of American
History, 247
National Museum of the American
Indian (NMAI), 248–251, 258
National Study of American Indian
Education, 94
National Tribal Chairmen's
Association (NTCA), 72, 121,
129, 131–133
Native American Church, 174–175,
192
Native American Communications
Council, 246
Native American Fine Arts Society,
Los Angeles, 183
Native American Grave Protection
and Repatriation Act (1990),
167–168

Native American Heritage
Commission (NAHC),
166–167, 239
Native American Languages Act
(1990), 177
Native American Renaissance
(1983), 202
Native American Rights Fund,
159, 160
Native American Studies, 205,
238–239
The Native Americans (1994), 258
*Native Americans in the Twentieth
Century* (1984), 27, 50, 71, 81
Natural gas resources, 139, 140,
142, 163–164
Navajo, 32, 56, 75, 84, 86, 87, 129,
142–143, 146–149, 156, 164,
185, 231, 239, 241
artists, 187, 188, 193, 196
economic development by,
140–141, 142–143, 152
education, 92–93, 94–97, 99
land dispute with Hopi, 146–148
Native American Church, 174
repatriation, 168
writers, 203, 217–218, 226
during World War II, 5, 6, 7,
8–10, 13–14, 19. *See also*
names of individuals
Navajo and Hopi Indian Relocation
Commission, 147
Navajo Community College,
95–97, 99
Navajo Community College Bill
(1971), 95
Navajo-Cornell Field Health
Project, 84
Navajo Curriculum Center, 95
Navajo Historical Preservation
Office, 168
Navajo History (1971), 95
Navajo-Hopi land dispute,
146–147
Navajo-Hopi Land Settlement Act
(1974), 147
Navajo Nation Film Office, 260

Navajo reservation, 6, 14, 18, 56,
94, 125, 139
Navajo Special Education Program,
92
NCAI Sentinel, 107
Nebraska, 28, 30, 40, 41
Nehalem, 181
Neighborhood Youth Corps, 58
Nelson, Ralph, 253
Nevada, 142, 143, 145, 180
The New Indians (1968), 114,
237–238
New Mexico, 6, 13–14, 15, 17, 19,
29, 38, 40, 47, 58, 60–61, 65,
75, 80, 87, 94, 95, 100, 109,
110, 116, 123, 142, 146, 151,
210, 221, 225
The New Trail, 54–56, 70–71
New York, 28, 29, 72, 94, 98,
108–109, 124, 125, 148,
152–153, 155, 161–162, 220,
233, 245–246, 248, 250–251, 259
New York (1961), 195
Newlands Reclamation Project, 145
Newspapers, Native American, 125,
153, 220
Nez Perce, 59, 146, 181
Nez Perce National Historic Park,
Idaho, 181
Niatum, Duane (Klallam), 216, 220
Nichols, Mark (Cabazon), 154
Nichols, John, 35
Nightwing (1979), 255
Nike corporation, 151
Nisqually, 112
Nisqually River, Washington, 114
Nixon, Richard M., 64–70, 72, 74,
123, 126, 127, 133–134
Noble savage image, 2–3,
234–235, 251–253, 254, 255,
257, 260, 261
Nooksack, 216–217, 219, 242
Nordwall, Adam (Chippewa), 122
Norick, Frank, 167–168
North American Indian Ecumenical
Movement, 172
North Carolina, 62, 151

North Dakota, 80, 97, 141, 145, 212
Northern Cheyenne, 172, 180, 245
  economic development by, 125, 140, 141, 145
  education, 102
  environmental protection, 143
  opposition to termination policy, 53, 56
  repatriation issue, 168–169. See also names of individuals
Northern Exposure, 260
Northern Paiute, 66
Northwest Indian Fisheries Department, 116
Northwest Native American Writers Association, 213–214
Northwest Passage (1940), 4, 251
Novels and novelists, 201, 203–212. See also names of individuals
Nuclear wastes, storage of, 146
Nuvamsa, Peter, Sr. (Hopi), 233

Oakes, Richard (Mohawk), 122
Oakland, California, 47, 120
Oates, Joyce Carol, 237
O'Connell, Barbara, 168
O'Connor, Sandra Day, 163
Offering the Pipe (1978), 192
Office for Indian Progress (1967), 58
Office of American Indian Trust, 74
Office of Economic Opportunity (OEO), 56–57, 65, 94
Ogallalah (1911), 2
Oglala Lakota College, South Dakota, 90
Oglala Sioux, 121, 122, 125, 129–135, 246, 247
Oglala Sioux Civil Rights Organization (OSCRO), 130, 135
Oglala Sioux Nation, 133, 135
Ohio, 47, 125
Ohlone, 159, 167, 177
Ohlone-Muwekma, 159
Oil resources, 139, 140–142

The Ojibway Conquest (1850), 220
Oklahoma, 7, 18, 28, 47–49, 58, 68, 97, 110, 140, 154, 155, 168, 186, 196, 205, 206, 213
Oklahoma City, Oklahoma, 47
Old Coyote, Barney (Crow), 6
Old Pascua Village, Arizona, 173
Old Person, Earl (Blackfeet), 42
Oliphant v. Suquamish Tribe of Indians (1978), 72
Oliver, Emmett (Quinault), 179
Olson, James S., 27, 50, 71, 81
Omaha, 122, 167, 260
Omnibus Bill (1966), 116–117
One Flew Over the Cuckoo's Nest (1962), 235–236, 255
One Flew Over the Cuckoo's Nest (1975), 255
Oneida, 72, 176
Oregon, 16, 32, 34, 40, 41, 45, 65, 67, 151–152, 158, 159, 177, 181
Organization of Petroleum Exporting Countries (OPEC), 139, 144
Ortiz, Simon J. (Acoma Pueblo), 223–224, 225
Osage, 42, 140, 145, 203, 239
Osage with Van Gogh (1975), 196–197
Other Destinies (1992), 203
Otoe-Missouria, 215
Ottawa, 68, 158
Otter, Lucille (Salish), 160
The Outsider (1961), 253
Owens, Louis (Choctaw / Cherokee / Irish), 203, 207, 211, 238

Padilla Bay, Washington, 151
Paiute, 66, 68, 110, 151–152, 158, 181, 253
  economic development by, 151
  land claims, 66
  water resources, 145. See also names of individuals
Palmer, Delbert, 160
Palouse, 239

Pan-Indian movement, 119, 125, 171, 182–183, 211
Papago. *See* Tohono O'odham
Parfit, Michael, 182
Parliament of World Religions, 175
Pasadena, California, 248
Pascua Yaqui, 155
Passamaquoddy, 68, 150, 177
Patagonia corporation, 151
The Path on the Mountain (1918), 220
Patton, George, 6
Pawnee, 71, 145, 186, 215
Peabody Coal Company, 140, 141, 143
Peabody Museum, Harvard University, 167
Pearl Harbor, Hawaii, 4, 5, 6
Peattie, Donald C., 12
Peltier, Leonard (Sioux), 135
Pennsylvania, 90, 108, 124–125
Penobscot, 68, 150
People v. Woody (1964), 174–175
Peoria, 68, 158
Pequot, 154, 251
Pera, D. Martin (Apache), 260
Peso, Fred (Mescalero Apache), 146
Petroleum resources, 139–140, 141–142
Pewewardy, Cornel (Comanche / Kiowa), 183
Peyotism, 174–175, 192, 233
Phelps-Dodge copper mine, Arizona, 13
Phillips, Rick (Eastern Cherokee), 246
Phoenix, Arizona, 47, 142, 181
Pickernell, Albert Clarence (Quinault), 94
Pierce, Harriet (Seneca), 108
Pima, 16, 17–18, 89, 150–151, 180, 253
Pine Ridge Sioux, 42, 80, 121, 173
Pine Ridge Sioux reservation, South Dakota, 13, 16, 58, 69, 130–136, 246
Pino, Amaldo (Tesuque Pueblo), 10
Pit River, 38, 124

Plymouth Rock, Massachusetts, 124, 125, 245
Pocahontas (1995), 260
Pocahontas image, 2, 260
Poems and poetry, 201, 203, 219–226. *See also* names of individual poets
Pomo, 166, 176, 181
Population, Native American, 82, 88–89
Posey, Alexander (Creek), 220
Poston, Arizona, 16
Potawatomi, 40, 122, 239, 247, 252
Poverty, 28–29, 45, 46, 75, 77–81
Powers, William K., 230
Powhatan, 69, 235, 239, 260
The Powwow Highway (1990), 256–257
Powwows, 182, 212, 245
Pratt, Richard Henry, 90
Preferential hiring, in Bureau of Indian Affairs, 68–69
Problems of Indian Administration (1928). *See* Meriam Report
Public Health Service (PHS), 58, 82, 83
Public Law 280 (1953), 41–42, 113
  repudiated, 61–62
Pueblo, 26, 29–30, 80, 173, 205
  All-Pueblo Council, 15, 29–30
  artists, 185, 187, 188
  Blue Lake struggle, 38, 65, 69, 123
  traditional form of government, 63, 71
  water resources, 145
  during World War II, 5, 10, 14
  writers, 208–209, 213, 223–225. *See also* names of individuals
Pulitzer Prize, 201, 225
Puvungna, California, 166
Puyallup, 112, 113, 114
Puyallup River, Washington, 114
Pyle, Ernie, 12
Pyramid Lake, Nevada, 145

Quaker Oats cereal, 150
Quaker policy, 26, 29
Quillayute River, Washington, 114
Quinault, 63, 94, 179

Ramah, New Mexico, 95
Rapid City, South Dakota, 130,
    131, 247
Reagan, Ronald, 73
Red Earth Theatre, 259
Red Power, 116, 119, 229,
    237–238
Reifel, Ben (Sioux), 49
Religion, 11, 15, 26, 27, 30, 34, 63,
    74, 164–165, 194, 240, 241,
    255
    Christianity, 173–174
    peyotism, 174–175
    repatriation issue, 165–169
    revival of traditional, 171–173
    world religions, 175. *See also*
    Sacred sites, Medicine men
Relocation policy, 46–50
Removal policy, 24–25
Renaissance of Native American
    literature, 201–203, 229, 261
    novels, 203–212
    short stories, 212–219
    poetry, 219–226
Renegade Tribe (1986), 239
Reno, Janet, 75
Repatriation issue, 165–169, 204,
    232, 250
Reservation policy, 25–26
Resource and Patient Management
    System (RPMS), 85
Returning the Gift (1994), 202
Rhode Island, 159, 196
Rhode Island School of Design, 196
Ridge, John Rollin (Cherokee), 203
Riesman, Paul, 237
Riley, Nancy Richardson (Karuk),
    178
Rios, Steven (Juaneño), 166
Risling, David (Hupa / Yurok), 94,
    166
Riverside, California, 181

Roberts, Mickey (Nooksack),
    216–217, 219, 242
Robinson, Ernie (Northern
    Cheyenne), 180
Rocha, Vera (Gabrielino), 248
Rockefeller Foundation, 189–190
Rocky Boy School, Montana, 95
Roger, Robert, 4
Rooks, Irma (Oglala Sioux), 133
Roosevelt, Franklin D., 4, 16, 30,
    186
Rose, Wendy (Hopi / Miwok), 202
Rosebud Sioux, 86, 107, 171
Rosebud Sioux reservation, South
    Dakota, 58, 125, 224–225, 233
Rough Rock Demonstration
    School, Arizona, 94–95, 226,
Rousseau, Jean Jacques, 2
Royalties, from mineral extraction,
    140–142
Rube, Calvin (Yurok), 162
Runningfox, Joseph, 258

Sac and Fox, 38, 122
Sacred sites, protection of, 142,
    143, 146, 147, 175
    Bear Butte, 164–165
    Medicine Wheel, 172
    Point Conception, 163–164
    Puvungna, 166
    San Francisco Peaks, 164
    Siskiyou Mountains, 162–163
Sahmaunt, Herschel (Kiowa), 99
Saint Regis Mohawk reservation,
    New York, 125
Sainte-Marie, Buffy (Cree), 115, 258
Salinan, 177
Salish, 160
Salamanca, New York, 161–162
Salt Lake City, Utah, 46
Sampson, Will, 255
San Carlos Apache, 42, 80
San Carlos Pueblo, 225
San Diego, California, 87, 166
San Diego American Indian Health
    Center, 87
San Felipe Pueblo, 145

San Francisco, California, 47, 85,
122, 126, 177, 194, 207,
232–233, 247, 259
San Francisco Peaks, Arizona, 143,
164
San Francisco State University,
California, 122
San Ildefonso Pueblo, 185
San Jose, California, 47, 167
San Jose State University, California,
167
Sand Creek Massacre (1864), 253
Sanitation, 78–81, 83–84, 85
Santa Clara Pueblo, 71, 187
Santa Clara Pueblo v. Martinez
(1978), 71
Santa Fe Indian School, 187, 188,
190
Santa Fe, New Mexico, 60, 61, 100,
109, 116, 171, 185, 187, 218,
233
Santee Sioux, 165
Satiacum, Robert (Puyallup /
Yakama), 113, 114
Saubel, Katherine (Cahuilla), 181
Scholder, Fritz (Luiseño), 190,
191–192, 193, 196, 197, 209
Scovell, Joe (Tillamook), 181
Seals, David, 229–230, 241,
256–257
Sears, Vickie (Cherokee), 218
Seaton, Fred, 46
Seattle, Washington, 14, 85, 124,
126, 259
Secakuku, Ferrell (Hopi), 157
Segregation, in the armed forces,
6–7
Sekaquaptewa, Abbott (Hopi),
146–147
Selective Service Act (1940), 5, 6
Self-determination policy, 53,
87–88, 98–99, 110, 117, 121,
123, 139, 144, 171, 175, 261
Clinton administration, 74–75
Ford administration, 70
Johnson administration, 60–63
Nixon administration, 64–70

Reagan and Bush administrations,
73–74
Seminole, 38, 153
Seneca, 28, 108, 161–162, 176,
252
A Separate Reality (1971), 237
Serviceman's Readjustment Act
(1944). *See* GI Bill of Rights
Shamans. *See* Medicine men
Shared Visions (1991), 188
Shawnee, 38–39, 176
She Wore a Yellow Ribbon (1949),
252
Sheen, Martin, 255
Shell Oil Company, 141
Shickel, Richard, 257
Shinnecock, 245–246
Shiprock, New Mexico, 94, 196
Shoalwater Bay, Washington, 161
Shongopovi, Arizona, 143, 152
Short stories, 201, 212–219
Shoshone, 14, 26, 145, 181, 195,
216, 253
Shoshone-Bannock, 94, 183, 216
Sierra Club, 162
Sijohn, Henry (Spokane), 156
Siletz, 158
Silko, Leslie Marmon (Laguna
Pueblo), 208–209, 211, 220,
225
Silverheels, Jay (Mohawk), 252, 259
Sinte Gleska College, South Dakota,
97, 99, 224, 241
Sioux, 25, 34, 35, 86, 107, 125,
146, 158, 171, 245, 253, 255,
256
activists, 121–122
education, 97, 100
exempted from allotment policy,
28
opposed termination policy, 42,
64
peyotism, 233
relocation policy, 49
sacred sites controversies,
164–165
unemployment, 80

Wounded Knee occupation, 129–136
writers, 240–241
during World War II, 5, 13, 14, 15, 16, 18. *See also* names of individuals
Siskiyou Mountains, California, 162
Sitting Bull (Sioux), 25, 158, 245
Sitting Bull (1954), 253
Six Rivers National Forest, California, 162
Skeletal remains, repatriation of, 165–169
Slagle, Allogan (Cherokee), 159
Smartlowit, Stanley (Yakama), 94
Smith, Alfred, 175
Smith, Janue Quick-to-See (Cree / Shoshone), 195
Smith, John, 235
Smithsonian Institution, 166, 183–184, 247, 248–251
Snake Ceremony, 152
Snoqualmie, 244
Snyder Act (1921), 82
Soldier Blue (1970), 253
Sonoma, California, 181, 244
The Sot-Weed Factor (1960), 235, 236
South Dakota, 13, 15, 34, 57, 61, 69, 80, 97, 99, 105, 124, 125, 130–136, 145, 158, 164, 165, 171, 173–174, 220, 224, 233, 246, 247, 256
South Dakota Review, 220
Southeast Asia, war in, 63, 120, 232, 236, 253
Southwest Indian Art Project, 189–190
Southwest Museum, Los Angeles, 166
Southwestern Indian Polytechnic Institute, 100
Southwestern Regional Youth Conference (SRYC), 109
Sovereignty, 71–72, 75, 117, 123, 126, 133, 135–136, 142, 149, 155, 156, 157–158, 240

Space Technology Applied to Rural Papago Advanced Health Care (STARPAHC), 85
Spalding, Idaho, 181
Spider Woman's Granddaughters (1989), 213
Spock, Benjamin, 127
Spokane, 155–156, 213–214
Sports Illustrated, 245
Sprague, Lee (Huron Potawatomi), 247
St. Louis, Missouri, 47
St. Paul, Minnesota, 14, 120, 126, 183
St. Pierre, John (Yankton Sioux), 34
St. Regis Mohawk reservation, 13, 153
Stagecoach (1939), 1–2, 4
Standing Rock Sioux, 35, 240–241
Standing Rock Sioux reservation, South and North Dakota, 15, 97, 158
Stanford University, California, 167, 182, 205, 221, 242
Stars, Lorenzo, 242
Steiner, Stan, 114, 237–238
Stensgar, Ernest (Coeur d'Alene), 161
Stewart, James, 252
Stockbeson, Henry, 160
Story, Dillon, 9
Strickland, Rennard, 188, 193, 195
Student Nonviolent Coordinating Committee (SNCC), 118, 127
Studi, Wes (Cherokee), 257, 258, 262
Studio style, 187–188
Suicide, among Native Americans, 77, 81, 90, 150
Sun Dance, 26, 125, 171, 253
Sundown (1934), 203
Sunrise Ceremonial, 173
Sun Tracks, 220
Suquamish, 71–72, 161
The Surrounded (1936), 204
Swastika, 7
Swinomish, 151
Syracuse University, New York, 243

Szasz, Margaret Connell, 91, 92, 98

Tait, Norman (Nisga'a), 179
Talking Leaf, 183
Talking Leaves (1991), 213
Taos Pueblo, 38, 65, 69, 123, 225
Tax, Sol, 109
Taxation, 14, 41, 42, 45
Teaching American Indian History
(1993), 239
The Teachings of Don Juan (1968),
237
Tell Them Willie Boy Is Here (1969),
253
Tenorio, Frank (San Felipe Pueblo),
145
Termination policy, 35–46, 53–56,
73, 83, 92, 116
abandonment of, 59–63, 64–68,
75
Texas, 10, 25, 40, 47, 158
Textbooks and the American Indian
(1970), 242
Textbooks, images of Native
Americans in, 93–94, 242
They Died With Their Boots On
(1941), 3
Thom, Melvin (Paiute), 110, 111,
113–114
Thompson, Hildegard, 93
Thompson, Morris (Alaska
Athapaskan), 67
Thornton, Russell (Cherokee), 89,
238
Thorpe, Grace (Sac and Fox /
Potawatomi), 122
Thorpe, Jim (Sac and Fox), 122, 253
Three Mile Island accident (1979),
146
Thunderbird Lodge, Arizona, 152
Tillamook, 181
Tlingit, 100
Tohono O'odham (formerly
Papago), 42, 85, 150–151, 155
Tohono O'odham reservation,
Arizona, 13, 16, 18
Tokonga. See Black Legs Society

Tolakwe (Point Conception,
California), 163
Tolowa, 162, 178
Totem-pole carving, 179
Tourism, 151–153
Tournament of Roses, California,
248
Trachoma, 78, 82, 83
Tracks (1988), 212
Tracy, Spencer, 4
Trade and Intercourse Act (1790),
150
Traditional culture, 11, 12, 15, 112,
142, 152
fine arts movement, 184–197
literature, 205–226
material culture, 178–180
preservation of traditional
languages, 175–178
programs to promote, 180–182
revival of Native religions,
171–175. *See also* related
topics
Traditional Kickapoo, 159
Trafzer, Clifford E. (Wyandot), 87,
213, 238–239
Trail of Broken Treaties (1972), 69,
125–129, 133, 135, 210, 241
Trail of Tears, 25
Tree Full of Leaves Which Are Stars
(1990), 225
Tregaskis, Richard, 11
Tribal Assets (1990), 157
Tribal courts, 63, 70–72
Tribal governments
challenged by activists, 120, 123,
124, 126, 130–136
during Collier era, 30–31, 34
Indian Civil Rights Act, 62–63
Indian Self-Determination and
Education Assistance Act,
70–72, 75, 106–108, 117
termination policy, 41–46, 59,
87–88
Tribally controlled colleges, 97, 99,
241. *See also* names of individual
colleges

Tribally Controlled Community
College Assistance Act (1978),
99
Tribes and Masses (1978), 239
Trickster of Liberty (1988),
210–211
Trimble, Charles (Oglala Sioux),
125
Trinity River, California, 153
Truckee River, Nevada, 145
Truman, Harry, 36, 39
Tsewenaldin Inn, California, 153
Tubatulabal, 178
Tuberculosis, 78, 81, 82, 83, 84,
88, 89
Tucson, Arizona, 84, 142, 173, 220
Tulalip, 179
Tulsa, Oklahoma, 47
Turner, Ted, 244, 258–259
Turner Broadcasting System (TBS),
258
Turner Network Television (TNT),
258, 259
Tuscarora, 94, 108–109
Two Hawk, Webster (Sioux), 129
Two Horn Priest with Maiden
(1978), 193
Two Rivers Resort, Washington,
155–156

Udall, Stewart, 55, 60, 116
Umatilla reservation, Oregon, 146
Umpqua, 159
The Underground Reservation
(1985), 239
Unemployment, 45, 77–81, 120,
150
The Union Pacific (1939), 3
United Nations, 133, 158
United Native Americans, 120
University of Alaska, 176
University of Arizona, 189–190,
205, 220
University of California, Berkeley,
167–168, 178, 209, 239
University of California, Davis, 239
University of California, Los
Angeles, 86

University of California, Riverside,
238–239
University of Chicago, 29, 109
University of Illinois, 243
University of Michigan, 80
University of Minnesota, 97, 167,
168, 209, 218
University of Nebraska, 167
University of New Mexico, 109,
188, 205, 221
University of Oklahoma, 140, 203,
243
University of Saskatchewan, 204
University of South Dakota, 57
University of Utah, 57
University of Washington, 260
Uranium resources, 139, 140,
145–146
Urbanization, 14–15, 17–18, 119,
205
pan-Indian identity, 182–183
relocation policy, 46–50. *See also*
names of individual cities
Utah, 13, 40, 46, 57, 67, 140, 142
Utah International Corporation,
140
Ute, 14, 26, 145

Vanishing American, image of, 234
Velarde, Pablita (Santa Clara
Pueblo), 187
Velie, Alan, 211, 219–220
Vera, Agnes (Yowlumni), 178
Vera, Matt (Yowlumni), 178
Vidor, King, 4, 251
Vietnam War, 63, 120, 232, 236,
253
Vivelo, Frank, 220
Vivelo, Jacqueline, 220
Vizenor, Gerald (Chippewa),
209–211, 239
Voices from Wah'Kon-Tah (1974),
221
Voting rights, of Native Americans,
19

Wade, Edwin L., 193, 195
Walker, John, 231

Wal-Mart (discount store), 164
Walker Lake, Nevada, 145
Walker River Paiute, 180
Walters, Anna Lee (Pawnee / Otoe-Missouria), 215–216
War Relocation Authority (WRA), 39
Warm Springs, 151, 151–152, 177
Warm Springs reservation, Oregon, 65
Warrior, Clyde (Ponca), 110–112, 116, 118, 119
Warrior image, of Native Americans, 2–4, 8–10, 234, 251–252, 253, 260–261
Warrior Society, 155
Wasco, 177, 203, 217
Washington, 14, 49, 59, 65–66, 85, 94, 97, 112–116, 118, 124, 126, 146, 151, 155–156, 159–160, 160–161, 179, 203, 238, 244, 259
Washington, D.C., 109, 126–129, 166, 168, 183–184, 210, 238, 244–245, 248–251
Washington Redskins (football team), 244–245
Washington State Board of Education, 244
Washington v. McCoy (1963), 113
Washo, 178
Water Bird (1980), 192
Water resources, 29–30, 72, 108–109, 125, 142, 143–145, 150–151, 161
Watergate scandal (1974), 69
Waterson, Sam, 255
Watkins, Arthur V., 40–41
Watt, James, 73
Wauneka, Annie (Navajo), 84
The Way to Rainy Mountain (1969), 206, 223
Wayne, John, 252
We Talk, You Listen (1970), 240
Webb, Chris (Nez Perce), 181
Weisl, Edwin L., Jr., 115
Welch, James (Blackfeet / Gros Ventre), 207–208, 211, 222

West, Richard (Cheyenne), 186–187
West, W. Richard, Jr. (Cheyenne / Arapaho), 250–251
Westerman, Floyd (Sioux), 258
The Western Gate (Point Conception, California), 163–164
Western Union (1941), 3
Westmoreland Resources Company, 144
Westmoreland, William, 236
Wheeler, Burton K., 30
Wheeler-Howard Act (1934), 30–33
When Coyote Leaves the Res (1980), 194
White Deerskin Dance, 153
The White Man's Indian (1978), 235
White Mountain Apache, 58, 90, 151, 155
White Painting (1971), 195
White, Robert H., 157
Whitehair, Mary (Navajo), 260
Whitesinger, Pauline (Navajo), 147
Whitish, Herb (Shoalwater Bay), 161
Whole Earth Review, 232
Wild West shows, 3, 236–237
Willetto, Carla (Apache), 225–226
Wilson, Darryl Babe (A-Juma-We / Atsuge-We), 214
Wilson, Raymond, 27, 50, 71, 81
Wilson, Richard (Oglala Sioux), 130–131, 133, 134–136
Wilson, Terry P. (Potawatomi), 239
Wind from an Enemy Sky (1978), 204
Windwalker (1980), 255
Wingate Elementary School Poetry Calendar (1989), 225
The Winged Serpent (1946), 220
Winnebago, 75, 243–244
Winter in the Blood (1974), 228
Winters v. United States (1908), 145
Winters, Yvor, 221
Wintun, 156, 178, 194, 250

Wiping the Tears of the Seventh
Generation, 172–173
Wisconsin, 40, 41, 43–45, 67
Witt, Shirley Hill (Akwesasne
Mohawk), 110–111, 113
Wolffe, Geoffrey, 238
The Woman Who Owned the Shadows
(1983), 213
Women, Native American, 34, 42,
47–49, 59, 75, 84, 133, 140,
167, 173, 176, 178, 181, 182,
183, 184, 260
activists, 110–111, 113, 122, 146
artists, 185, 187, 194–195
entertainers, 115, 258
scholars, 238, 242, 247, 250
tribal leaders, 59, 67, 73, 74, 75,
157, 246
during World War II, 6, 14, 15
writers, 203, 211–212,
213–214, 214–215, 216–218,
219. *See also* names of
individuals
Woodenlegs, John (Northern
Cheyenne), 102
Woodward, Dennis (Mescalero
Apache), 182
Woody, Elizabeth (Wasco / Navajo),
203, 217–218
Woody, John, 174–175
Wordcraft Circle of Native Writers
and Storytellers, 238

Work Incentive projects (WIN), 58
World War I, 5, 7, 19, 29
World War II, 4–20, 23, 39, 47, 49,
50, 77, 82, 91–92, 107, 109,
140, 187, 193, 205, 209, 230,
231, 248, 261
Wounded Knee, occupation of
(1973), 69, 105, 129–136, 139,
157, 241
Wyandot, 68, 87, 158, 176, 213,
238–239
Wyoming, 145, 172

Ya-Ka-Ama Center, California, 181
Yakama (formerly Yakima), 65–66,
94, 113, 114, 146
Yakima Chief, Dave (Sioux), 256
Yakima River, Washington, 114
Yankton Sioux, 34, 188
Yaqui, 155, 173, 214–215, 237
Yazzie, Etheloo (Navajo), 95
A Yellow Raft on Blue Water
(1989), 240
Yellowbank, James (Winnebago),
243–244
Youth Opportunity Campaign, 58
Yowlumni, 178
Yurok, 94, 162–163, 166, 178, 183

Zah, Peterson (Navajo), 75, 147,
149
Zuni, 17, 145, 185